ECOCIDE

ECOCIDE

A Short History of the Mass Extinction of Species

Franz J. Broswimmer

Pluto Press

LONDON • STERLING, VIRGINIA

First published 2002
by PLUTO PRESS
345 Archway Road, London N6 5AA
and 22883 Quicksilver Drive,
Sterling, VA 20166–2012, USA

www.plutobooks.com

British Library Cataloguing in Publication Data
A catalogue record for this book is available from
the British Library

ISBN 0 7453 1935 1 hardback
ISBN 0 7453 1934 3 paperback

Library of Congress Cataloging in Publication Data
Broswimmer, Franz.
  Ecocide : a short history of the mass extinction of species
/ Franz Broswimmer.
      p. cm.
Includes bibliographical references and index.
  ISBN 0–7453–1935–1 — ISBN 0–7453–1934–3 (pbk.)
  1. Nature—Effect of human beings on. 2. Extinction (Biology) 3.
Biological diversity conservation—Social aspects. I. Title.
  GF75 .B73 2002
    333.95'22—dc21
                                                    2002003085

10   9   8   7   6   5   4   3   2   1

Designed and produced for Pluto Press by
Chase Publishing Services, Fortescue, Sidmouth EX10 9QG
Typeset from disk by Stanford DTP Services, Towcester
Printed in the European Union by Antony Rowe, Chippenham, England

For my parents

CONTENTS

TABLES

ACKNOWLEDGEMENTS

This book would not have been possible without the help of a large number of people, too many to list here by name. I would like to acknowledge the key role played by the Globalization Research Center (GRC) at the University of Hawai'i -Manoa in making the publication of this book possible: first, by having the vision to see how my doctoral work fits in with the research mission of the GRC; second, by giving me time off from my other duties as a researcher and editor with the GRC during the summer of 2001 to revise the manuscript, while continuing salary support; and third, by providing me with the manuscript preparation skills of Sally Serafim. Moreover, upon my request, GRC made it possible for me to work with my good friend and colleague Manfred B. Steger. His editorial expertise and hard work on behalf of this publication have been invaluable.

A number of people have read all or parts of the book manuscript at various stages and offered important suggestions. In particular I wish to thank Peter Manicas for his unfailing support and insightful comments throughout the project. I thank my doctoral committee members Emanuel Drechsel, Leslie Sponsel, Alvin So, David Swift, and my Chair Herb Barringer for giving me free rein in pursuing my interests during the dissertation research, which provides the basis for this book. A note of thanks also goes to my colleagues and friends at the University of Hawai'i for freely sharing new ideas and resources, and to Kayomi Kaneda, whose good spirits enabled me to bear with the rather depressing topic of this study.

Finally, I want to express my thanks to the East-West Center at the University of Hawai'i-Manoa for granting me a Visiting Fellowship in the summer of 2000, which enabled me to develop relevant ideas and resources. I am grateful to the many others who have provided feedback, data, or simply old-fashioned encouragement and support. In alphabetical order, they include among others Ann and Ron Kirk, Anneliese Moore, Arthur Getz-Escudero, Anthony Medrano, Barry Barnes, Barry Smart, Carole and Shi-jen He, Charles Luce, Chris Barker, David Goalstone, Deanna Donovan, Devin Joshi, Dorothy and Rom Goldsborough, Eric and Margaret Dornauer, Floro Quibuyen, Glen Dolcemascolo, Hermine Landstaetter, Jennie Peterson, John and Rene Gutrich, Joseph and Renate Sanladerer, Kit Collier, Leopoldine and Franz Ambichl, Lynn Ann Mulrooney, Manfred Henningsen, Manfred Junghans,

Mark Valencia, Perle Besserman, Rosarita and Johann Sonnleitner, Yow Suen Sen, Stephen Philion, Tian Chenshan, Val Burris, Vinod and Manju Mishra, and Wolfgang and Susan Sperlich. A *mahalo nui loa* also goes to the Department of Sociology at the University of Hawai'i at Manoa for providing me with the assistance to make this study possible. Despite the assistance and advice I received from numerous individuals in the course of this project, all remaining flaws of this book are my sole responsibility.

INTRODUCTION

Homo sapiens has become the most dominant species on Earth. Unfortunately, our impact is devastating, and if we continue to destroy the environment as we do today, half the world's species will become extinct early in the next [twenty-first] century.... *Homo sapiens* is poised to become the greatest catastrophic agent since a giant asteroid collided with the Earth sixty-five million years ago, wiping out half the world's species in a geological instant. (Richard Leakey and Roger Levin, *The Sixth Extinction*)[1]

And they were sawing off the branches on which they were sitting, while shouting across their experiences to one another how to saw more efficiently. And they went crashing down into the deep. And those who watched them shook their heads and continued sawing vigorously. (Bertolt Brecht, *Exile III*)[2]

THE PROBLEM

The problems arising from the current acceleration of mass species extinction and the global destruction of habitat are only now acknowledged as being of fundamental importance for humanity. Still, the fundamental importance of the Earth's remaining biodiversity remains under-studied and under-appreciated. At the beginning of the twenty-first century, only a fraction of the estimated diversity of life has been identified. Numbers vary considerably, with the most conservative assessment at about 5 million species worldwide, and more generous estimates at about 30 million to 50 million.[3] Of the 1.7 million species that are presently catalogued, only 5 per cent can be considered well known and the relationships between many of them are still a mystery.[4]

What we *do* know, however, is that planet Earth is losing species at a rate unparalleled in human experience. In the late modern era, the normal trickle rate of extinction has become a gushing hemorrhage as 100 species or more disappear every day.[5] The current wave of extinction is rivaled only by the three large cataclysmic mass extinctions of the remote geological past.

The first crisis of mass extinction occurred on land and in shallow water environments some 250 million years ago, marking the close of the Permian period. Being the oldest, this event is still poorly understood, and its causes are largely unresolved. Paleontologists believe that it was brought about by a slow but inexorable change in climate and sea level occurring when forces of continental drift caused the Earth's great continents to merge together slowly into a single, gigantic super-continent. When the continents had

1

finally separated from their tectonic embrace, more than 90 per cent of the Earth's species had died. This great extinction swept away most of the marine and land-living animal life, ending a 200 million-year-long evolutionary history that geologists have named the Paleozoic era.[6]

The second major crisis arose about 200 million years ago, just when the world's ecosystems reorganized themselves into a series of stable marine and terrestrial communities. The land fauna prior to this second cataclysmic period was a mix of newly evolving dinosaurs, large crocodile-like animals, with a few mammal-like reptiles. Most of these creatures disappeared from Earth, together with coral reefs and most shelled ammonites. The cause of this mass extinction event was not a single, rapid event, but a series of environmental catastrophes occurring in a close sequence spanning about 100,000 years or less. The two main causes are most likely a 1- to 5-mile-wide meteor colliding with the Earth, leaving a 70-mile-wide crater in Quebec, and the eruption of great lava flows beneath what are now the jungles of the Amazon River valley. In addition, the planet's climate changed dramatically. All of these events combined to create environmental change sufficient to produce this second wave of mass extinction. Yet, this catastrophe opened the way for the dinosaurs that emerged as the great winners at the end.[7]

The third great mass extinction took place 65 million years ago, annihilating the terrestrial dinosaurs along with hundreds of thousands of other land and aquatic species. Like its predecessor, this event was caused by several factors, including climate changes and a sudden change in sea level. But the culmination of this mass extinction, and by far its most dramatic element, took place when a giant, 6-mile-wide asteroid or comet crashed into the surface of the Earth near the Yucatan peninsula. The collision produced a fiery hell of burning forests over much of the Earth's surface, accompanied by giant tidal waves and great volumes of poisonous gas.[8] But even more lethal were the months of darkness that enveloped the planet after the comet's impact. Millions of tons of earth and extraterrestrial debris blazed upward and blocked the sunlight, producing an endless ecocidal night. On land, and even more so in the oceans, plants died, leading to the starvation of many creatures that fed upon them. Well over 50 per cent of all species on Earth perished.[9]

In the 65 million years since the last of the dinosaurs perished, the surviving species and their descendants have multiplied to levels of diversity unseen during previous ages. Yet, with the emergence of behaviorally modern humans a new major crisis of mass extinction arose. It has been unfolding for millennia, and, unlike the greenhouse effect, global warming, or holes in the ozone layer, it is visible without sophisticated imagery or complex computer modeling. It is real, and it is happening all over the globe, most glaringly in the tropics.

I chose the term "ecocide" to refer to this most recent crisis of mass extinction of species. Ecocide indicates the horrifying scope and cumulative effects of the human-induced crisis of mass extinction and habitat destruction. The aim and purpose of this study is to sharpen our historical and sociological understanding of ecocide and to explore possible emancipatory alternatives. My central objective is to examine the sociological underpinnings of this global predicament. Adopting an interdisciplinary approach to investigate the social, political, and ideological forces that lead to ecocide, the book is part of recent efforts to bridge the social and the natural sciences. This interdisciplinary framework also contributes to a more holistic understanding of ecocide. As paleontologist Stephen Jay Gould notes, "we need a broad perspective on this most portentous of all ecological and evolutionary disasters."[10] Ultimately, this study is about one aspect of globalization, that is, the global processes leading to the colonization and destruction of our planet's life-support systems.[11] I hope to offer a sociological critique of ecocide as an exceedingly damaging global configuration, showing it to be a conditional historical product of human agency. Paleobiologists – scholars who study the consequences of the death of individual species in the historical record – distinguish two types of species extinction: background extinction and mass extinctions. The ordinary background extinction of species occurs all the time, usually after a prolonged period of "success" during which neither species nor their ecological niches change significantly. Unlike the random disappearances of species "gradually" through background extinction, mass extinction brings about cataclysmic changes in the distribution and number of species. Gould states that "mass extinction must, by four criteria, be reinterpreted as ruptures not the high points of continua. They are more *frequent*, more *rapid*, more *profound* (in numbers and habitats eliminated) and have effects more *different than those* of normal times."[12]

Extinction is the ultimate fate of every species. Just as an individual is born, lives out its time on the Earth, and then dies, so too does a species come into existence, exist for a number of years (usually counted in millions), and then eventually become extinct. Like the obituary page of a newspaper, the fossil record reflects background extinctions taking place throughout time. But paleontologist David Raup and other researchers have shown that the rate at which these random extinctions have taken place through geological time is remarkably low. According to Raup's calculations, the background extinction rate during the past 500 million years has been about one species going extinct every five years.[13] In contrast, Norman Myers, one of the earliest scientists to warn of a current mass extinction, has estimated that, for the past 35 years, four species per day have been going extinct in Brazil alone.[14]

Harvard biologist E.O. Wilson estimates that before humans existed, the species extinction rate was (very roughly) one species per million species per year (0.0001 per cent). Estimates for current species extinction rates range from 100 to 10,000 times that, but most hover close to 1,000 times prehuman levels (0.1 per cent per year), with the rate projected to rise, and very likely sharply.[15] If one considers that the forests and other habitats of the

Earth's remaining 25 biological hotspot areas have already been reduced to
as little as 10 per cent of their pre-human levels, and most are at immediate
risk of disappearing,[16] and that species extinction is increasingly enhanced
by pollution, climate change, and the growing flood of invasive species, the
foregoing estimates of mass extinctions based on habitat reduction are,
"sadly, minimal and modest."[17]

Homo sapiens has only been in existence for little more than 130,000
years.[18] Yet, it would take somewhere between 10 million and 25 million
years for the natural process of species evolution to rectify the devastation
of the Earth's biodiversity unleashed by human societies over the past
millennia, and particularly by recent generations.[19] The human-induced
changes to the global biosphere are unprecedented. They include the
worldwide disruption of biochemical cycles, rapid climate change, massive
soil erosion, extensive desertification, and the unchecked release of synthetic
toxins and genetically modified organisms.

The globalization of environmental degradation and mass extinction
demands a re-examination of human hierarchical traditions and social
practices. Ever since agriculture began and class society emerged, the socialization (humanization) of nature has been subject to new rules, defined by
struggles over surplus production. Modern industrial societies in particular
distinguish themselves by their unprecedented capacity to transform nature,
including the historically unique capacity to destroy species habitats on a
planetary scale. Yet, the prevailing spirit of late modernity seems to
distinguish itself by a conspicuous denial, or at least obliviousness to the
ecological consequences of human social behavior. Many social scientists
have been largely complicit in this project, for they have tended to be
concerned with abstract structures rather than with real-life processes.
Frequently, they have been preoccupied with abstract collectivities rather
than with interacting individuals and their concrete material conditions;
with discursive shell games rather than with observable behavior in a real
and particular historical environment; with statistical manipulation of
aggregated data and maps rather than with normative study of ongoing
social-ecological processes.[20]

In contrast, the goal of this study is to direct critical attention to the
historical nexus of ecological and social relations, leading to progressive
ecocide. I argue that the apparent social success of humans in eliminating
other living species is turning into a severe handicap. The self-destructive
record of some 480 generations since the Neolithic revolution deserves more
scrutiny on both social and ecological grounds. The tendency of humans to
eliminate other living species – at times unwittingly or accidentally – is an
indicator of the extent to which we are transforming nature in a self-
defeating way. The globalizing capitalist economy exacerbates these
problems by threatening to destroy the entire biosphere, inflicting grievous
and irreparable injury on an intricate life-supporting system. Complex
ecosystems are undermined to the point of collapse. Practices of over-grazing,

deforestation, and brush clearing extend the deserts, a factor now accelerated by climate change. Coastal wetlands are being drained for agricultural purposes, allowing toxic chemicals to spill into the sea, where they add to already-accumulated industrial pollutants and sewage.

Late modern societies have been losing ground on important environmental issues in part because they have allowed these issues to disappear from the public's intellectual radar screens. After all, organized efforts undertaken by vested interests systematically seek to undermine critical public support for the environment.[21] The glacial pace of negotiations related to the globalization of environment degradation over the past decades can similarly be attributed to broad and well-organized corporate opposition. But ecocide is not, as some commentators have suggested, a "morbid exaggeration," "gloomy invention," or "melodramatic disaster scenario of alarmist academics" or "eco-quack environmentalists." In fact, if daily news broadcasts were informed by ecological realism, then people around the world would hear evening after evening something like the following announcement:

Also today as many as 100 animal and plant species have become extinct, some further 50,000 hectares of tropical rainforests have disappeared; the deserts have expanded worldwide by another 20,000 hectares; the global economy has consumed today the equivalent of 22 million tons of oil and we will consequently have collectively released during the same 24 hours another 100 million tons of greenhouse gasses into the atmosphere...

Indeed, already gone forever are the European elephant, the European lion, and European tiger. The Labrador duck, the giant auk, and the Carolina parakeet will never again grace this blue planet. Lost for all time are the Eurasian woolly mammoth and the woolly rhinoceros, the musk-ox and the giant Irish elk of the ice age. Gone are the enormous mammoth and mastodon, the giant bison and the saber-toothed tiger, the giant beavers, the giant sloth and the large short-faced bear, the camel, the tapir, the horse, the stag-moose and the half-ton lion of North America. Gone are the dwarf elephant and pygmy hippo of Cyprus and Crete and ancient Egypt; the New Caledonian crocodile, the half-ton elephant bird, the dwarf hippo, the giant iguana, the giant tortoise and the gorilla-sized giant lemur of Madagascar; the giant ground sloth of the West Indies; the Nauman's elephant and giant deer of Japan; the giant koala, the giant emu-like genyornis, and the giant wombat of Australia; the spiny anthe and giant guinea pig of South America; the antlered giraffe of nascent Africa; the Eurasian musk; the flightless rails, ibises, and a variety of waddling giant ducks and geese of Hawai'i ; the 13 or more species of the New Zealand/Aotearoa moa, flightless wrens and small petrels, and the dodo of Mauritius; the spiny anteater and wolf of Tasmania; the North American passenger pigeon, great auk, and the Atlantic gray whales; the Biscayan right whales and the stellar sea cow. Future generations will never look upon the California condor in the wild or watch the Palos Verde blue butterfly dart from blossom to blossom.

We have already forgotten that, only two centuries ago, billions of passenger pigeons, once the most abundant bird on the planet, still adorned the landscape now known as the United States. That 60 million bison once roamed the North American plains. Walrus once mated and bred along the coast of Nova Scotia.[22] Between 30 million and 50 million 500-pound giant sea turtles once flourished in the Caribbean sea.[23] A mere hundred years ago, the white bear populated the forests of New England and the Canadian Maritime Provinces. Now it is called the "polar" bear because that is where it now makes its last stand. Like the ruins of a medieval castle, contemporary "nature" is a mere vestige of its past glory.

The above list of impressive megafauna is but a small fraction of the species-diversity spectrum that is currently being irreversibly destroyed by human societies. Given the mounting evidence of our cataclysmic historical record, it might be time to rename our species "*Homo esophagus colossus*" – the creature with a gigantic esophagus capable of devouring entire ecosystems.[24]

WHY BOTHER?

Why should social scientists be concerned about mass extinction and loss of biodiversity? Why bother to develop an explanatory sociological account of the social and historical roots of ecocide? Why expend a great deal of energy to save species? Why should this matter be of collective concern to humans? The answers to these questions can be developed along several different lines. A short response would emphasize collective existential imperatives and concerns. Like all species, we collectively depend on other species for our existence. Some of the most obvious ways are that other species produce the oxygen we breathe, absorb the carbon dioxide we exhale, decompose our sewage, produce our food, maintain the fertility of our soil, and provide our wood and paper. Humans are not only part of biodiversity, but also profoundly dependent on it.

Another good reason pertains to the irreversibility of extinctions. Loss of species is final. When an ecosystem is destroyed, re-creating it is either impossible or extremely difficult. Some environmental problems, such as the increasing concentrations of chlorofluorocarbons or carbon dioxide in the atmosphere, can be reversed. However, once an element in biodiversity vanishes, it is literally "as dead as a dodo."[25] Each species and ecosystem adds to the richness and aesthetic beauty of life on Earth. Each species is unique and has a right to exist. Each species is worthy of respect regardless of its cash value to human beings. These claims are recognized in the World Charter for Nature, adopted by the United Nations in 1982. Nine years earlier, the US Congress passed the official Endangered Species Act in recognition that species of animals and plants "are of aesthetic, ecological, educational, historical, recreational, and scientific value to the nation and its people."[26]

Therefore, many naturalists have argued that the extermination of species represents a spiritual and intellectual impoverishment for humanity. A world without other earthly companions would not merely be a more dangerous place, it would also be much lonelier and more desolate.[27] What is to become of the human spirit when the inspirited creatures we have invoked over millennia in our most enlightened cultural traditions are gone? The power of human dreams, as philosopher Elias Canetti argues, is tied to the multiformity of animals. With the disappearance of dreams, people's imagination and creativity dry up as well.[28]

However, many of the dominant rationales against progressive ecocide and loss of biodiversity are not aesthetic or sentimental but practical and utilitarian. One of the most compelling rational-utilitarian arguments is that of collective self-interest. In addition to the basics of food and shelter, the natural world provides countless medical, agricultural, and commercial benefits. Besides the plants and animals that we use for food, shelter, raw materials, decoration, and companionship, there are thousands of species whose natural products are literally lifesaving. Biological products and processes, for example, account for 45 per cent of the world economy, and the annual economic and environmental benefits of biodiversity in the United States alone total approximately $300 billion.[29]

In 1997 an international team of researchers from the University of Maryland's Institute of Ecological Economics published a landmark study of the importance of nature's services in supporting human economics.[30] The study provided, for the first time, a quantification of the economic value of the world's ecosystem services and natural capital. The researchers synthesized the findings of over 100 studies to compute the average per hectare value for each of the 17 services that the world's ecosystems provide. They concluded that the economic value of the world's ecosystem services is in the neighborhood of $33 trillion per year, exceeding the global GNP of $25 trillion.[31]

Species do not simply contribute to commerce by virtue of the potential commodities they supply. Species also provide so-called "ecological services," such as purifying water, cycling nutrients, and breaking down pollutants. Species make up the fabric of healthy ecosystems – such as coastal estuaries, prairie grasslands, and ancient forests – which we depend on to purify our air, clean our water, and supply us with food. When species become endangered, it is an indicator that the health of these vital ecosystems is beginning to fail. The US Fish and Wildlife Service estimates that losing one plant species can trigger the loss of up to 30 insect, plant, and higher animal species. Species evolve to fill particular niches or habitats. Many species depend on each other in intricate ways for survival. This ecological insight has been exemplified by the classical extinction example of the dodo. This flightless bird, whose name is synonymous with extinction, formerly lived on the island of Mauritius. The dodo was exterminated and disappeared in the seventeenth century, most likely through the use of its eggs rather than direct hunting. At least one tree species became extinct following the extermination of the Dodo due to its ecologically strategic role as a species as a seed distributor or germinator. The extermination of the dodo was followed by destruction of half of all land and freshwater bird species of Mauritius in the wake of the island's colonization by Europeans.[32] Worldwide, some 40 per cent of all prescriptions written today are either based on or synthesized from natural compounds from different species. Not only do these species save lives, they contribute to a booming pharmaceutical industry worth over $40 billion annually.[33] For example, the Pacific yew, a slow-growing tree found in the ancient forests of the Pacific Northwest, was historically considered a "trash" tree and was burned after clear cutting. A substance in its bark – taxol – was identified as one of the most promising treatments for ovarian and breast cancer. More than 3 million American heart disease sufferers would find their lives cut short within 72 hours without digitalis, a drug derived from the purple foxglove. The American Cancer Research Institute identified 3,000 plants that contain active ingredients against cancer; 70 of them originate in the tropics.[34]

More than half of all medicines today can be traced to wild organisms. Chemicals from higher plants are the sole ingredients in one-quarter of all prescriptions written in the United States each year. Many of the organic compounds currently being used can be obtained more cheaply from their natural sources. However, despite their rich rewards, only 5 per cent of the world's plant species have been investigated for their pharmaceutical applications.[35] From the tropical rosy periwinkle one can extract vincristine, a drug that is a critical component in the treatment of pediatric leukemia and Hodgkin's disease. Chitin, the substance in the shell of crabs and other crustaceans, is being used to produce a suture material that promotes the healing process. Dolstatin 10, derived from the sea hare, a fist-sized shell-less mollusk, has been hailed as a new anti-cancer drug.

Genetic diversity is also of vital importance in breeding crops and livestock.[36] Each species is of potential value to humans, as are healthy ecosystems. The global collection of genes, species, habitats, and ecosystems provides for human needs and is essential for human survival in the future. The loss of biodiversity with regard to crop species cultigens has potentially disastrous implications for global food security and economic stability.[37] Crop breeders need a diversity of varieties in order to breed new varieties that resist evolving pests and diseases. Many crops have been "rescued" with genetic material from wild relatives or traditional varieties. Biodiversity represents a living library of options for adapting to local and global change.

Even so, amplified by economic-structural factors such as patterns of rapid urbanization, only a small percentage of humankind has any direct, daily, active engagement with other species of animals and plants in their habitats (other than domesticated species or pets). Few people are in the position to validate from personal experience that mass extinction of species and progressive ecocide ultimately run counter to their own long-term interests. But even among those individuals who recognize the danger, only a few are in a position to translate environmental insights into meaningful and effective measures.

Public policies that halt ecocide must be connected to a comprehensive effort to rethink historical, social, and economic models in which culture is celebrated in a Promethean manner and nature is devalued as "passive." Contrary to conventional wisdom, most of the value and sustenance in the world economy does *not* come from pulling things out of nature, but from the proper functioning of rivers, forests, and fields.[38] Humans are only part of the evolutionary process. Nonetheless, we have taken on a major role in shaping its future course. We are cutting the cords of nature's safety net even as we depend on it to support the world's growing population.

ETIOLOGY OF ECOCIDE

The first critical step in the etiology of the present disaster occurred some 60,000 years ago. The defining marker of ecocide was the development of language and an unprecedented expanded human capacity for culture. These novel features of *Homo sapiens sapiens* allowed for the rise of the conscious intentionality that humans bring to their projects. Reflected in the vastly improved capacity for language, conscious intentionality led to an explosion of innovation – manifest in a proliferation of artifacts – at the end of the Pleistocene era some 35,000 to 50,000 years ago. The emergence of conscious intentionality made possible the extension of human biological evolution by cultural means – including the species-specific capacity for conscious adaptive or maladaptive changes in social organization. By about 13,000 BCE, this development path resulted in the human colonization of all continents with the grave consequence of the worldwide destruction of most of the existing megafauna.

The second critical step in the etiology of ecocide was the establishment of sedentary agriculture, culminating in the Neolithic revolution some 10,000 years ago. Anthropologist Mark Cohen explains it as an unintended consequence resulting from the extermination of megafauna, whereby mass extinction combined with climatic and demographic changes to produce the "food crisis in prehistory." It forced people to change their social organization wherever conditions such as a favorable climate, water, and fertile soil, and species that could be domesticated, were present.[39] As Jean-Jacques Rousseau noted as early as 1755, the transition to agriculture gave rise to what has long since become a series of fateful assumptions: first, human life requires strict hierarchy, the extensive division of labor, and social inequality. Second, improved modes of organization and technological innovation are capable of addressing human needs and wants. Third, *Homo sapiens sapiens* is entitled to dominate the natural order and this dominance can be achieved without costs.[40] These assumptions, stemming from the increasingly class-stratified and conflict-ridden social contexts of city-states emerging in Mesopotamia, Egypt, India, China, and Mesoamerica remain very much part of modern consciousness.

The third critical step in the etiology of ecocide was the rise of modernity, characterized by three related features: the increasing division of labor, the capitalist mode of production, and the emergence of the modern nation-state. Individual enterprise and commercial competition were promoted as the beneficial engines of progress and enlightenment.[41] Ideologically, this vision drew from Judeo-Christian interpretations of God giving the land to the industrious and rational in order to improve humanity. The "free market" was exalted as the natural and most efficient vehicle for the coordination of complex societies. The rational-legal nation-state was celebrated as the final form of political organization.[42] The exploitation of nature was universalized and commodified. In the end, the imperatives of late modernity produced the global framework in which ecocidal tendencies greatly accelerated. The loss of biodiversity is particularly felt in the global South.

CHAPTER OUTLINE

The five chapters of this book explore the critical milestones and turning points in human social evolution and associated changes of society–nature relations that led to the loss of biodiversity and progressive ecocide.

The beginning of the book introduces the reader to the problem and the general historical and sociological approach taken to explain the etiology of ecocide and mass extinction of species. Chapter 1, titled "The Human Odyssey: From Biological to Cultural Evolution," explores the turning points in human evolution that led to the emergence of culture and language as the defining marker of our species. It argues that, in order to understand how human-caused ecocide and mass extinction of species occurred, it is necessary to understand how and when the genus *Homo* reached the *sapiens* stage of evolution. The first major recorded ecological impact of the human species is explored with reference to the worldwide megafauna mass extinction of the late Quaternary. This chapter aims to show that the unique combination of biological attributes possessed by our species does not necessarily determine human social behavior, except to lay the foundation genetically for virtually unlimited variations of human behavior. In other words, "human nature" – the sum of biological attributes of our species – is analytically distinct from human behavior – the sum of social and cultural attributes of our species.

Chapter 2, titled "Problematic Society–Nature Relations before the Modern Era," explores the impact of pre-modern societies on the environment. The Neolithic transition to sedentary agriculture some 10,000 years ago is presented as another major turning point and milestone in human society–nature relations. It is explored as an unintended consequence of the megafauna extinction and climatological changes during the late Pleistocene. The implications of sedentary food production and domestication are discussed, and particular attention is given to the economic boom and ecological bust cycles – "ecological blunders" – of select societies in antiquity. Case studies include China, Mesopotamia, the ancient Greeks and Romans, the Chaco Anasazi, the Mayas, and the Easter Islanders. The purpose of the study is to explore articulations of ecological depredations in pre-modern societies as precursors in the etiology of modern ecocide.

Chapter 3, titled "The Modern Assault on Nature: The Making of Ecocide," provides a historical and sociological overview of the etiology of ecocide and mass extinction of species in the early modern era. The emergence of capitalism, the associated rise of scientific and technological thinking, and the increasing commercial assault on species are traced as a worldwide phenomenon. Three case studies are presented to illustrate the unprecedented ecological impact of humans in this new global social context: the over-exploitation and destruction of fur animals due to the commercial fur trade; the mass slaughter and near extermination of the North American bison; and the overexploitation of marine species due to the rise of industrial whaling. The acceleration of biodiversity loss in the modern era is explored as a movement from commercial overexploitation of species in the early modern era to large-scale habitat destruction in more recent times. The aim of the chapter is to illustrate and explain the globalization of environmental degradation and making of ecocide in the early modern era.

Chapter 4, titled "The Planet as Sacrifice Zone," explores the sociological processes that I call the "juggernaut of modernity," reflecting developments in the modern industrial era. The chapter opens with a discussion of the ecological and social implications of the enclosure of the commons as a global phenomenon. Nature in this new context is progressively reduced to an assortment of exploitable resources, all negotiated in the open marketplace. The global enclosure movement is analyzed as a guiding metaphor for understanding conflicts and contradictions generated in the modern era. The massive loss of biodiversity and the heightening of environmental degradation progressively turned the planet into a species sacrifice zone. The chapter focuses in particular on the role of the modern industrial war economy and the huge increase in human populations as causal parts of the global ecocidal predicament.

Chapter 5, titled "Ecocide and Globalization," analyzes the social and historical processes that account for the accelerating mass extinction and progressively ecocidal nature of the post-World War II era. I pay special attention to corporate-driven neoliberal forms of globalization, structural adjustment programs, and the ideological and institutional mechanisms by which related practices continue to be reproduced on a global scale. The chapter then sketches some countercurrents to globalism, in particular the movements for ecological democracy and attempts to envision an equitable global commons. In my view, the creation of ecological democracy is a practical and ethical imperative for a more socially just and ecologically sustainable planet. The book concludes with a final observation about what it means to live in an age of ecocide.

1 THE HUMAN ODYSSEY: FROM BIOLOGICAL TO CULTURAL EVOLUTION

Humanity is nature achieving self-consciousness. (Elisée Reclus, *L'Homme et la terre*)[1]

Without some knowledge of evolution one cannot hope to arrive at a true picture of human destiny. (Julian Huxley, *Evolution in Action*)[2]

BEGINNINGS

Life is planetary exuberance, a solar phenomenon. It is the transmutation of Earth's air, water, and sun into cells. In order to appreciate the severe consequences of ecocide, it is necessary to examine the tenuous nature of biological evolution. Briefly, how did planetary life, including human life, evolve? Astrophysicists tell us that our universe came into being some 20 billion years ago with a "Big Bang." Five billion years ago, our planet formed. Life on earth evolved around 1 billion years later. Single-celled organisms found by paleontologists in ancient rocks suggest that simple life was flourishing as early as 3.8 billion years ago. These first biological organisms were able to use the water vapor, nitrogen, methane, and ammonia that made up the Earth's atmosphere for food and energy, probably through a process facilitated or catalyzed by metals such as iron and magnesium. Between 3.3 and 3.5 billion years ago, blue-green algae appeared. These single-celled organisms had the ability to convert energy from the sun into chemical energy through photosynthesis using hydrogen sulfide. Between 1 and 2 billion years ago, some bacteria adapted the use of water in photosynthesis. Oxygen, which is released as a byproduct of H_2O photosynthesis, gradually appeared in Earth's atmosphere, and in turn facilitated the evolution and diversification of subsequent life forms. For billions of years, simple creatures like plankton, bacteria, and algae ruled the Earth. Then, suddenly, around 550 million years ago, the evolution of life accelerated, gaining in diversity and complexity.[3]

Born into the most biodiversity-rich evolutionary epoch in Earth's history, and genetically nearly indistinguishable from the bonobo chimpanzee, the earliest human predecessors make their appearance on the evolutionary scene in southern and central Africa around 4.5 million to 6 million years ago, belonging to the genus *Aridipecus* and *Australopithecus*.[4] These first human ancestors *Homo habilis* and *Homo erectus*, emerging in Africa merely some 2.5 million and 1.6 million years ago, succeed these ape-like early hominid creatures. Equipped with a unique combination of biological and social attributes, hominids developed an upright stance with bipedal locomotion, prehensile hands with opposable thumbs, stereoscopic binocular vision, audio and vocal tract anatomy, and the largest and most complex brain of any hitherto existing primate. The biological creation of the ancestors of modern humans is a remarkable achievement of evolution by natural selection, which brought with it a new dimension to the evolutionary process – cultural evolution.

Any attempt to explain modern ecocide is necessarily based upon some historical understanding of how and when *Homo* reached the so-called *sapiens* stage of evolution. The purpose of this chapter is to show that the unique combination of biological attributes possessed by our species does not necessarily determine human social behavior except that it lays the foundation genetically for virtually unlimited variations of human behavior. In other words, "human nature" – the sum of biological attributes of our species – is analytically distinct from human behavior – the sum of social and cultural attributes of our species. My central argument is that, with regard to *Homo sapiens*, natural selection alone is not a sufficient explanation for the evolution of our species into *Homo esophagus colossus*. As some evolutionary biologists emphasize, biological evolution in the case of humans works to preserve and augment the human ability to create, absorb, and transmit culture. This surely does not mean, however, that we employ our cultural capacity only for the benefit of life on Earth. We obviously don't, and my underlying question is precisely how to explain this ultimately self-destructive tendency. As we will see in later chapters of this study, it is only when human biology combined with particular social organizational and institutional behavior that the danger arose of creating a global ecocide.[5]

The narrative connecting the subsections of this chapter is very much constituted by a number of historical questions, important for our understanding of the causal social mechanisms of ecocide. For example, when and how did primates begin to acquire complex language and culture? When did humans develop the social and technological capacities for both habitat creation and destruction? Why did agriculture and fixed settlements replace nomadic hunting, scavenging, and gathering? Of course, a discerning response to these questions must be predicated upon a clear understanding of what we mean by "human beings."

It seems obvious that humans are unlike other animals. Molecular genetic studies have shown that we continue to share 98.3 per cent of our DNA with the bonobo chimpanzee, our closest ape relative in the animal kingdom.[6] The total genetic distance between chimpanzees and us is even smaller than the distance between such closely related bird species as North American red-eyed and white-eyed vireos.[7] Bonobo chimpanzees have rudimentary elements of culture[8] and a sense of self that entails basic linguistic elements.

They are far more vocal than any other of the great apes and much more peaceful than other chimps. They have never been seen to kill their own relatives and they possess the ability to read basic emotive stages on the faces of their kind, a feature shared by all higher primates. They pat each other on the hand to show affection or kiss or embrace each other; they have menopause, develop lifelong friendships, and grieve for their dead babies by carrying them for days or weeks; they have the ability to perform simple calculations and they communicate using signs. Bonobos are also the most sexual of all primates, a distinctive behavioral feature that Dutch ape researcher Frans de Waal sees as an important social function, not as a mere means of species reproduction.[9]

However, even between humans and the great apes lies a seemingly unbridgeable gulf when we separate ourselves from such "animals." This difference is reflected in our socio-cultural capacities that have been responsible both for our present biological success and failures. Humans are learning creatures with a massively expanded capacity for culture. Flexibility and learning are the hallmarks of human biological and cultural evolution.[10] We talk, write, and build complex machines. We fundamentally depend on complex social organization and institutions for survival. For example, we cook, steam, fry, roast, smoke, pickle, or freeze our foods, and we brew alcoholic and non-alcoholic beverages in myriad variations. Most of us wear clothes, enjoy art, and many believe in some form of religion. We are scattered across the entire planet, and we have even begun to explore outer space.

FROM TREE SHREWS TO PRIMATES

Primates have their earliest evolutionary ancestry in tree-shrew-sized proto-mammals that evolved in the shadow of dinosaurs about 200 million years ago. Only after their disappearance 65 million years ago did our (then barely larger than rat sized) mammalian ancestors slowly begin to evolve into primates. In the early part of their evolutionary history, most primates looked much like the modern-day tarsiers or lemurs. About 40 million years ago, however, new primate families arose: the monkeys. As the world cooled and forests increasingly gave way to grasslands, monkeys had to either adapt or disappear. They did disappear from North America, and they became largely restricted to tropical forest environments in equatorial regions. Africa was largely forested as late as about 15 million years ago, but soon afterward, its great tropical forests shrank. Between 5 million and 7 million years ago, the global climate gradually became warmer and drier. Forested areas began receding, making way for grassland savanna environments. Northern Africa gradually grew drier, while regions to the east and south became dominated by a savanna landscape. Indeed, the Mediterranean completely dried out 6 million years ago, and a great drop in the sea level occurred during that period, lasting for about 1 million years.

Eventually, the African primates that would evolve into *Homo sapiens* were forced down from the trees and made the open savanna their home. From paleontological work carried out over the last two or three decades we know that primates occasionally began to walk upright in the African savanna 5 million to 6 million years ago.[11] It is important to emphasize the human "family tree" does not proceed in a straight line. Paleoanthropologists Ian Tattersall and Jeffrey Schwarz have presented convincing evidence that over 15 different species of humans or hominids have existed over the 6-million-year sojourn of the hominid family – and many of these species have existed simultaneously. Even at the beginning of the human sojourn there were at least three separate species of these early now-extinct ancestors.[12] Thus, the diversity of extinct humans – and the consecutive number of hominid species – is much broader than many scholars have thought it to be.[13]

The earliest hominids were chimp-sized creatures that lived in the Ethiopian forests between 5 million to 6 million years ago. These earliest hominids were essentially tree-dwelling creatures, but they had developed an upright posture; its arms and shoulders, as well as its relatively small brain, show that it was still living a semi-arboreal life. In all likelihood, our early ancestors spent much of the daylight foraging on the ground in open semi-woodlands, seldom straying far from the safety of the trees. And, like modern chimpanzees, they still retreated to the trees at night. Slow and occasionally walking upright in an awkward gait, they would have been at the mercy of a variety of predators had they remained on the ground in the darkness.

At first blush, bipedalism just does not make sense. For our early ancestors, it would have been slower than walking on all fours, while requiring the same amount of energy. Several theories have been suggested to explain bipedalism and upright gait. Anthropologists Henry McHenry and Peter Rodman, for example, champion the idea that climate variation was part of the picture after all. When Africa dried out, they argue, the change left patches of forest widely spaced between open savannah. The first hominids lived mostly in these forest refuges but could not find enough food in any one place. Learning to walk on two legs helped them travel long distances overground to the next woodsy patch.[14] Paleontologist Maeve Leakey, a member of the world's most famous fossil-hunting family, suspects the change in climate rewarded bipedalism, since a drier climate made for more grassland. Our ancestors, she argues, spent much of their time not in dense forests or on the savannah but in an environment with some trees, dense shrubbery, and a bit of grass. If a creature has to move into open country with grasslands and bushes, foraging on fruits and berries on low bushes, there must have been a strong advantage to being able to reach higher.[15] A third explanation is offered by anthropologist Owen Lovejoy. He speculates that males who were best at walking upright would get more sex, leading to more offspring with those genetic advantages. Over time, female apes would choose to mate only with those males who brought them food — presumably the ones who were best adapted for upright walking.[16] In short, there exist a variety of explanations for bipedalism.

Physical evidence for these distant relatives of our biological family was found in the Olduvai Gorge in Tanzania and consisted of the fossil relics of about 20 individuals. Subsequently, further physical evidence discovered at a site near Lake Rudolf in northern Kenya and later discoveries at Olduvai added to our sparse understanding of the activities of our ancestors. For example, we know that they used elementary tools, a notable step in the control of the environment. Tools found in Kenya are the oldest such evidence and consist of stones crudely fashioned by striking flakes off pebbles to give them a sharp edge. Frequently, the pebbles seem to have been transported purposefully and selectively from one site to another where they were further refined. In short, the conscious creation of tool implements had begun. About 1 million years ago, simple pebble choppers of the same type spread all over the Africa and Eurasia.[17]

In discussing the evolution of archaic humans, we must bear in mind that the period of 2.5 million years before the present marks the onset of the great climatic perturbations that culminated in the ice ages. For anthropologists, this period is characterized by a great diversification of hominids. Geological evidence indicates that massive layers of ice began to cover Antarctica. Eventually, great ice regions formed at the North Pole as well. Ice sheets began to move across North America, Europe, and Asia, until as much as a third of the area of those continents was buried under ice 1 mile thick. Huge glaciers descended from the great north–south mountain chains as well, and the Earth's climate changed rapidly. Rain forests dried, deserts became wet, and species began to die. Apart from the obvious effects on animals and plants, the severe cold locked up large quantities of sea water in ice sheets: sea levels fell, establishing a land connection between Britain and Europe, as well as between Indonesia and the Asiatic mainland. Periods of intense cold were interrupted by interglacial, usually warm, periods that produced heavy tropical rainfalls.

Climate change, in short, also figured in important ways in the evolution of other hominids. According to paleoecologist Stephen Stanley, the Isthmus of Panama was lifted up by movement of the planet's tectonic plates 2.5 million years ago. A new land bridge connected North and South America for the first time, causing major disruptions in the flow of the ocean currents and leading to a major ice age. In Africa, the climate grew cooler and drier, and the formerly large areas of open woodland began to disappear, forcing our ancestors to become ground dwellers. The results were predictable. *Australopithecus* died out, along with a large number of other species that were adapted to the woodlands. While the crisis eliminated many of the early hominids, it also freed them from an evolutionary dead end. As a result, at least one hominid group rapidly evolved into something new – an upright, large-brained hominid that could survive on the ground. From that group derived the genus *Homo* and, eventually, modern humans.[18]

In Africa, several new species of land-dwelling hominids appeared. Growing in stature, these creatures developed a distinct taste for meat.[19] One of the most important stages of human evolution was reached: the appearance of *Homo erectus* ("man that walks upright"). So far, the earliest remains of a *Homo erectus* specimen are estimated to be about 1.5 million years old. Many signs point to its African origin and hence to its spread through Europe and Asia some half a million to a million years ago. Apart from fossils, a special tool used by *Homo erectus* helps us to plot the distribution of the new species by defining areas into which *Homo erectus* did not spread as well as those into which he did. This is the so-called stone "hand-axe," whose use may well have been mainly as a scraper and dresser of other materials.[20] There can be no doubt of the historical success of *Homo erectus*, but the ecological impact of *Homo erectus* or other species through predation was comparatively minimal.[21]

Nevertheless, *Homo erectus* had an unprecedented capacity to manipulate the environment. Beside hand-axes, *Homo erectus* left the earliest surviving traces of constructed dwellings – huts, sometimes 50 feet long, built of branches, with stone-slab or skin floors – the earliest worked wood, the first wooden spear, and the earliest container, a wooden bowl. The existence of such artifacts hints strongly at a new level of mentality, at a preformed conception of the objects and perhaps an idea of process. Some researchers have argued that *Homo erectus'* early form of conscious intentionality might be viewed as the first budding of an aesthetic sense.[22] *Homo erectus* – considered the proverbial missing link between apes and humans – was a bipedal creature, a social omnivore who could hunt and kill prey. Like modern humans, *Homo erectus* bore helpless young, and thus infant care was essential and the infant's brain could continue to expand during the first year. However, it has been firmly established that *Homo erectus* possessed only rudimentary linguistic abilities.[23]

FIRE USE AND DIETARY CHANGES

The most remarkable innovation of *Homo erectus* is undoubtedly the use of extrasomatic energy, in order to accomplish human ends outside the body. The most important source of extrasomatic energy, by far, is fire.[24] Hominid hunter-gatherers and scavengers used the somatic energy of fire for the provision of warmth, the clearing of forests, the hunting of game, self-defense, and cooking. It has been estimated that the *per capita* use of extrasensory energy in the form of fire in early hunter-gatherer societies amounted roughly to the same quantity that flows through human organisms themselves as somatic energy.[25]

Learning to manage fire represented a remarkable technical and cultural advance for anatomically pre-modern hominids. It brought the possibility of warmth and light and therefore a double extension of the human environment into the cold and the dark. In physical terms, one obvious expression of this was the occupation of caves. Animals could now be driven out and kept out by fire. Technology could move forward: spears could be hardened in fires and cooking became possible, with indigestible substances such as seeds becoming sources of food, and distasteful or bitter plants becoming edible. And cooking must have stimulated attention to the variety and availability of plant life.

Moreover, the use of fire influenced the evolution of reflexive mentality. Around the hearths after dark gathered a community almost certainly aware of itself as a small and meaningful unit against a chaotic and unfriendly background. Language, of whose specific origins we still know little, would have been shaped by a new kind of group intercourse. At some point, fire-bearers and fire specialists appeared – beings of awesome and mysterious importance, on whom depended life and death. They carried and guarded the great liberating tool, and the need to guard it must sometimes have made them masters. Fire began to break up the iron rigidity of night and day and even the discipline of the seasons. It thus carried further the breakdown of the great objective natural rhythms that bound *Homo erectus*. Hominid behavior, as historian J.M. Roberts notes, now could be less routine and automatic.[26]

The harnessing of fire was also a prerequisite of big game hunting, another of the significant achievements of *Homo erectus*. Any meat eating was a great effort as game had to be followed and killed; hominids became dependent upon other species, including the megafauna, as a food source. Organized hunting provided concentrated protein and therefore released meat-eaters from their incessant nibbling on a variety of vegetarian products. Although elephants, giraffes, and buffalo were among the species whose meat was consumed at Olduvai, scholars emphasize that the bones of smaller animals vastly preponderated in the archaeological excavations.[27]

Still, the ecological impact of anatomically pre-modern hominids such as *Homo erectus* appears to have remained small. Complex stone tools that appear at the end of the Pleistocene were still unknown to both *Homo erectus* and early *Homo sapiens* about 130,000 years ago. There were no bone tools, no ropes to make nets, and no fishhooks. All the early stone tools may have been held directly in the hand; they show no signs of having been mounted on other materials for increased leverage, as we mount steel axe blades on wooden handles.[28]

The routine argument in the past has been that we have been successful big game hunters for a long time. The supposed evidence comes mainly from three archaeological sites occupied around half a million years ago: a cave at Zhoukoudian near Peking containing bones and tools of *Homo erectus* ("Peking Man") and bones of many animals, and two non-cave (open-air) sites at Torralba and Ambrona in Spain, with stone tools plus bones of elephants and other large animals. It is usually assumed that the same people who left the tools killed the animals brought their carcasses to the site and ate them there. However, all three sites also have hyena bones and fecal remains, which means hyena could equally well have been the hunters. The bones at the Spanish sites in particular appear to have come from a collection of scavenged, water-washed, trampled carcasses such as one can find around African water holes today, rather than from human hunters' camps. While early humans ate some meat, we do not know how much meat they ate, or whether they got it by hunting or scavenging. Not until much later, around 100,000 years ago, do we have good evidence about human hunting skills, and it's clear that humans even then were still very inefficient big game hunters.[29]

The archaeological evidence of big game hunting or its effectiveness in *Homo erectus* and early archaic *Homo sapiens* populations remains scarce, and, given the absence of elaborate technologies in protohuman species, their impact on other species and ecologies must have been negligible. Nevertheless, this is an epoch of crucial significance with respect to human evolution. Culture and tradition were slowly replacing the importance of genetic mutations and natural selection as the primary source of change among hominids. The group with the best memories of effective adaptive techniques would be favored in the evolutionary process.

Selection also favored those hominid groups whose members had not only good memory but also the increasing power to reflect upon it in language. We know still very little about the history of language. Modern types of language only appeared with anatomically modern humans, long after *Homo erectus* disappeared.[30] What system of communication early hominids possessed may never be known, but one plausible suggestion is that they began by breaking up calls akin to those of other animals into particular sounds capable of rearrangement. This process would create the possibility of different messages and thus constitute the root of grammar. Once more, there can be no separation of social and biological processes. Better vision, an increased physical ability to deal with the world as a set of discrete objects, and the use of tools developed simultaneously with the refinement of linguistic capacities over a long period. Ultimately, these factors combined to contribute to the further extension of abstract conceptualization.

THE RISE OF MODERN HUMANS

The meteoric ascent of early humans a quarter of a million years ago in East Africa had little ecological impact. Still, early *Homo sapiens* did look rather different from earlier *Homo erectus*. Climatologically, the era was characterized by shifting ice age conditions.

The precise origin of *Homo sapiens* is not yet fully resolved. Two different models have been proposed. According to the first, called the "multiregional hypothesis," the distribution of anatomical traits in modern human populations in different regions was inherited from local populations of *Homo erectus* and intermediate "archaic" forms. This model holds that all modern humans evolved in parallel from earlier populations in Africa, Europe, and Asia, with some genetic intermixing among these regions. Support for this view comes from the similarity of certain minor anatomical structures in modern human populations and preceding populations of *Homo erectus* in the same regions.

The second model proposes that a small, relatively isolated population of early humans evolved into modern *Homo sapiens*, and that this population succeeded in spreading across Africa, Europe, and Asia, displacing and eventually replacing all other early human populations. This scenario views the variation among modern populations as a recent phenomenon. Part of the evidence to support this theory comes from molecular biology, especially studies of the diversity and mutation rate of nuclear DNA and mitochondrial DNA in living human cells. From these studies, an approximate time of divergence from the common ancestor of all modern human populations can be calculated. This research has typically yielded dates around 200,000 years ago. Molecular methods tend to point to an African origin for all modern humans, implying that the ancestral population of all living people migrated from Africa to other parts of the world. Hence the name of this model, the "Out of Africa hypothesis." Which model is correct has not been conclusively determined. However, it appears that the earliest fossil evidence for anatomically modern humans in Africa is about 130,000 years old, and there is evidence that modern humans lived in the Near East sometime before 90,000 BCE. During this period, two closely related protohuman forms – Cro-Magnon and *Homo sapiens neanderthalensis* – had emerged out of Africa and coexisted in various places for some time.[31]

Neanderthals are generally considered a subspecies of *Homo sapiens*. Their fossil remains were first found in Neanderthal, Germany, in 1856. The so-called classic Neanderthals were robust and had a large, thick skull, a sloping forehead, and a chinless jaw. Their brains were somewhat larger than those of most modern humans, but this is probably due to their greater bulk. Neanderthals were the first humans to adapt to cold climates, and their body proportions are similar to those of modern cold-adapted peoples: short and solid, with short limbs. Men averaged about 168 cm (5 feet 6 inches) in height. Their bones are thick and heavy, and show signs of powerful muscle attachments. Neanderthals would have been extraordinarily strong by modern standards, and their skeletons show that they endured hard lives. The Neanderthals' culture included stone tools, fire, and cave shelters. They were formidable hunters and are the first people known to have buried their dead.

Neanderthals were initially thought to have been limited to Western Europe, but their remains have also been discovered in Morocco, in the northern Sahara, at Mount Carmel in Israel and elsewhere in the Near East and Iran. This highly successful species has also been traced to Central Asia and China, where the earliest specimens go back as far as 230,000 BCE. Neanderthals must have been creatures adapted to the cold, but they did not migrate any farther north than Northern Europe, the Ukraine, and the Caspian Sea. The first penetration of Siberia and the Arctic was left to later, fully modern humans. The Neanderthals were meat-eaters and they fashioned quite advanced tools. They buried their dead and worshiped bears. Their burial rituals show that they were capable of thinking abstractly and that they communicated with each other in a highly developed way.[32]

Neanderthals were the first species to leave undisputed evidence of regular use of fire, and they were the real inventors of cooking, a cultural practice that became much more ambitious with the appearance of the Cro-Magnon.[33] Food probably was scarce, because it was difficult to hunt in frozen environments. The spring and autumn were particularly difficult times for hunters because of the difficulty of moving over the slushy snow. There is no evidence that the Neanderthals knew of snowshoes or skis to help them cross the snow. Around their winter caves archaeologists found the remains of large mammals, such as cave bears, ibex, and rhinoceros, as well as many smaller animals such as birds and snails. This suggests that Neanderthals were pressed for food and would eat virtually anything.

In such conditions, cooking takes on a particularly important function. After all, advanced methods of cooking make supplies go further. Evidence suggests that Neanderthals developed quite sophisticated cooking techniques that helped keep alive members of the group who were apparently either very elderly or lifelong invalids. Probably they were able to prepare soup-like food dishes by cooking meat within prepared animal skins, an early practice in many parts of the world that was still used in Ireland as late as the sixteenth century.[34] Perhaps because they lacked the physiological capacity for advanced speech, Neanderthals perished some 30,000 years ago.[35]

Cro-Magnons first appeared in Europe some 10,000 to 40,000 years ago. They are one of the best-known examples of early modern human populations. Remains of this most recent late-Stone Age ancestor were first found in France in 1868 and then throughout other parts of Europe and Western Asia. Their skeletal remains show a few small differences from modern humans, but they are still generally classified as the earliest known representatives of the same subspecies, *Homo sapiens sapiens*. Cro-Magnon features differed significantly from Neanderthal, including a high cranium, a broad and upright face, and a cranial capacity about the same as that of modern humans but smaller than that of Neanderthals; the males were as tall as 6 feet. Their geographic origin is still unknown.

Cro-Magnon culture was markedly more sophisticated than Neanderthal. They used a wider variety of raw materials such as bone and antler to produce novel implements for making clothing, engraving, and sculpting. They produced fine artwork in the form of decorated tools, beads, ivory carvings of humans and animals, shell jewelry, clay figurines, musical instruments, and polychrome cave paintings of exceptional vitality. Cro-Magnons were without any doubt skilled hunters of game of all sizes, exploiting their environment to the limits. Fish and bird bones are present at various Cro-Magnon sites, and it is clear that these people regularly exploited the migratory movements of other vertebrates to their advantage. Campsites were often quite elaborate, and the making of complex fire hearths and the use of heated stones to heat up water in skin-lined pits show that cooking had become much more sophisticated.[36] They constructed shelters similar to tents in which several families lived. They also created sophisticated weapons such as spear tips, harpoons, and animal traps. They even created a crude lunar calendar to keep track of the seasonal movements of game animals. In essence, Cro-Magnons were nomadic hunters and gatherers with a sophisticated material culture.

Like all other hominids, *Homo sapiens* originally evolved in – and migrated out of – Africa. Our species had already reached Israel some 100,000 years ago, and 40,000 years later had conquered the whole of Europe and the Asian continent. Humans entered Australia as early as 60,000 years ago, and, some 13,000 years ago, climatic variations enabled them to enter the Americas, the last uninhabited continent. Crossing from Asia somewhere in the region of what is now the Bering Strait, they moved southward for thousands of years as they followed large animals. Equipped with unprecedentedly expanded cultural and linguistic capacities, *Homo sapiens*' ecological record and impact on fellow species were unlike those of other hominids. A new order of conscious intentionality expressed itself in the creation of new cultural and technological means to control and change the environment.

A few thousand years sufficed to produce art, trade, mythology, pearls,[37] sculpture, cave painting, and a plenitude of tools. Representative art appeared in the form of clay and stone sculptures, along with simple but often strikingly beautiful paintings on cave walls. Ice age archaeological remains from 30,000 years ago in Sungir, Russia, show people bedecked in woven garments decorated with thousands of ivory beads. Like contemporary humans, these people had art, religion, and a social structure.[38] In some parts of Europe, an archaic form of literacy became established as early as 32,000 years ago, as illustrated by the Chauvet cave paintings in the Rhone Valley in France.[39] This important form of expression and communication consisted of scratches on ornaments, pieces of bone and clay, and stones. The scratches were arranged through repeated motifs into descriptive classes such as meanders, fishlike images, and parallel lines. All these inventions appeared near the end of the anatomical evolution of *Homo sapiens*.[40] Moreover, during this period, increases in the technical sophistication of tools, flute-like instruments carved of sawbones, appear in the archaeological record of humans. For more than a million years, the universal repertoire of tools of hominids had been stone scrapers and simple blades. Now, spear points made of mammoth tusks, drilled fox and wolf teeth, and deer horn and bone needles for sewing on leather appear in large numbers.

THE MEGAFAUNA EXTINCTION

We have seen above that from approximately 100,000 to 50,000 years ago, anatomically modern humans were confined to Africa, plus the warmer areas of Europe and Asia. After that, our species underwent a massive geographical expansion that took us to Australia and New Guinea around 50,000 to 60,000 years ago, then to Siberia and most of North and South America, and finally to most of the world's oceanic islands only around 2000 BCE.[41] We also underwent a massive expansion in numbers, from perhaps a few million people 50,000 years ago to about 150 million around 2000 BCE.[42]

Our capacity as a social species to transform nature dramatically increased during this early phase in human social evolution due to the development of language and the associated expansion of our symbolic and social organizational capacities. This crucial turning point in the biological and social evolution of the human species essentially marks the continuation of biological evolution by cultural means. It is precisely at this conjuncture that humans begin to pose a global environmental risk. The cultural and geographic implications of this profound evolutionary transformation are first manifest in what Jared Diamond refers to as the "Great Leap Forward" – that is, our species' terrestrial expansion to and colonization of all major ecosystems, and the accelerated evolution of technological and artistic innovations.[43] This was soon followed by the development of gardening and farming, and, 10,000 years ago, by the emergence of sedentary agriculture. The invention of metallurgy and use of metal tools arose around 6,000 years ago.

Human–animal relationships changed dramatically. Surpassing our archaic predecessors anatomically and behaviorally, modern humans of the late Pleistocene acquired unprecedented skill as big game hunters.[44] The impressive testimony of these changes is manifest in the leitmotivs of the flourishing cave art. Leopards and hyenas, hitherto unknown in Paleolithic cave art, were depicted in conjunction with images of lions, rhinos, bears, owls, mammoths, bison, ice-age horses, Irish elk, and extinct deer with giant antlers.[45]

Homo sapiens developed a keen understanding of their new prey. As a food historian suggests, big game hunting was history's first, but not last, "war on subsistence."[46] New technologies and socially expanded intelligence became manifest in newly created material culture and ingeniously designed weaponry for catching prey including such instruments as harpoons, fish gorges, bows and arrows, spear throwers, pit traps, dead falls, blals, and arrow poison.[47] These devices and more tightly coordinated hunting techniques must have considerably increased food supplies. *Homo sapiens* were now socially coordinated enough to collectively dismember and carry away the remains of large mammals such as great mastodons and woolly mammoths. They were able to encircle great numbers of animals and drive them over a cliff. This enormous wastefulness in hunting was to become a chief characteristic of anatomically and behaviorally modern humans' attitude toward their food supplies.

Indeed, the extermination of the megafauna in the late Pleistocene should be taken as the first indicator of the greatly expanded transformative capacities of modern humans on the planet's species and ecosystems.[48] The term "megafauna" refers mainly to large herbivores such as mammoths, mastodons, huge ground sloths, cave bears, and woolly rhinoceros, as well as the carnivores that fed on them, such as dire wolves and saber-toothed cats. This pre-industrial form of ecocide represents a prelude to what was to evolve, under the aegis of the modern industrial era, into a collectively species-threatening pattern of global ecocide. The human-induced megafauna extinctions of the late Quaternary occurred in many different parts of the world, and involved at least 200 genera.[49]

For example, at Solutre, France, at the bottom of a cliff used by ice-age big game hunters to massacre stampeding animals, one can find a vast accumulation of bones estimated to contain the remains of more than 100,000 horses.[50] Even allowing for the relatively vast time period of the Paleolithic or Old Stone Age, it seems obvious that these ancient hunters killed more game than was necessary.[51] In the Pacific Northwest, pre-modern people created elaborate devices to drive herds of white-tailed deer into enclosures in the forest where they were slaughtered. Native American people have been recorded to have burned forests to force out elk and deer, creating gusts of hot wind, soot, and smoke powerful enough to make temperate October days feel like mid-summer. On the Great Plains, some tribes drove bison over cliffs, creating heaps of fur and meat far greater than their needs. Mounds of remains, discovered by archaeologists at the foot of cliffs, show that the animals were left to rot.[52] There is also evidence from bones that before *Bison antiquus* became extinct, the species suffered stress, which may well have been caused by overhunting.

The megafauna mass extinction of the late Quaternary is now generally acknowledged by paleontologists and physical anthropologists to have occurred largely without the impact of global catastrophes such as sudden climatic change.[53] In most cases, the megafauna extinctions began shortly after the first arrival of prehistoric humans. If we compare the number of genera of large mammals lost on the various continents, we find that Australia lost 94 per cent, North America 73 per cent, Europe 29 per cent, and Africa south of the Sahara 5 per cent.[54] The first humans encountered animals that had evolved in the absence of human predators, and the animals were probably easily vanquished. Therefore, the most plausible explanation is that these extinctions were caused over the course of centuries and millennia by over-exploitation of relatively few, but growing numbers of big game hunters. Let us examine these extinctions in several geographical regions.

In Africa, early humans were not as carnivorous as their descendants in other parts of the world were. However, it is now well documented that more recent accelerated extinctions in Africa did coincide with the rise of advanced, early anatomically and behaviorally modern human Stone Age hunting cultures. Africa lost its giant buffalo, giant wildebeest, and the hipparion, a giant horse. Although Africa still has more large animals than any other place on Earth, even there, the megafauna that we see today is only about 70 per cent of the genera that were present in mid-Pleistocene. About 50 genera disappeared about 40,000 years ago.[55]

In Eurasia, there is good evidence that the megafauna extinctions occurred a few thousand years earlier, with most animals becoming extinct about 12,000 to 14,000 years ago.[56] Late Pleistocene megafauna in Europe

Included the woolly mammoth, woolly rhinoceros, musk ox, giant deer (the "Irish elk"), bear, bison, and the cave lion. Many of these species became completely extinct. In the case of extinction patterns in Southern Europe, it has been pointed out that all the large fauna of the Mediterranean disappeared soon after human arrival between 4,000 and 10,000 years ago. Most scholars agree that the megafauna extinctions in Europe were mainly due to "the over-extension of human hunting after major changes had taken place in the prey population."[57]

The arrival of humans in Australia resulted in the extinction of most of the large animals on this continent. Australia lost all of its very large mammals, including marsupial mammals much larger than present ones, such as giant wombats as big as grizzly bears and giant kangaroos. Lost, too, were Australia's giant snakes and reptiles, and half of its large flightless birds.[58] About 85 per cent of the Australian animals weighing more than 100 pounds disappeared.[59] Humans burned vast areas of the outback, a practice that proved to be extremely destructive for what was then already a rather fragile and dry environment.[60] According to paleobiologist Tim Flannery, Australia's original inhabitants were the world's first group to over-exploit their environmental resources. Australian aborigines eliminated 95 per cent of their continent's large mammals by about 20,000 BCE, long before the onset of the most recent ice age.[61]

On the islands of Aotearoa (New Zealand), the situation was only nominally different. Here, large flightless birds dominated the megafauna and anthropogenic extinction of species is a much more recent affair, beginning about 1,200 years ago. Again, humans were clearly responsible.[62] But not only birds such as the giant Moa, flightless wrens and small petrels suffered range reductions or extinctions in the prehistoric era. Other affected species included sea mammals, reptiles, amphibians, insects, and, to a lesser extent, fish, molluscs, and crustacea.[63] The zoological impoverishment of the region followed soon after, after a second wave of social colonization, with European whaling and sealing leading to widespread environmental degradation from the North Island to the furthermost South.

Of all continents, the megafauna mass extinction data are clearest for North America, where 70 species (95 per cent of the megafauna) disappeared about 11,000 to 14,000 years ago. This is exactly the time when North America was colonized by humans, and their arrival and skill as hunters at that time are documented by the appearance of artifacts.[64] In some cases, accurate dating methods have shown that certain species became extinct at exactly the times that humans arrived.[65] Giant ground sloths and mountain goats in the Grand Canyon both went extinct 11,100 years ago, the same time that human hunters arrived. The mammals that disappeared in North and South America included all of the following: mammoths, mastodons, various kinds of horses, tapirs, camels, four-horned antelopes, ground sloths, peccaries, giant beavers, dire wolves, giant jaguars, and saber-toothed tigers.[66] The carnivores on the list were probably not hunted directly, but, as they were dependent on the large herbivores for food, they followed them to extinction. South America was also colonized by humans about 11,000 years ago, and since that time it has lost 80 per cent of its genera of large mammals, including ground sloths, horses, and mastodons.[67]

In the Pacific islands there is no reasonable doubt that the arrival of humans caused megafauna and, in particular, bird extinctions.[68] For example, archaeologist team Storrs Olson and Helen James argued that of the 68 endemic Hawaiian birds, 44 became extinct before they could be recorded by ornithologists.[69] The coincidence of timing of extinction with first human arrival is equally convincing for Madagascar and for the Caribbean.[70] Madagascar has yielded subfossil bones of giant lemurs and elephant birds and cow-sized hippos. The island is believed to have been settled by humans only recently, around 500 CE, and all these species were apparently extinct by the time that Europeans began describing Madagascar's animals in the seventeenth century. In the case of the Caribbean, it is important to note that, until first human colonization, as early as 7,000 years ago, Cuba and the other islands that constitute the Greater Antilles were home to a number of mammals found nowhere else. In Cuba they ranged in size from the island's behemoth, a ground-living sloth, estimated at 400 pounds, to monkeys[71] as large as any living in the forests of Brazil today. Among the other large vertebrates were enormous, flightless owls, giant tortoises, and monk seals. Except for a few fragments, this part of the megafauna is gone.[72] No one has ever tried to guess the number of plants, invertebrates, and lizards exterminated by prehistoric human habitat destruction.[73]

Still, the impact of our species on late Pleistocene ecosystems was rather small in many ways, compared to our cataclysmic social ecological impact in the modern era. Calculations suggest that a mere 20,000 humans lived in France around 30,000 BCE in Neanderthal times. The pre-European population of the Americas during this period has been estimated at something less than 1 million, and the human population of the Australasian continent was probably between 300,000 and 600,000.[74] All in all, there were not more than 5 million to 10 million humans in the whole world. The evolutionary playground or setting and locale of *Homo sapiens* during the Old Stone Age, in one scholar's description, was "a human desert swarming with game."[75] People still predominantly lived by hunting and foraging, but a lot of land was needed to support a tribal group or clan or family.

The progressively detrimental impact of *Homo sapiens* and the global expansion into previously uninhabited habitats is, therefore, historically a very recent and unprecedented phenomenon. Before moving into a more elaborate discussion of humanity's more recent ecocidal activities, I wish to re-emphasize the pivotal role of language in the evolutionary odyssey of humans.

THE PIVOTAL ROLE OF LANGUAGE

Language is central to our historical understanding of the cultural, social, and ecological developments of the past 50,000 years. The capacity for speech, progressively enhanced only relatively recently, produced a huge change in the behavior of our species. With language, it took only a few seconds to communicate a big game hunter's message: "Turn sharp right at the fourth tree and drive the male antelope, moa, or mastodon toward the reddish boulder, where I'll hide to spear it." Without language, that message could not be communicated at all. Without language, two protohumans would be incapable of brainstorming together about how to devise better tools, or about what a cave painting might mean. Without the enhanced representational repertory of language, people would have difficulty thinking for themselves how to devise a better tool. The "Great Leap Forward" in the cultural evolution of human species took place as soon as the mutations for altered tongue and larynx (and pharynx) anatomy arose.[76] And, as Jared Diamond adds, "it must have taken humans thousands of years to perfect the structure of word order and case endings and tenses and to develop vocabulary."[77]

The evolutionary expansion of human communication capacities is intricately interwoven with the eventual global spread and terrestrial colonization of the planet. Humanity was fully modern in anatomy, behavior, and language by 40,000 years ago.[78] Until then, human culture had developed at a snail's pace for millions of years. That pace was dictated by the slow nature of genetic change. In the last 40,000 years, however, there has been far more cultural evolution than in the millions of years before.

Language is the key to understanding human history and our species' capacities. Language enabled people to store precise representations of the world in their minds, allowing them to encode and process information far more sufficiently than can any other animal. Without language, human beings would never have undertaken the great leap forward in cultural development and global terrestrial expansion.[79] Our capacity for language provided the foundation for both social reflexivity and our transformative capacities in social organization. As linguist Derek Bickerton notes, no other species has ever revolutionized its social organization in the midst of its evolutionary journey. The role of language was crucial.[80]

To be sure, humans are animals and everything we do is both constrained and enabled in some sense by our biology. However, culture enormously expanded the range of these possibilities. As philosopher Stephen Toulmin states, "culture has the power to impose itself on nature from within."[81] People are in a sense both part of nature and apart from nature. This paradox underlies the history of our civilization and our dreams of progress and protection of the planet. Human societies change most drastically by cultural evolution, not merely as a result of biological alteration. For example, there is no evidence for biological change in brain size or structure since *Homo sapiens* appeared in the fossil record more than 50,000 years ago.

Human cultural evolution is the greatest transformative force that our planet has experienced since its crust solidified nearly 4 billion years ago. Biological evolution continues in our species, but, compared with cultural evolution, it is incomparably slow and its impact upon the history of *Homo sapiens* has been small.[82] Cultural evolution can proceed so quickly because it operates not by the inheritance of acquired characteristics, but through learning. Whatever one generation learns, it can pass to the next through writing, instruction, inculcation, ritual, tradition, and a host of methods that humans have developed to assure cultural continuity. Biological evolution, on the other hand, is an indirect process: genetic variation must first be available to construct an advantageous feature, and natural selection must then preserve it. Since genetic variation arises at random, the biological process works slowly. Cultural evolution is not only rapid, it is also readily reversible because its products are not coded in our genes.[83]

Hence, culture and language have enormously expanded the range of human possibilities. By means of our uniquely expanded biological capacity for culture, *Homo sapiens* acquired the awesome power to impose itself on nature from within. But this power is a double-edged sword: it both creates and destroys. Ecocide constitutes the destructive dimension of cultural evolution.

2 PROBLEMATIC SOCIETY–NATURE RELATIONS BEFORE THE MODERN ERA

I am committed to this enterprise: to climb the mountain to cut down the cedar, and leave behind me an enduring name. (Gilgamesh, *The Epic of Gilgamesh, King of Uruk in Mesopotamia, c.* 3000 BCE)[1]

We are the absolute masters of that which the earth produces. We enjoy the mountains and the plains, the rivers are ours. We sow the seed and plant the trees. We fertilize the earth ... we stop, direct, and turn the rivers, in short, by our hands we endeavor, by our various operations in this world, to make, as it were, another nature. (Cicero, *c.* 106–43 BCE, Roman statesman and writer, describing the Roman world-view)[2]

THE NEOLITHIC REVOLUTION[3]

The transition from hunting-gathering and scavenging to agricultural production of some 10,000 BCE is undoubtedly one of the major events in human history, an event which has been revolutionary in the sense that it entailed radical changes in people's relationship to nature and among themselves.[4] This transformation, known as the Neolithic revolution, was actually comprised of many revolutions, taking place in different times and places.[5] For at least 99 per cent of the duration of their existence, members of the omnivorous genus *Homo* had lived by hunting and gathering. This nomadic way of life, supplemented by scavenging, was presumably also shared by earlier hominids. Living in bands of well under 100 members, pre-neolithic societies had comparably low population density with fewer than two persons per square mile.[6] At their own low level of material needs and wants, our hunter-gatherer and forager ancestors lived a decent life of original affluence.[7] Although they had few material possessions, which are heavy and hampered mobility, they enjoyed exceptional abundance and leisure.[8] As can be judged from anthropological findings, they were well nourished, and probably spent relatively few working hours to secure their subsistence.[9] One hunter-gatherer could feed four or five people; thus, he was as "efficient" as an American farmer in 1870 or a French one in 1938, though he needed much more space.[10] Prehistoric people shared with each other the means of life, and would surely have been shocked at the modern idea that food represents a commodity to be bought and sold on the free market.

This mode of subsistence procurement represents an excellent system as long as the climate is warm enough and as long as the world remains a thinly populated place. However, given a number of changing climatic and social factors, the existential framework of the species changed, resulting in gradual demographic and geographic expansion. During this process of expansion, human societies depleted their local and regional natural environments, and were forced to change their mode of existence.[11] Sedentary and intensified forms of agriculture emerged in part as a response to wildlife scarcity.[12] This revolution in food procurement generally followed the collapse of the big-game hunting cultures in northern Europe and the Americas, initiating what is generally known as the Mesolithic period or "Middle Stone Age," during which people obtained necessary protein from fish, shellfish, and forest deer.

In the Middle East, where the age of the big-game hunters had ended much earlier than in the Northern Hemisphere, the pattern of food procurement became even more diversified. People turned from hunting giant wild cattle and red deer to preying on smaller species such as sheep, goats, and antelopes, and paying increasing attention to fish, crab, shellfish, birds, and snails. The expansion of human food procurement systems to marine ecosystems is thus a very recent historical occurrence.[13] Moreover, Neolithic humans selectively collected acorns, pistachios, and other nuts, wild legumes, and wild grains, a practice that would eventually lead to more conscious forms of agriculture.[14]

The general historical trend in the Late and Middle Stone Age has been from abundance to scarcity of big game animals, with humans hunting ever further down the food chain.[15] This led not only to an intensification of efforts on the part of hunters and incipient agriculturists, but also to reduced biodiversity on our planet.[16] At the same time, I must emphasize that the beginning of sedentary modes of food production – the intensified domestication of plants and animals – was a momentous occurrence in human prehistory. Imagine, 10,000 years ago almost all human societies lived by hunting and gathering; 8,000 years later, hunter-gatherer societies were a distinct minority.[17] These new subsistence strategies of the Neolithic resulted in more stable food supply, but only at the cost of greater energy expenditure.

There are several theories about the origins of sedentary food production. One suggests that human population pressure was an important factor, forcing people to turn to agriculture only when there was no other alternative.[18] The transition from gathering to cultivation of root crops may have been almost unconscious, for many tubers are easy to grow. Cutting off the top and burying it, for example, can result in the germination of the African yam. Hunter-gatherer bands familiar with such plants cultivated them to supplement food supplies only in times of shortage. After tens of thousand years of digging up wild edible roots with wooden sticks, it would have been an easy step to use the same stick for planting seeds.[19]

Early animal domestication may have been a similar step. Several types of animals amenable to taming – including dogs, goats, sheep, and wild oxen

– were widely distributed throughout the Old World during the Upper Pleistocene.[20] In the case of dogs, the process probably began at least 12,000 years ago. It is not difficult to imagine how an alliance between humans and canids may have originated. At the end of the Pleistocene ice age, people and canids were competing for the same food. A particularly placid or submissive canid pup scavenging around a human camp might have survived to adulthood accepting the human group as its pack.[21] Domestic animals constituted the original "slaves," upon which the ownership of other living beings was subsequently based.

By taking up sedentary food growing, people began to alter the biosphere in ways that, in the long run, would prove much more far reaching than megafauna extinction and just as irreversible.[22] A contemporary observer could not have perceived the destructive potential of small groups of people settling on one place to cultivate species of plants that would come to be known as crops. The original enterprise of food domestication was small in scale and not always successful.[23] By the time large-scale civilizations flourished, extensive tracts of natural systems in temperate and subtropical regions of Europe, Asia, and the Americas had been replaced by human-directed systems, sometimes called agro-ecosystems.[24] Within the last two millennia, large portions of Africa and the Americas have similarly been converted to agriculture. The introduction of food procurement systems based on farming has been followed by loss of biodiversity through processes of intensified predation and habitat displacement.[25]

Environmental sociologist Marina Fischer-Kowalsky refers to this new social setting and dynamic as a form of "terrestrial colonization."[26] This novel social adaptation to transformed landscape following the mass extinction of the late Pleistocene and early Holocene was accompanied by increasingly hierarchical forms of social life. Ancient civilizations finally emerged out of early city-states and institutionalized forms of inequality and violence. The exploitation of domesticated animal power and the domestication of plants species are at the root of "civilization," playing an important role in subsequent population growth and geographic distribution of humans.[27] Animals pulled the plow, animals carried produce to market, and animals provided a protein-rich complement to a grain-based diet. Although wind power was utilized to carry cargo by water, fire remained nonetheless the most important source of extrasomatic energy. It made possible the creation of artifacts we normally associate with the civilizing process such as ceramics and metal objects.[28]

Division of labor emerged with craft specialization, and so did individual ownership. Pre-modern class structures arose during the past six millennia, based primarily on slave and tributary relationships. Urbanization became a significant factor in providing the cultural bonds necessary for complex societies. Tradition and kinship remained very important in this context, but we must also recognize the beginnings of a social process that slowly separated the institutional spheres of politics and economics.

The emergence of upper classes with privileged access to food and administrational powers is a characteristic of Neolithic adaptations that have stayed with us to this very day. There is good reason for believing that sedentary agriculture led to the development of private property and "work" as distinct categories of life, separate from other spheres and activities. As political philosopher Hannah Arendt points out, the word for "tilling" later came to mean "laboring" and this association implies servitude on the part of humans. Sedentary agriculture, as is well documented, also provided the historical framework for social stratification, violence toward women and animals, and the destruction of wilderness areas.[29] As the European philosophers, beginning with Jean-Jacques Rousseau clearly saw, the Neolithic rise of private property in both its pre-modern and modern forms amounted to mutual slavery:[30]

The first man, who, having enclosed a piece of ground, bethought himself saying "*this is mine*" and found people simple enough to believe him, was the real founder of civil society. From how many crimes, wars, and murders, from how many horrors and misfortunes might not any one have saved mankind by sullying up the stakes, or filling up the ditch, and crying to his fellows: "Beware of listening to this imposter; you are undone if you once forget that the fruits of the Earth belong to us all, and the Earth itself to nobody."[31]

The social condition described by Rousseau began historically with the Neolithic revolution. However, the real disaster in the making was much broader than even Rousseau imagined. The problem was not merely intrasocial in nature but, most important, also interspecies. In short, the adaptations in human food-procurement systems strengthened human ecocidal tendencies, a development reflected in all major civilizations of the pre-modern era.

ECOLOGICAL BLUNDERS OF ANTIQUITY

Human history is replete with accounts of the early ecocidal activities of great empires such as Babylonia, Egypt, Greece, Rome, ancient China, and Maya, all of which destroyed their forests and the fertility of their topsoil, and killed off much of the original fauna through a combination of "their linear thinking and their insatiable drives for material wealth."[32] The most flourishing lands of antiquity were sites of civilizations that remained powerful and wealthy for great periods of time, but they are now among the poorest regions of the world.[33] Large parts of these areas are now barren deserts, most of the ancient cities are abandoned, and local people now often have little historical awareness of their social and ecological past. To be sure, civil strife, warfare, famine, and disease contributed to the demise of ancient civilizations, but one of the primary causes of their decline was the depletion of their biological resources. Exhaustion of water and climate change dealt, in many instances, the final blow.

The demographically and ecologically stressed Mayan civilization, for example, collapsed following a brief dry period, and Mesopotamian civilizations disappeared after their systems of irrigation were destroyed by the Mongols. As many as 3,700 years ago Sumerian cities were deserted by their populations because the irrigated soil that had produced the world's first agricultural surpluses had become saline and waterlogged. But these environments had begun to degenerate long before this final disaster.[34]

Further east, philosopher Meng Tze (Mencius) was acutely aware of environmental degradation in Asia, warning the rulers of imperial China of the unsustainable use of resources and land.[35] A section of Meng Tze's book *Mencius* describes the environmental degradation of Ox Mountain, a geographical feature close to his residence:

There was a time when the trees were luxuriant on the Ox Mountain. As it is on the outskirts of a great metropolis, the trees are constantly lopped by axes. Is it a wonder that they are no longer fine? With the respite they get in the day and in the night, and the moistening by the rain and dew, there is certainly no lack of new shoots coming out, but then the cattle and sheep come to graze upon the mountain. That is why it is as bald as it is. People, seeing only its baldness, tend to think that it had never had any trees. But can this possibly be the nature of the mountain? ... When the trees are lopped day after day, is it any wonder that they are no longer fine? ... Hence, given the right nourishment there is nothing that will not grow, and deprived of it there is nothing that will not wither away.[36]

Unfortunately, Meng Tze's advice was not heeded. A major force in decimation of both plants and wildlife during Meng Tze's life was the expansion of agriculture into undeveloped land. In the two centuries before, the ox-drawn iron plowshare had come into use, supplementing human labor with a major new source of energy. Advanced agricultural tools and methods of fertilizing had been invented. Thus, it is not surprising that Meng Tze spoke of the increase of cultivated land at the expense of the wild. His contemporary, the legalist Shang Yang, urged rulers to take measures to cultivate wasteland as a deliberate policy to increase population. Rulers often ordered the cultivation of wasteland to increase agricultural production and combat famine.[37] Moreover, they frequently squandered their states' resources on ostentatious new palaces, tombs, self-indulgence, and, above all, military campaigns. From the fourth century BCE onward, economic crises and famines plagued China.[38] Deforestation and associated patterns of ecological degradation, such as soil erosion and biodiversity loss, were key factors in the destruction of early Chinese civilization. Based on classical literary texts such as *The Book of Poetry*,[39] several Chinese environmental historians have traced the etiology of the decline of this once-productive ecosystem.[40] This part of China had emerged as the civilizational cradle of China partly because of its climatic and agricultural virtues. The land was predominantly flat, and covered by one of the most fertile and loose soils to be found on earth. Hence, it was easily turned into farmland and the available crops flourished. Today, the Loess Plateau has become one of the poorest regions in the country, its residents poorly educated in comparison to other parts of China.

The most important three reasons for deforestation in Chinese history, according to geographer Jin-qi Fang, are land use for agriculture and road repair, firewood collection, and construction of houses.[41] Because of the thick layer of loess in the plateau, soil erosion initially did not affect fertility. But it did turn the flat surface of the plateau into a landscape of hills and ravines, thus making water conservation ever more difficult.[42] Originally, there were at least 27 large lakes in the region, all of which have disappeared today.[43] According to geographer S.Y. Tian, a great number of springs also dried up within a few centuries. As a result, ground water tables fell to unprecedented levels.[44] The severe soil erosion led to an increasing flooding of the Yellow River. Clearing the river's irrigation channels and tributaries of heavy sediment became an increasingly difficult task, requiring hundreds of thousands of laborers. Ultimately, the scope of these undertakings devoured enormous economic and social resources that could have been put to better use elsewhere. George Borgstrom, a widely respected authority on world food problems, has ranked the deforestation of China's uplands as one of the three worst ecological blunders in history, closely followed by the destruction of Mediterranean vegetation by livestock, which left once fertile lands eroded and impoverished, and, in modern times, the disaster of the Dust Bowl in the southern Great Plains of the United States in the early twentieth century.[45]

Living in the same century as Meng Tze but almost 5,000 miles to the west, Plato used remarkably similar language to describe the deforestation of the hills of Attica. Trees were cut down for fuel and the soil eroded because of overgrazing. In ancient Rome, too, there were warnings about crop failure and soil erosion as a result of wasteful animal husbandry practices. The history of pre-modern societies is thus full of examples of social collapse brought on by a combination of localized forms of ecocide and political conflicts. These early societies were especially vulnerable to regional degradations of the environment that occurred often because of human interventions designed to extract a larger surplus product. Such accumulative practices raised the specter of ecological collapse whenever the extremely narrow limits of sustainable production were crossed.

As we will see in this chapter, the first large civilizations of antiquity were made up of societies that had moved beyond a low level of agricultural development and arrived at a stage characterized by state structures and class hierarchies. Control over the land and its produce was exercised through the extraction of tribute from peasant producers by economic means. Ancient Egypt, feudal Europe, and the Aztec Empire are all examples of such tributary societies. Although the timing of its emergence varied across the globe, the tributary form of production was part of a universal path of development.[46] It constituted the most developed type of economic formation over the course of the more than 5,000 years that stretched from the emergence of Sumer in Mesopotamia, the first literate society in world history, to the rise of capitalism in the late fifteenth century.

1. The Mesopotamians, Southwest Asia: 3700 BCE to 1600 BCE

The first known case of ecological collapse of a civilization occurred during the Bronze Age, several thousand years ago, in the valley of the Tigris and Euphrates rivers in what is now Iraq and part of Syria. This Mesopotamian culture, known as the Sumerian civilization (3500–1600 BCE), was one of the first human societies to have produced what some archaeologists refer to as "big tradition."[47] Mesopotamian civilizations utterly depended on irrigation from the two great rivers. With an assured water supply and the invention of the plow, early sedentary agriculturists could grow much more food than they needed for their own kin group. The availability of surplus grain opened the door not only to the development of cities but, in time, also to social inequality and stratification.[48] However, the exploitation of land and people by means of irrigation led to disastrous results over the centuries: dams and canals silted up, and the land became infertile due to waterlogging and salt accumulation. Even today's societies, with the most modern technologies, find it difficult to prevent such deterioration of the soil, as farmers from California to the Aral Sea know only too well.

Settlement in the Tigris–Euphrates valley dates back to at least 6000 BCE. Like the Egyptian civilizations later, first settlers in Mesopotamia developed a hunting economy, supplemented by harvesting of wild grain.[49] Indeed, the culinary achievements of the Mesopotamians and the Egyptians are very similar. Cheese, butter, and buttermilk enriched the palate of the upper classes in both societies. The great gardens of Babylonia, some of them raised on terraces, harbored many of the vegetables that were later to become staples of the Western kitchen, such as carrots and fennel. Though quantities of Mesopotamia's river fish were not equal to those of Egypt, there were plenty of birds to be caught in the marshes between the rivers. Long-tailed sheep grazed in the fertile marshes between the rivers of Babylon. Grapevines grew abundantly, but the consumption of wine was usually limited to the rich.[50]

The oldest city in the region was Eridu, suggested to have been the original site of the biblical "Garden of Eden." Other city-states, including Ur, Lagash, Nippur, and Kish, were also founded around the same time. These early city-states were ruled by priest-kings who were elected by the people. Later changes in the constellation of social power allowed rulers to assume the throne through birthright. In short, early Mesopotamian civilization was a loose collection of agricultural city-states that developed into centrally controlled empires.

Mesopotamia lacked protection by natural boundaries, encouraging constant migrations of semi-nomadic Indo-European people from areas located between the Black and the Caspian seas. The influence of neighboring countries and regions was great. Military expeditions occurred frequently after the harvest, when the farmers were available as soldiers, and thus warfare contributed to the movements of people in this region. These constant migrations led to cultural diffusion, a process whereby an existing society adopts the traits of another and the two eventually merge to produce a new culture.[51] Mesopotamia's cultural heritage, religious-mythological systems, and scientific accomplishments are of great significance to the formation of the modern world. Sumerians invented the wheel in about 3700 BCE; they also developed a system of mathematics based on the number 60 that became the basis for measuring time in the modern world. They formulated the earliest concepts of algebra and geometry, and their system of weights and measures was used in the ancient world until the Roman period. In addition, the Sumerians mapped many of the celestial constellations in great detail.

Social historian Karl Wittfogel coined the term "oriental despotism" when describing the tributary and slave-based mode of production in Mesopotamia.[52] The upper classes consisted of nobles, priests, government officials, and warriors. Merchants ranked below, followed by traders and artisans, who made up a thin middle or "freeman" class. Serfs, slaves, and subsistence farmers made up the majority of the population and were responsible for all manual labor, most importantly the agricultural labor necessary for building and cleaning the irrigation canals, dams, and reservoirs. The high yields produced by Mesopotamia's irrigation-based agricultural system made possible the freeing of up to 10 per cent of the population from agricultural work.[53]

Ownership of agricultural land was divided among private individuals, temples, and the state.[54] Typically, peasants rented land from a temple, which controlled it on behalf of the gods. Land under temple or state ownership was cultivated, and a portion of the produce was provided as remuneration to the different classes of state personnel.[55] An important later development in Mesopotamian city-states was the extension of the concept of ownership to apply not only to land, material objects, and animals but also to other humans. The practice of slavery was pervasive. Most slaves were captured during raids into the hills flanking the Tigris and Euphrates valleys, but others were taken in the frequent scuffles between the cities.[56] The concept of ownership even came to apply to the members of a married man's family. In Ur, for example, a man could avoid bankruptcy – that is, he could avoid being sold into slavery – by selling his wife or children in order to pay off his debts.[57]

The combination of organized and hierarchical exploitation of human labor and a productive environment over time created a distinctive and potent mode of production which transformed nature so completely that almost nothing remains today of the original alluvial landscape.[58] Nature, in other words, became progressively "humanized." With the Pleistocene megafauna largely extinct, the social formation of early Mesopotamian civilizations led to the extermination of much of what remained of larger mammal species and birds. As usual, the first species to go were those that represented a threat to existence for early humans in the newly colonized territories, for example, large predators such as lions and tigers. Impressions taken from southern Mesopotamian cylinder seals show a hairy image of the deity Endiku, Gilgamesh's companion, holding up two vanquished lions.[59] Other wildlife once flourishing in the region, but now regionally extinct, include the rhinoceros, the elephant, and some species of antelope.

Mesopotamia's irrigated agriculture became increasingly vulnerable, as it was critically dependent upon a "good flood." Waters cresting too high would destroy settlements and grain stores; waters too low would yield poor crops, food shortages, and famine. Moreover, there always lurked the threat of river and irrigation channels changing their course, which occurred periodically as sedimentation raised the height of diversion canals. Most of the water carried by the Tigris and Euphrates never reached the sea, but evaporated in the flat alluvial marshlands. This led to another problem, that of salinization. As river water evaporated, it left behind its mineral contents, leading to increasingly saline soils. These soils reduced crop yields and eventually made cultivation impossible.[60]

Initially, Mesopotamians kept salinization at bay by alternating years of cultivation and allowing weeds to grow during the fallow years. The practice lowered the level of saline groundwater. However, it did not provide a permanent solution. Carbonized grains and textual sources prove that Mesopotamians were forced to switch from the cultivation of wheat to more salt-tolerant barley. Eventually even barley yields declined, and there is frequent mention in Sumerian texts of land abandonment due to salinization. The resulting agro-ecological crisis was instrumental in bringing about a switch in political power from southern to northern Mesopotamia, where saline soils were less prevalent.[61]

In discussing the decline of agricultural production at the end of the Ur III period in 2100 BCE, Robert Adams concludes that an abundance of water provided by an expanded canal system led to over-irrigation, shortened fallow cycles, and salinization.[62] However, the eventual collapse of Mesopotamian civilization was not simply a matter of the inherent instability of hydraulic irrigation agriculture. Extensive deforestation over millennia in a region known for its extensive cedar forests contributed to an ecological degradation that was heightened by the ecological impoverishment stemming from the secondary effects of soil erosion and siltation. The precise effect of deforestation on the biodiversity and flourishing of wildlife of the region remains unclear, but it is reasonable to suggest that it must have been extensive.

Deforestation has a long history in a region once known for its extensive cedar forests. Archaeological work indicates that deforestation was a factor in the collapse of an even earlier sedentary Neolithic community in the Near East region. According to Anne and Paul Ehrlich, Mesopotamian civilization was heading for an ecological catastrophe from the outset.[63] For example, there is ample evidence that deforestation caused the collapse of communities in the southern Levant as early as 6000 BCE.[64] Environmental historian

Richard Grove observes that this collapse "may well have been related not to climatic change but to the effect of human activities on the environment." In particular, trees were used as fuel for the production of lime plaster as a building material. Environmental damage in this instance was also exacerbated by herds of goats eating seedlings, saplings, and shrubs, thereby preventing re-growth and exposing steep hillsides to rapid soil erosion.[65]

Militarization and imperial endeavors also played a major role in the destruction of Mesopotamia's primary forests. The progressive deforestation of the region was closely correlated with the steadily growing capacity of Mesopotamian states to consume timber both for construction and for military purposes, in particular for naval shipbuilding.[66] Massive quantities of wood were also required for commercial shipbuilding, bronze and pottery manufacturing, and building construction, including palaces and administrative offices.[67] Thus, environmental sociologist Sing Chew argues that the crisis in agricultural productivity has to be understood within a wider context of the political-economic and ecological relations of Mesopotamia. The stratified centers of Mesopotamia pursued intensive socioeconomic activities to produce a surplus for domestic consumption as well as for export (in the form of grains and woolen textiles) to the Persian Gulf and beyond. The scale and intensity of economic activity required extensive deforestation, maximal utilization of agriculture, and animal husbandry. Furthermore, with a state structure requiring tax payments, the farmers were required to produce increasing surpluses to meet the reproductive needs of the system.[68] Population increases led to state policies of establishing new towns that engaged in a range of economic practices requiring heightened utilization of resources. The end result was an intensification of agricultural production that pushed the ecological sustainability of the lands to the limit.[69]

Around 4,400 years ago, the city-states of ancient Sumer faced an unsettling dilemma. Farmland was gradually accumulating salt, the byproduct of evaporating irrigation water. Almost imperceptibly, the salt began to poison the rich soil, and over time harvests tapered off. Until 2400 BCE, Sumerians had managed the problem of dwindling yields by cultivating new land (reclamation-works), thereby producing the consistent food surpluses needed to support their armies and bureaucracies. But within a few centuries, they had reached the limits of agricultural expansion. The accumulating salts drove crop yields down more than 40 per cent, resulting in shrinking food reserves for an ever-increasing population. Sumerian agriculture effectively collapsed in 1600 BCE, causing this once glorious civilization to fade into obscurity.[70]

2. The Greeks, Mediterranean: 770 BCE to 30 BCE

The ancient Mediterranean is a paradigm of the abuse of natural resources in pre-modern Europe. Ecological mismanagement, combined with endemic warfare, military escapades, and conquest, was responsible for the deterioration of agriculture around the Mediterranean basin in the world of antiquity.[71] During the second half of the Holocene, there evolved a diverse range of Mediterranean cultures based on agriculture or pastoralism. Their hierarchical form of social relations changed relations of humans with their environment in several important ways. It meant, for example, that the maximization of economic output replaced the mix of social and economic goals that characterized communal peasant farming societies. Agricultural output was maximized by improving the productivity of existing farmland or by increasing the cultivated area. The latter led to clearance of woodland and draining of marshland but also included cultivation of marginal land that was susceptible to soil erosion and other forms of ecological degradation.

The advent of complex agricultural societies distanced and often weakened the link between people and nature. Nature became less the "habitat" for the farmer than a set of economic resources to be managed and manipulated by the dominant group.[72] This was particularly true of cultures where the ruling classes were urban-based, as in Greco-Roman antiquity. Indeed, the Greeks, and later the Romans, were not much more successful than the Sumerians in producing an ecologically sustainable civilization. When the Mesopotamian civilizations at the eastern end of the Fertile Crescent had faded, the Mediterranean basin was still a relatively well-watered land, mostly covered with thick forests. Corsica, for instance, had tall trees crowding its shores, their branches extending far enough to occasionally break the masts of the ships of the first settlers. Vast Mediterranean forests covered rich soils that would one day support the granaries of the Roman Empire.[73] However, the ecological abundance of this region proved to be rather short-lived. The ancient Greeks produced the first civilization of antiquity to inflict ecological damage to the Mediterranean landscape. The demographic and economic expansion of the Greek city-states led to the progressive destruction of rich pine and oak forests which satisfied the insatiable appetite for lumber, firewood, and charcoal. Moreover, the Greeks destroyed forests simply in order to create more pasture lands for their domesticated animals.[74]

The impact of Greek city-states (polis) like Athens on the natural environment produced environmental problems prefiguring many modern ones, including the destruction of ecosystems in the surrounding countryside. Athenian citizens had to make difficult decisions regarding land use and urban planning. Although democratic citizenship in Athens meant that small producers were to a great extent free of the extra-economic extractions to which direct producers in pre-capitalist societies have always been subject, for the most part the mobilization of labor in Greek society was based on an enslaved segment of the population, who, together with women, were excluded from democratic participation.[75] Different categories of land use and ownership were recognized, and specific laws and administrative arrangements were applied to them.

Athens had grown haphazardly around the majestic heights of the Acropolis. Streets were a jumble of narrow passages yielding only to the

Sacred Way, a wide ceremonial road, as well as to the open space of the
Agora, where trade and political affairs were conducted. Within the city walls
resided some 100,000 people, including a large number of resident aliens.
City-dwelling Athenians had little space, and Athens suffered from crowding,
noise, air and water pollution, the accumulation of wastes, plagues, and
other dangers to life and limb. No wonder Socrates preferred to hold his con-
versations with young Athenians along the tree-shaded banks of a stream
flowing outside the city.[76] But the effects of urbanization on the natural
environment were not limited to the city's immediate neighborhood, since
the city drew upon the resources of a large part of Greece and even more
distant lands such as Egypt and the Black Sea coast.[77]

Greek philosophers like Plato and Aristotle thought of the *polis* as a self-
sufficient unit, harboring all the natural resources needed for its population.
This vision of autonomy was never achieved in classical Athens, however.
A city could be self-sufficient only if it managed to establish a sustainable
mode of subsistence within its local ecosystems. Bent on expansion, the
leading political figures of Athens would not accept such spatial limitations
based on ecological imperatives. The economic needs of a militarily powerful
city could be met only by pushing beyond existing limits by means of trade
and conquest.[78]

Classical Greek city-states prefigured modern democracies in achieving
domestic pacification through imperialistic, expansionist policies toward
their neighbors. Such forms of imperialism have severe ecological consequences. Large-scale wars lead to wholesale destruction of nature due to
intensive utilization of resources to produce weapons and to mount the
military campaigns. In ancient Greece, the combination of military activity,
state building, and deforestation is even more evident than in Mesopotamia.
For example, the seemingly unending Peloponnesian War between Sparta
and Athens consumed large quantities of wood for the construction of
warships.[79] The result was the severe deforestation of mainland Greece and
Asia Minor.[80] Large areas of countryside were transformed into relatively
barren wastes, and there are indications that much-increased soil erosion
and flooding resulted.[81] These changes made a considerable impression on
contemporary observers, and particularly on Theophrastus of Eurasia,
Aristotle's biographer and a botanical gardener. Based on his observations
of the deterioration of local forests, Theophrastus developed a theory that
linked deforestation to the decline in rainfall which, he believed, was taking
place in Greece.[82] There is very little evidence, however, that Theophrastus'
remarkable theoretical innovation stimulated any serious government
restrictions on forest cutting.[83]

By the mid-fifth century BCE, the land surrounding Athens was largely
deforested. Erosion depleted the mountain soils, deposited silt along the
coastlines, and dried up many springs. The result was a declining agricultural production and a chronic shortage of wood and other forest products.[84]
Environmental historian Donald Hughes explains Athens' aggressive foreign

policy in this way:[85] Athenian diplomats sought advantageous timber deals in treaties with forested lands such as Macedonia. Groups of Athenian clerics or colonists were dispatched to the tree-bearing coasts of Chalcidice and Italy. Timber towns like Antadros were forced into the Athenian Empire, and the timber trade became an issue in conflicts with other maritime cities such as Corinth. As a major argument in favor of the ill-fated military expedition to Sicily, the Athenian general Alcibiades specifically mentioned access to the island's forests. By the end of antiquity Sicilian woodlands had been depleted. Thus, the decline of Athens can be correlated with its failure to maintain the forest ecosystem.

Regeneration of the Greek forests was made impossible by a combination of severe soil erosion and overgrazing by goats. These "horned locusts" proved to be engines of ecological destruction, wiping out all but the most resistant and least accessible vegetation. Goats have made a ruinous impact on much of the Earth, but the "goatscapes" they helped create in the Mediterranean basin are perhaps their greatest monument.[86] Plato seemed to understand what was happening to the land under the impact of human ecocidal activities: "What now remains compared with what then existed is like the skeleton of a sick man, all that fat and soft earth having wasted away, and only the barest framework of the land being left."[87]

The failure of the ancient Greeks to adapt their economy to existing ecosystems in a sustainable fashion turned out to be one of the important causes of their civilization's decline. Placing too great a demand on the available natural resources, Greek citizens failed to maintain the balance with their own environment that is necessary for the long-term survival of any human community. Ecological failure, as Hughes notes, interacted with social, political, and economic forces to ensure that classical Greek society would be altered beyond recognition in a process that represented in many respects a disastrous decline in the level of civilization.[88]

3. The Romans, Mediterranean: 500 BCE to 500 CE

The Romans were even less environmentally aware than the Greeks and showed scant concern for the ecological consequences of their activities. Like the Christian civilization that succeeded them, the Romans evinced a possessive view of our planet: it was the property of *Homo*, to be exploited for human purposes.[89] At the height of its power the Roman Empire was vast, stretching from the deserts of Africa to the borders of northern England. Over a quarter of the world's population lived under the rule of the Caesars. During the Roman Empire, too, deforestation caused by the Roman agricultural system spread from the hills of Galilee to the Taurus Mountains of Turkey to the Sierra Nevada of Spain.[90] The imperialism of Roman institutional culture prefigured the contemporary era of mass extinction. The study of Roman writings combined with scientific investigations of deposits of silt from erosion and ancient grains of pollen has led many social historians to conclude that environmental factors were important causes of the decay of Roman economy and society. The results of environmental deterioration are evident in the landscape; impressive Roman ruins are often surrounded by desolate environments.[91] Roman intellectuals variously took note of the degradations of their environment. Seneca, for example, remarked:

If we evaluate the benefits of nature by the depravity of those who misuse them, there is nothing we have received that does not hurt us. You will find nothing, even of obvious usefulness, such that it does not change over into its opposite through man's fault.[92]

Pliny the Elder, too, noted that human beings sometimes abused "Mother Earth," but he and most Romans saw the abuse simply as a failure of intelligent husbandry.[93] This attitude still dominates Western thinking about land use and management.

In Chapter 1, I indicated that late Paleolithic and early Neolithic peoples were determined hunters of big game, responsible for the extinction of large animals such as the lions of Greece and the pygmy hippos of Upper Egypt. But the Romans far outdid their predecessors in hunting for meat, skins, feathers, and ivory.[94] In addition, the Romans captured countless animals for use in gladiatorial games. They ransacked their empire for bears, lions, leopards, elephants, rhinos, hippos, and other live animals to be tormented and killed in public arenas until there were no more to be found.[95] The scale of these brutal entertainments, pitting animals against one another and against humans, is hard to grasp from a distance of two millennia. Emperor Titus dedicated the Colosseum with a three-month series of gladiatorial games in which 9,000 beasts were killed. The celebration of Emperor Trajan's conquest of Dacia (modern Romania) involved games in which 11,000 wild animals were slaughtered.[96]

However, these numbers indicate only a fraction of the real extent of the destruction. The poor conditions of capture, transport, and housing of these animals must have meant that for every animal that died entertaining the masses, dozens or even hundreds of others must have perished before reaching the arena. The Roman Empire was probably responsible for the greatest annihilation of large animals since the Pleistocene megafauna mass extinction.[97] Already in the first century CE, the empire had exhausted ivory supplies in northern Africa, having decimated local populations of elephants. Regions as remote as southeast Asia supplied ivory to the Romans.[98] While there is no clear evidence that any species of large animals was wiped out by the Romans, numerous populations were destroyed or decimated, and the ranges of many species were therefore severely destroyed or decimated.[99]

These extinctions also affected agriculture in unsuspected ways. B.D. Shaw, an expert on Roman North African history, observes:

The tens of thousands of animals purposefully hunted down for the gladiatorial games in the arena were, of course, a small proportion of the total that yielded to more mundane processes such as the systematic destruction of their habitat by the expansion of agricultural settlement. With each species that is extirpated, the closer the ecosystem verges upon collapse, so by hunting and capturing animals for slaughter in the arena, the Romans were weakening their economies in the long run.[100]

Non-agricultural industry in the Roman Empire was minuscule by contemporary standards, but it nonetheless resulted over time in an astonishingly widespread environmental legacy. The physical evidence of industry in antiquity is still visible in the Mediterranean landscape, such as the scars of ancient mining and quarrying. The demands on forests for timber and fuel for mining, smelting, metallurgy, and firing of ceramics, were a particularly destructive force in Roman antiquity, translating not merely in large-scale patterns of deforestation in the Mediterranean basin, but producing fantastic pre-modern patterns of pollution.[101] Lead pollution has been one of the best-documented instances of eco-toxic pollution in pre-industrial times – although it should be noted that the Romans were by no means the first people exposed to this predicament.[102] Analysis of the Greenland ice core shows a dramatic increase in lead levels between 500 BCE and 300 CE. These measurements reflect tropospheric pollution of the Northern Hemisphere caused by Greek and Roman lead and silver mining and smelting activities long before the Industrial Revolution.[103] These traces of lead in the Greenland ice core have provided scientific evidence that mining and smelting of lead first peaked during the Greco-Roman civilization before rising again in more recent times.

In addition, Mediterranean rivers were polluted by sewage, which seeped into the ground water and made drinking water unsafe, especially in Roman cities. The Roman *Cloaca Maxima*, or "main drain," discharged pollutants into the Tiber River that threatened not only those living downstream but the city itself – especially when the river flooded and untreated sewage spilled into the streets.[104] Typically, toilet and garbage pails were emptied out of windows, rotting into sludge so deep that, in places like Pompeii, stepping-stones were provided for pedestrians. Such wastes attracted vermin and provided breeding grounds for epidemics, such as the severe plagues during the reigns of emperors Marcus Aurelius and Justinian.[105]

Why did the Romans fail to maintain a sustainable balance with the Mediterranean ecosystem within which they lived? Hughes argues that the main reason lies in the general Roman attitude toward the natural world.[106] In the early days of the Republic, Romans considered nature to be the sacred space of the gods. They avoided actions that would anger their deities, such as killing deer in temple precincts, and tried to please the gods by planting trees. These practices contained some ecological wisdom, but, as the Republic grew, Roman religious practice tended to deteriorate into empty rituals that lost their intimate connections to natural processes. In the name of economic expediency, prominent citizens like Cato the Elder advised the gods through prayers before cutting down trees or turning sacred groves into agricultural farmland.[107]

During the days of the empire, Stoic and Epicurean philosophy prevailed, at least among the upper classes. Adherents of these views rejected the traditional gods as explanations for the world, even if they continued to make offerings on the official altars of the state. Rome had conquered the world and subdued the peoples of the Mediterranean. These thinkers did ask some questions that today would be termed ecological, but their answers were based on the doctrines of the particular schools to which they belonged, and were of limited application to practical environmental problems. It was simpler utilizing, for most part, human and animal power and, to some extent, non-polluting water power. However, even simple technologies dependent on wood and charcoal for energy often result in loss of biodiversity. Ironically, the technological achievements of the Romans that we admire most are usually the ones that were the most damaging to the environment.[108]

As in the case of Greek civilization, frequent warfare constituted a major threat to the environment. The well-known *Pax Romana* may have lasted for almost 200 years, but it was not uninterrupted and it did not end wars on the frontiers. The military anarchy of the third century CE followed close on its heels, with 50 years of warfare that left no province untouched. Taxes for military expenditures were collected mainly from farmers, and reduced their ability to invest in the production of crops. Military campaigns devastated the countryside, slaughtered farmers and their families, and requisitioned or destroyed crops and buildings. Army agents conscripted farmers, who often spent years fighting instead of caring for the land, inevitably neglecting terraces and irrigation works.[109] Roman generals frequently used deliberate "environmental warfare" that destroyed the enemy's natural resources and food supplies.[110]

Following a common socio-cultural pattern in other stratified civilizations that emerged in the wake of the Neolithic revolutions, Roman society prominently exhibited status- and prestige-driven patterns of conspicuous consumption. The lavish lifestyle of the upper classes was reflected in their fondness for food, both as gourmets (persons given to eating "fine" food) and as gourmands (persons who eat excessively). The Roman social ruling stratum developed a reputation for overeating, debauchery, and overindulgence.[111]

But with the over-expansion of the Roman Empire, problems with regard to the quantity and reliability of food supplies arose. Rome was predominately a grain-based empire, sustained largely by slave labor. Subject to diverse social-military, ecological, and climatic stresses, the main Roman grain supply areas moved over time from Egypt to Sicily, and then from Sicily to Morocco. Indeed, grain was so precious that Roman military camps were full of specially built granaries. They were well-constructed buildings with ample ventilation.

Growing food imports caused economic crises and contributed to the strains which led to the eventual decline of the Roman Empire. The import of spices and luxury articles from India and the colonies, for example, was very costly and was partly financed by the export of wine. Although Rome shipped large quantities of wine to India, they were not enough to settle the balance of payments. The remainder had to be paid in gold and silver. The outflow of gold to India resulted in a severe economic crisis. Roman emperors could no longer finance the customary free distribution of food. Unable to pay its soldiers, Rome was no longer capable of stopping the "barbarian incursions" in the north. Ultimately, the overextended and financially strapped empire collapsed.

Just as the Mesopotamians paid a high price for their inability to adjust cultural and social achievements to the existing ecological framework, so the Romans suffered for their shortsighted exploitation of the environment. The decline and fall of the Roman Empire was the consequence of a combination of factors including intra-social forms of exploitation (slavery); military and fiscal overextension; environmental degradation, including soil erosion and deforestation; and foreign invasions. All these variables contributed to the eventual eclipse of the empire.[112]

Based on exploitative and stratified social-ecological relations, Rome failed to adapt its economy to the environment in sustainable ways and placed an insupportable demand on the available natural resources. Thus, Rome failed to maintain the balance with nature that is necessary to the prosperity of a human community. The empire depleted the lands of the ancient Mediterranean world, and in so doing it undermined its own ability to survive.[113] The Romans left succeeding civilizations a chilling monument to their ecological folly: the fertile wetlands of North Africa that once supplied the empire's granaries had turned into deserts.[114]

4. The Chaco Anasazi, Northwestern New Mexico: 700 CE to 1300 CE

The ancient Anasazi civilization in the American southwest was a farming society that created one of the grandest regional and social political systems in prehistoric North America. "Anasazi" is a Navajo name that is usually, and romantically, translated as the "ancient ones," also "ancient strangers." A better translation, according to anthropologist team David Stuart and Susan Moczygemba-McKinsey, would be "ancestors of our enemies," a frank description of the social relationships that once prevailed between local Navajo bands and the village-dwelling farmers of the late prehistoric Southwest.[115] Generally, the Anasazi people lived for centuries on mesa tops. Later some of them moved to cliff dwellings with protective overhangs such as Colorado's Cliff Palace.

The earliest North American ancestors of the Anasazi were the Clovis hunters of some 10,000 to 5,000 years ago. As discussed in Chapter 1, these archaic ancestors had over-hunted the immense game animals of the later ice ages and contributed to their extinction.[116] The first great transformation leading to the Chaco Anasazi society occurred around 5000 BCE to 2000 BCE, when their Neolithic ancestors took up agriculture as an adaptive response to climate change, loss of big game animals, and population growth. This newly emerging mode of livelihood was based on more work, more stored food, greater sedentariness, and accelerating changes in technology.[117] These early ancestors grew in numbers and their cultural forms of knowledge expanded as well. Eventually, their success created the interconnected, open community of Chaco Anasazi.

At its height in the eleventh century, the Chaco Anasazi culture dominated 40,000 square miles of a scrubby, semi-arid region roughly the size of Scotland.[118] Anasazi civilization consisted of 10,000 to 20,000 farming hamlets and nearly a hundred spectacular district towns, called "great houses" or "pueblos," that integrated the surrounding farmsteads through economic and religious ties. Hundreds of formal roadways linked the population areas. Chaco Canyon, now a national park in New Mexico, was both the heart and soul of this domain. At the bottom of the canyon, Anasazi people built 650-room dwellings that were five stories high, 650 feet long, and 315 feet wide, making them the largest buildings ever erected in North America, only surpassed by steel skyscrapers in the late nineteenth century. It took the Anasazi farmers more than seven centuries to lay the agricultural, organizational, and technological groundwork for the creation of a flourishing civilization that lasted about 200 years and then collapsed in a span of only a few decades.[119] What happened to change the landscape so dramatically? Mounting archaeological evidence points to the Anasazi culture itself.[120]

Archaeologists have put together a convincing case of man-made environmental disasters engineered by pueblo-dwelling Anasazi Indians 800 years ago. The Anasazi, who lived in what is now New Mexico and Arizona, built an elaborate complex of roads, irrigation channels, and five-story stone and wooden beam pueblos, some containing as many as 800 rooms. All were abruptly abandoned around 1200 CE. Originally, Chaco Canyon was covered by pinyon pines and junipers. We know this from the fossilized remains of wood rat middens dated back to the period between 8000 BCE and 1200 CE. These ancient refuse heaps created by packrats living after 1200 CE have preserved an accurate historical record of a human-induced environmental disaster. The heaps contain leaves, twigs, and other odds and ends collected within a short distance of the rats' home burrows; glued together with the rats' urine and sheltered below ground from the weather, they provide a time capsule of local vegetation. The packrat heaps contain an abundance of pinyon needles and juniper twigs – until 1200 CE, that is. At that point, all traces of juniper and pinyon suddenly vanish.

At the peak of the Anasazi civilization, between 1075 and 1100 CE, people relied heavily on the use of timber to build their gigantic pueblos. As large portions of the surrounding area became denuded, Anasazi were forced to travel longer distances to procure timber. In addition, they cut down trees and bushes for firewood. Heavy use of timber for construction and firewood meant severe deforestation. The increase in population further placed a tremendous strain on the resources of the area. As the land could no longer support the population, Anasazi culture collapsed, together with the ecological habitat on which it was based.[121] Archaeologists had long suspected that the abandonment of Chaco Canyon was the result of climatic change. More recent research, however, makes it clear that the environmental disaster that befell the Anasazi was largely self-inflicted.[122] The social organization of this society played a key role, ultimately facilitating the collapse.

Chaco society was stratified into two major classes: the Chaco farmhands, living in farmsteads, and Chaco elites, living in big houses or pueblos. Daily life in the great houses contrasted dramatically with the customary realm of the farmstead. For most Chaco Anasazi, the daily regime was based on hard work and few luxuries.[123] Elites fared much better. Studies of burial populations indicated that both great-house males and females were on average 1.8 inches (4.6 cm) taller than their small-house cousins living as close as 500 to 1,000 yards away. A child's chances of living to age 5 were a sobering three times better in a great house than in the farmsteads within sight of it.[124]

Until 1090, the stratified system seemed to have worked well. But Chaco society carried within its hierarchy the seeds of its own destruction. Having quickly expanded into virtually every possible farmland location after 1000 CE, Anasazi farmers soon ran out of additional farmland.[125] The real calamity began with a combination of drought and a shortage of farmland in the face of burgeoning population in the 1080s and 1090s. A second major drought occurring 30 years later spelled the end of the Chaco civilization. The Anasazi, as Stuart points out, were "seduced by growth and power." They overreached and Chacoan society became so fragile that events that would have sparked few consequences in the first 8,000 years of southwestern prehistory – two droughts about 30 years apart – undid it completely.[126] How had they become so vulnerable?

One of the decisive causes for the Chaco Anasazi collapse, according to Stuart, was the elites' power and their formulaic response to the crisis: "roads, rituals, and houses."[127] In a stunning but final building frenzy, the Chacoan elites erected their grandest buildings in an effort to "pump up the economy." Many hundreds of thousands of ponderosa pines had been cut to support the roofs of the canyon's proliferating great houses. Immense logs, up to 30 feet long, were carried 20 to 30 miles from outlying forests. They were also carried on formal roads constructed after 1050. About 400 miles of roadway 12 to 30 feet wide have so far been documented.[128]

Over-planting and over-building were clearly two distinguishing features of the Chaco Anasazi response to the crisis. But apparently the Pueblo elite also failed to realize that, without the small farmers to produce corn, their society was not viable. That point was forcefully driven home by the second drought. Stuart sees in the late eleventh-century great houses of Chaco Canyon archaeological evidence of their short-term power but the ultimate futility of psychological denial and social myopia.[129] It must have taken hundreds of millions of working hours to build the great houses and the more than 400 miles of roads of Chaco Canyon. But the society depended upon the tens of thousands of working hours it took to plant farm plots that supplied the daily food, to carry water and firewood, to grind corn, to make tools and cloth and fabulous pottery to trade, as well as to produce cotton cloaks and rabbit fur and turkey feather blankets for the winter.[130] The Chaco did not fail because they ran short of pueblos, turquoise, or macaws, which they prized; they failed because their exaggerated growth pattern could not be sustained. In the end, they lacked sufficient water, corn, meat, and fuel to meet their increasing demands.[131] Heightened violence and vicious civil wars accompanied the collapse of Chaco Anasazi society between 1150 and 1200.

Ascending civilizations often create vast infrastructural networks and produce remarkable quantities of manufactured objects in a relatively short period. The social and ecological over-extension of the Chaco Anasazi was facilitated by its stratified social structure and its dependence on getting maximum results from a subsistence system; they made no allowance for long-term hazards. As anthropologists David Stuart and Susan Moczygemba-McKinsey suggest, Chaco's failure can be pinpointed in their inability to adapt to the consequences of rapid growth.[132] The Chaco Anasazi elites seem to have been seduced by their own power. Like many civilizations before and after, this advanced society committed a series of ecological blunders that proved to be the source of their ruin.[133] Over 800 years later, the woodlands of Chaco Canyon have not returned.

5. The Mayas, Mesoamerica: 200 CE to 900 CE

Ever since the discovery of Mayan ruins in the Honduran jungle during the mid-1800s, the remnants of this majestic civilization have lured archaeologists, anthropologists, and linguists from around the world. By 900 BCE the Mayan civilization had spread across the region we now know as Mexico's Yucatan Peninsula, Belize, and the northern half of Guatemala. Between 250 CE and 900 CE, Mayan civilization reached its zenith, producing great intellectual achievements in the arts, mathematics, and astronomy. Moreover, the Mayas evolved the only elaborate writing system native to the Americas. Without metal tools, horses, oxen, or even the wheel, they were able to construct vast cities across a huge jungle landscape with an amazing degree of architectural perfection and variety. Their massive pyramids across Central America have become modern-day monuments to their cultural legacy. Their great cities were dominated by brightly decorated royal palaces that gleamed in the tropical sun, and the grandeur of the greatest of all Mayan centers, the 123-square-kilometer metropolitan town of Tikal, rivaled that of Rome, Alexandria, and the great centers of China. Their cultural legacy has survived in spectacular fashion there and also at places like Palenque, Tulum, Chichen Itza, Copin, and Uxmal. The Mayas created elaborate and highly decorated ceremonial architecture, including temple pyramids, palaces, and observatories. They were also skilled farmers, who cleared large sections of tropical rainforest, and, where groundwater was scarce, they built sizable underground reservoirs for the storage of rainwater. The Mayas were equally skilled as weavers and potters, and they built roads through jungles and swamps to foster extensive trade networks with distant peoples.[134]

The ancient Mayan civilization occupied the eastern third of Mesoamerica, primarily the Yucatan Peninsula. The topography of the area varied greatly, from the volcanic mountains of the Highlands in the south to the porous limestone shelf known as the Lowlands in the central and northern regions. The southern portion of the Lowlands was covered by a rainforest with an average height of about 150 feet. Scattered savannas and swamps appeared sporadically, interrupting the dense forests. The northern Lowlands were also comprised of forests, but, because the area was drier than its southern counterpart, trees were small and thorny. February to May marked the dry season, characterized by intensely hot and uncomfortable weather. At this time of year, the fields were freshly cut and burned in a type of slash-and-burn agriculture. The skies filled with a smoky grit, making the air even more unbearable until the rains cleared the polluted atmosphere.

Originally, the region was blessed with abundant flora and fauna, including large predators like the jaguar and the caiman crocodile, and many species of poisonous snake. These animals threatened human invaders, who scavenged the forest for deer, turkeys, peccaries, tapirs, rabbits, and large rodents such as the peca and the agouti. Many varieties of monkey and quetzal also occupied the upper canopy. The climate of the Highlands greatly contrasted with that of the Lowlands, as it was much cooler and drier.[135]

Both the Highlands and the Lowlands possessed important economic value for the Mayan civilization. The Lowlands primarily produced crops for personal consumption, the principal cultigen being maize. But Lowland Mayas also grew squash, beans, chili peppers, amaranth, manioc, cacao, cotton (for light cloth), and sisal (for heavy cloth and rope). The volcanic Highlands, however, were the source of obsidian, jade, and other precious metals like cinnabar and hematite that the Mayas used for trade. Rainfall was as high as 160 inches per year in the Lowlands, with the water draining toward the Caribbean or the Gulf of Mexico in great river systems. These rivers were vital to the civilization, providing transportation for both people and materials.

The Mayan civilization survived as a cultural system for more than 1,000 years but vanished in the ninth century CE. Scholars have suggested a number of reasons for its sudden collapse: typhoons, diseases, or earthquakes were initially thought to have been responsible for this terrible "fate."[136] Others speculated that the Mayas were vanquished by the Vikings. Researchers at the University of Florida have presented a more convincing explanation based upon the analysis of 15 feet of sediment in Lake Chinancanab in the Yucatan Peninsula. The data suggest that the region underwent a prolonged drought. Researchers have found evidence of a sharp decrease in rainfall between 800 and 1000 CE, which was roughly the era of Mayan decline. According to paleontologist Scott Stine, it was one of the most severe climatic aberrations in 10,000 years. Stine cites recent evidence that suggests that the drought extended as far north as California.[137] Equipped with these findings, researchers were able to document the occurrence of severe climatic changes during this critical period.[138]

A dearth of water appears to have been one of the decisive elements in the collapse of Mayan civilization. At the time, an estimated 5 million people lived within close proximity in the Mexican Lowlands. Their food supply appears to have been extremely low during this period. Ever-larger sections of the rainforest needed to be cut down by farmers to keep pace with the sharply increasing population. By the eighth century, vast stretches of the jungle had been completely cleared and uprooted, and half of the harvest was going to the parasitic upper social classes in the urban centers.[139] The disappearance of the lush vegetation was a major factor in the ensuing climate change.

As this chapter shows, the predicament of Mayan civilization was shared by many other Neolithic civilizations: rapid population growth, incessant warfare, and sharp social inequalities combined with careless ecological practices to produce fundamental environmental changes that led to a serious social crisis and an eventual cultural collapse. These conditions often exacerbated human tendencies toward violence. A US research team found that within 50 years, the Mayan population dropped to 5 per cent of its previous level. The head of the team, archaeologist Arthur Demarest, notes that this collapse was due to ferocious warfare.[140]

The lessons to be drawn from the decline of the Mayan civilization is that societies based on growth economics – with elites demanding ever-higher levels of material well-being – eventually reach their limits.[141] Mayan civilization was caught in a spiral of escalating consumption driven by the society's elites and their penchant for pharaonic building projects and chronic warfare. The more temples that were built, and the more enemies that had to be vanquished, the more food had to be supplied to feed the builders, priests, and soldiers. The need for increased food production correspondingly required more farmers. Likewise, constant warfare stimulated population growth in response to the demand for soldiers.[142]

If this explanation is correct, then it is reasonable to conclude that the consumption patterns of the Mayan civilization exceeded the carrying capacity of their environment, especially during a prolonged period of drought.

6. The Easter Islanders, Rapa Nui: 700 CE to 1700 CE

Perhaps one of the most poignant examples of negative human impact on the environment and one of the most spectacular instances of social-ecological collapse in pre-modern times occurred between 700 CE and 1800

CE on Easter Island. Known by its original Polynesian inhabitants as "Rapa Nui," the island is located in the South Pacific over 2,000 miles off the coast of Chile.

Rapa Nui is among the most intensely studied places in the world. Archaeologists and natural scientists have speculated long and hard about the history of the island and the fate of its original inhabitants. Today, we have a better understanding of Rapa Nui's place in Polynesian prehistory and the dramatic environmental and social changes that unfolded on this small, remote island.

When European explorers first landed on the island in 1722, their first impression was not of a paradise, but of a wasteland: "We originally, from a further distance, have considered the said Easter Island as sandy; the reason for that is this, that we counted as sand the withered grass, hay, or both scorched and burnt vegetation, because its wasted appearance could give no other impression than of a singular poverty and barrenness."[143]

The island they beheld consisted largely of grassland, without a single tree or bush over 10 feet high. Modern botanists have identified only 47 species of higher plants native to Rapa Nui, most of them grasses, sedges, and ferns. The list includes just two species of small trees and two woody shrubs. Such sparse flora provided European sailors with no real source of firewood to warm themselves during Easter Island's cool, wet, and windy winters. Native animals they found included nothing larger than insects, and not even a single species of native bat, land bird, land snail, or lizard.[144] What these early European colonists did not know is that this bleak landscape was all that remained of a once biodiversity-rich and thriving ecosphere.

Rapa Nui's most famous feature is its huge stone statues, some as high as 65 feet and as heavy as 270 tons. More than 200 of these statues stood on massive stone platforms lining the coast. Most of them were carved in a single quarry and then transported to their final resting-places as far as 6 miles away. The sheer number and size of these monuments suggest a population much larger than the 2,000 people once estimated to have populated the islands during the height of their cultural achievements.[145] Excavations of Rapa Nui's prehistoric landscape prove that, during the early years of Polynesian settlement, the island was not a wasteland at all. Instead, it was a subtropical forest of tall trees and woody bushes towering over a ground layer of shrubs, herbs, ferns, and grasses. The forest trees included the rope-yielding hauhau tree, and the toromiro tree, which furnished dense, mesquite-like firewood. The most common tree in the forest was a species of palm now absent on Rapa Nui but formerly so abundant, researchers have found, that the bottom strata of the sediment column were packed with its pollen.[146] The palm was closely related to the still-surviving Chilean wine palm, which grows up to 82 feet tall and to 16 feet in diameter at the base. The tall, unbranched trunks of Easter Island palms would have been ideal for transporting and erecting statues and constructing large canoes. The palm would also have been a valuable food source, since its Chilean relative yields edible nuts as well as sap used to produce sugar, syrup, honey, and wine. Remnants of Rapa Nui's original animal world yield a picture as surprising as this image of abundance in the island's plant world. In addition to fish, Rapa Nui's waters housed large turtles that were hunted for their meat and shells. Archaeologists also found that Polynesian settlers of Rapa Nui feasted on sea birds. The isle's remoteness and lack of predators made it an ideal breeding site, at least until humans arrived. Among the prodigious numbers of sea birds that bred on Rapa Nui were albatrosses, boobies, frigate birds, fulmars, petrels, prions, shearwaters, storm petrels, terns, and tropicbirds. With at least 25 nesting species, Easter Island was once the richest sea bird-breeding site in Polynesia and probably in the whole Pacific. Archaeologists have also identified bones of at least six species of land birds, including barn owls, herons, parrots, and rails. Rapa Nui's inhabitants cooked bird stew seasoned with meat from the large numbers of rats, which Polynesian colonists had inadvertently brought with them. Easter Island is the sole known Polynesian island where rat bones outnumber fish bones in archaeological lists.[147] A few bones hint at the possibility of breeding seal colonies as well. Such evidence suggests that the island onto which the first Polynesian colonists stepped ashore some 1,600 years ago was a pristine, ecologically balanced paradise. What happened to it? The pollen grains and the bones yield a grim answer.[148]

Here, the story of Rapa Nui can be summed up as an all too familiar and rather brief tale of the rise and decline of a sophisticated civilization. The first Polynesian settlers enjoyed a high level of affluence, spending comparatively little time and effort on subsistence-related activities. Few hours were taken up with fishing and planting their introduced staple root crops.[149] Initially, it appears that people were not troubled about subsistence production or resource base maintenance, enjoying ample time and space for leisure. However, soon the small Polynesian settler community began to increase in size. As the island became more crowded, ecologically restricted, and internally stratified, more of the society's time and resources were invested in organized religious ceremonial activities. It is believed that Rapa Nui's notorious "statue builders' cult" religion emerged as a way to ensure good crops and fertility. Specialized masonry became ever more elaborate and mighty, producing ever-taller statues. As a result, the effort of social subsistence grew more laborious.

The drama of Rapa Nui culminates with the population growing to more than 20,000 people by the seventeenth century, with the achievements of the stone masons becoming ever-more elaborate and toilsome. Rapa Nui's colossal rock statues were manually carved and moved from the island's only central quarry. Ecological resources and means of subsistence on the island became increasingly scarce. The land no longer produced enough for all, and the forests of the island were soon all clear-cut.[150] Thus, the story of Rapa Nui ends with a demographic, ecological and social collapse, reaching its anticlimax with a now-familiar escalation of violence and warfare. By the time the fighting ended, Rapa Nui had become a severely degraded island ecologically and socially. The statue builders' religion collapsed as well, when the giant, multiple-ton rock statues on ceremonial grounds were thrown off their foundations. Rapa Nui's downfall was finally sealed with European arrival and terrestrial recolonization, first by Holland (1722), then by Spain (1770), and then by more than 120 years of Chilean occupation. The tragedy of Rapa Nui concludes with the virtual enslavement of the remaining population, gone to work as indentured laborers in Chilean mines. Following this concluding disaster, the population of the island had shrunk to 111 people.[151]

The ecological and social collapse of Rapa Nui constitutes yet another warning of problematic society–nature relationships in the pre-modern era. All of the examples presented in this chapter represent horrific accounts of progressive ecocide and the self-endangerment of our species. Still, the degree of devastation inflicted by pre-modern civilizations is dwarfed by that wrought by modern industrial societies. As the next chapter shows, modernity has allowed ecocide to escape its previously localized framework, turning it for the first time into a truly global phenomenon.

3 THE MODERN ASSAULT ON NATURE: THE MAKING OF ECOCIDE

So many goodly cities ransacked and razed; so many nations destroyed and made desolate; so infinite millions of harmless people of all sexes, states and ages, massacred, ravaged and put to the sword; and the richest, the fairest and the best parts of the world topsiturvied, ruined and defaced for the traffic of Pearls and Pepper. (Montaigne, 1533–1592)[1]

The war on other species reflected the dominance of commercial ends. The ecological effects of the mercantilist age of capitalism, however, were to be found not simply in the destruction of animal species for profit, but in the creation of a world system of cash-crop production based on the transformation of nature and the subjugation of human labor. (John Bellamy Foster, *Vulnerable Planet: A Short History of the Environment*)[2]

THE CAPITALIST SYSTEM: A BRIEF HISTORICAL AND SOCIOLOGICAL OVERVIEW

The emergence of the modern era in the sixteenth century is inseparable from the emergence of capitalism as a historically novel mode of social organization. Successful development of capitalism as a comprehensive system of social relations fundamentally depends on the accumulation and reinvestment of profits in a free market. New class relations based on the capitalist mode of production first took shape in Europe, following the disintegration of the feudal order of medieval society.

Beginning roughly in the fifth century CE, following the eclipse of the Roman Empire and continuing into the fourteenth century, social relations based on agriculture and caste prevailed in Europe. Feudalism can be defined as a social and economic system centered on land worked by serfs, who were working agricultural producers bound to the land. The land was held by vassals, who pledged fealty to the overlords, who were titled members of nobility. They ruled feudal states, conferring land holdings on vassals in return for military services. Within the feudal mode, which historically preceded capitalism in Western Europe, the relations of production were characterized by feudal landlords using political and legal power to extract profit from an unfree peasantry in the countryside. This dynamic of social relations between town and countryside, together with the development of trade and manufacturing in the towns, was an important element in the dynamics of the feudal mode of production and the transition from feudalism to capitalism.[3] This process intensified existing patterns of resource extraction. The Anglo-Saxons in Britain, for example, continued with the Roman practice of deforestation, leaving less than a tenth of the original forest that covered the island.[4] Indeed, the use of large trees for the masts of naval and merchant ships in the late Middle Ages accelerated the destruction of forest all over feudal Europe.

In the last few centuries, capitalism has worn many faces and taken many forms. The words we associate with capitalism reflect its elusive breath: private property, business, laissez-faire, profit motive, the pursuit of self-interest, free enterprise, open marketplace, the bourgeoisie. For Adam Smith, it was an economic system loosed from the shackles of feudalism – a natural liberty to make, buy, and sell things. For Karl Marx, it was a vicious class order in which a few owned the means of production and the rest sold their labor to stay alive. For Max Weber, capitalism was a "spirit" that emphasized hard work, accumulation, and economic rationality.[5] What separates capitalism sociologically from all the economic systems preceding it is not merely the unprecedented worldwide expansion of productive forces. The difference is also qualitative. Value is extracted through an impersonal economic mechanism based on the labor contract, whereas in all earlier societies the extraction of value took the form of a personalized system of tribute based on traditional, ascribed social relations.

All civilizations depend to some extent on the extraction of surplus labor. In feudal societies, exploitation is still direct and visible. Serfs were not only required to render services to a lord, but they were also attached to the lord's land. Profit extraction under capitalism, by contrast, occurs by economic means and is ideologically concealed in seemingly "free" relations of exchange. This novel mode of social production, its relations based on capital and labor, came to define a whole epoch and represented an altogether more efficient and more veiled form of exploitation. The transparency of economic phenomena in pre-capitalist societies on the one hand, and the concealment and opaqueness of exploitation under capitalism on the other, have led to the rise of the economic realm as an autonomous sphere. Whereas political forms of domination prevailed in early modern societies, market-based forms of authority emerged in later capitalist systems.

The expansion of agriculture in Britain in the seventeenth century was one of the determining factors in the first stages of capitalist development.[6] But it was only in Atlantic societies that capitalism developed into the global system that dominated the next four centuries. The ecological setting was not inconsequential. As environmental sociologist Enrique Leff notes, "the high resilience of temperate zones permitted an intensive agriculture to develop that in tropical regions might have led to premature depletion of the soils and a disequilibrium in productive ecosystems, blocking the structural changes undertaken in this determinant phase of primitive capital accumulation."[7]

Economic historians disagree about the decisive social factors involved in the development of capitalism. Marx identified two main factors in the formation of the capitalist mode: first, emergence of autonomous craft manufacturing in the feudal towns around which capital developed; and, second, the growth of overseas trade, particularly the emergence of British trade with the Americas in the sixteenth century leading to the rise of merchant capital.

By contrast, Max Weber laid great emphasis on political changes in Western European feudalism, particularly the contradiction between the centralizing tendencies of absolutism and the centrifugal forces associated with, and the local and regional power of feudal lords.

Yet both Marx and Weber associated capitalism with an outlook of a very specific kind: the continual accumulation of wealth for its own sake, rather than for the material rewards that it can serve to bring. Said Weber: "Man is dominated by the making of money, by acquisition as the ultimate purpose of his life. Economic acquisition is no longer subordinated to man as the means for satisfaction of his material needs."[8] Still, he emphasized the role of the Protestant ethic as containing the ethos and worldview of the newly emerging bourgeoisie.[9] The entrepreneurs associated with the development of rational capitalism combine the impulse to accumulation with a positively frugal lifestyle. Weber finds the answer in the "this-worldly asceticism" of Puritanism, focusing on the concept of "calling."[10] The notion of the calling, according to Weber, did not exist either in antiquity or in the Middle Ages; the Reformation introduced it.

Ultimately, feudalism was toppled by the expansion of markets and trade, together with the rise of a new ethos of the individual entrepreneur. Being first, English capitalism set a competitive challenge for others, compelling them – not least through England's military strength – to adapt to the new conditions. However, the existing conditions under which those countries had to compete with England differed greatly. In order to catch up with the more advanced and productive England, the rest of Europe was forced to utilize their absolutist systems as engines of capitalist development. This required a more centralized, concentrated, and interventionist pattern of development. The emergence of capitalism had given rise to the geopolitical and ideological social phenomena of nationalism. The stage was set for the competitive framework of nation-states competing on the capitalist "world market."

THE RISE OF SCIENTIFIC AND TECHNOLOGICAL THINKING

Underpinning the evolving capitalist system one finds scientific and technological assumptions about the world that encourage the exploitation of nature. The Enlightenment period saw nature as a dead and mechanical world, a view that permits people to think of ecosystems and their inhabitants as mere resources for human use. Scientists like Francis Bacon and Sir Isaac Newton and philosophers like René Descartes, John Locke, and David Hume supported a "scientific method" according to which living ecosystems become objects of detached analysis, observation, and experimentation.

Technological manipulation becomes central in the process of removing minerals, plants, and animals from their habitat in order to better understand the "laws" governing their behavior.[11] The ultimate purpose of this mode of thinking is absolute control over both living beings and material nature. Francis Bacon, for example, hoped to conquer and subdue nature and "to shake her to her foundations." What was needed was an all-out mobilization against what he referred to as "this common harlot." For Descartes, animals were "soulless automata" and their screams in death the mere clatter of gears and mechanisms. Indeed, in this view, nature itself is nothing but a machine. Newton saw the world as a giant clockwork, wound up by God, where the entrepreneur, merchant, industrialist, and scientist become God's counterparts – skilled technicians who use the same mechanical laws and principles that operate in the universe to assemble the stuff of nature and set in motion the industrial production of the modern age.[12]

It is critically important not to forget here that all these constellations of ideas and practices originally emerge out of a capitalist context. Within that framework, the institution of private property in land and nature becomes defined and institutionalized as a "natural and inalienable human right." Not only do people now regard their own bodies as "theirs," but they also define labor as "their own." By logical extension, that which is being appropriated through the use of people's labor becomes a private commodity. As philosopher John Locke put it, nature was given to "the industrious and rational." Locke viewed the whole of nature as a mere resource for commercial exploitation, arguing that "land that is left wholly to nature is called as indeed it is, waste."[13] The sanctification of private property in the hands of liberal thinkers has played a crucial part in the emergence of global capitalism. At its very core, the prevailing capitalist ethos and liberal world view of the modern industrial era remained expansionary and imperial, involving a calculated form of indifference to the social and ecological order.[14]

Indeed, the scale and nature of social and ecological transformations since 1500 CE are without historical precedent. It is incontestable that economic growth since the Industrial Revolution has been achieved at enormous costs both to the natural environment and to the autonomy of communities. The rise of the modern age has been described in the critical sociological literature as the making of a "runaway world," or a "juggernaut."[15] Demographically, the juggernaut nature of modernity is reflected in an explosive increase of world population. Militarily, the juggernaut becomes manifest in the increasingly deadly marriage of commerce and warfare, culminating in the destructive global configuration of modern industrialized war. Economically, the juggernaut generates massive global social inequality.[16] The ecological implications of these processes find their expression in the acceleration of environmental degradation and the unprecedented scope and pace of worldwide ecocidal activities.

As pointed out in Chapters 1 and 2, the social and ecological depredations associated with modernity are not unique or new. They are part of a larger historical movement that has continued for millennia. But capitalist social relations speed up ecocide and environmental degradation in two important ways: first, they push previously regional environmental catastrophes to a planetary level. Second, in reducing nature to the status of a mere commodity to be bought and sold on the free market, capitalism makes ecological exploitation universal.

THE CAPITALIST ETHOS: ECOLOGICAL AND SOCIAL VALUES

Capitalism is an evolving economic system that produces a complex culture. The latter consists of a core set of values and assumptions that provides continuing stability for the system. Environmental historian Donald Worster has summarized the ecological values contained in the capitalist ethos: first, nature must be seen as capital. It is a set of economic assets that can become a source of profit and advantage, a means to make more wealth. Trees, wildlife, minerals, water, and the soil are all commodities to be bought and sold in the marketplace. Thus, the natural world is desanctified and demystified. Functional interdependencies barely figure in the capitalist economic calculus. Second, humans have a right, even an obligation, to use nature and its products for constant self-advancement. Capitalism is an intensely maximizing culture, always seeking to get more out of the natural resources of the world that it did the day before. It is a system that must expand lest it destroy the conditions of its own existence.[17] The highest economic rewards go to those who make the best effort to extract from nature all they can. Private acquisitiveness and accumulation are elusive ideals, impossible to satisfy once and for all.[18] Third, capitalism generates an image of the self as an economic accumulating being. The pursuit of private vice, in the classical utilitarian formulation, is to render public benefits. The community exists merely to help individuals and economic corporations. Consequently, profits are privatized and the ecological and social costs are externalized.[19]

There are a couple of points relating to the capitalist ethos that deserve further critical attention. One relates to the systemic nature of exponential growth. Today there is every reason to believe that the kind of rapid economic growth that the system has demanded in order to sustain its very existence is no longer ecologically sustainable.[20] Many ecological critics would agree that, of all its core features, the systemic growth imperative is perhaps the most destructive dimension of the capitalist ethos. Another point that warrants further discussion concerns the centrality of autonomy in the capitalist ethos. It suggests that we are sovereign creatures, independent of the environmental restraints that plague other species. But, as Worster points out, this remarkable disregard for the interdependence of all beings has not been the view of most people in world history.[21] There have been few more important changes in human history than the abandonment of the last few seeds of the sense of intimate dependence on nature to the exaggerated feeling of absolute free will and human autonomy. "It is not too much to say," notes Worster, "that our entire industrial world was made possible by that change in outlook."[22]

Overall, capitalism contains a well-organized and rationalistic ethos, expressing supreme confidence in unending progress. It is unashamedly materialistic and utilitarian, critical of those who fail in the race for profits, and incredibly wasteful. In short, the capitalist ethos with regard to nature is both imperial and commercial.[23] None of its cardinal values include environmental humility, reverence for the diversity of life, or restraint. The desire for accumulation of wealth is the cultural impetus that originally drove Europeans into the New World, and then corporations into all corners of the earth in search of new markets and resources.[24]

SOCIAL AND ECOLOGICAL IMPLICATIONS OF THE "COLUMBIAN EXCHANGE"

"If I were required to pick a calendar date to mark the birth of the modern world," noted political economist Samir Amin, on the occasion of the American celebrations of the fifth centenary of Columbus, "I should choose 1492, the year in which the Europeans began their conquest of the planet – militarily, economic, political, ideological, cultural/ecological, and even in a certain sense ethnically." Sociologically, for Amin the world in question is also already the world of early capitalism.[25]

In the centuries that followed, thousands of miles of coastline were identified on European maps, oceans were named, the Americas were divided up by the European conquerors. Known as the "Columbian Exchange," the ensuing cultural and ecological interactions are of critical importance for the making of the ecological juggernaut of modernity. The apparent benefit of these exchanges was a worldwide improvement of dietary choices. It provided, in the worlds of ecological historian Alfred Crosby, "a second miracle of the loaves and fishes."[26] But while Columbus' voyage provided the starting basis for a veritable global revolution in dietary habits, its problematic social and ecological consequences involved an unprecedented disruption of native populations and ecosystems.

The events of 1492 put into motion the erosion of cultural and ecological diversity, whose importance would later be considerably amplified by the progressive subjection of all regions of the planet to industrial capitalism. For example, the genocide and ecocide that subsequently occurred in the Americas is unparalleled on a world scale. As Mark Twain wrote of the European conquerors, "first they fell on their knees, then on the Amerindians."[27] Indeed, one conservative estimate suggests that the number of indigenous peoples in the Americas was 112 million in 1492. In 1980, it had fallen to 28 million.[28] In retrospect, however, one might expand the remark in the following way: "First they fell on their knees, then on the Indians, and then on the continents' ecosystems and species."

The success of European imperialism often resided in the germs Europeans brought with them. Germs were the conquistadors' most devastating weapons; local populations were so racked by illness that they could offer little resistance to the European conquest. Europeans spread crowd diseases, which developed only within the past 10,000 years, such as smallpox, chicken pox, and measles, and treponemal diseases such as tuberculosis, syphilis, and typhoid. In Crosby's persuasively dark portrayal, European imperial conquest of the New World consisted of a series of violent biological exchanges.[29] European expansion, as he shows, consisted of a form of "ecological imperialism."[30] For example, smallpox and influenza arrived in Mesoamerica with the Europeans and swept across the land, killing millions of indigenous people.

In addition to deadly germs, other introduced European species proved to have ecologically devastating unintended consequences. Alien species began to transform the local ecosystems in profound ways. Within a century after the Spanish arrival in the Americas, hundreds of thousands of horses competed for grassland with herds of introduced cattle and European goats, sheep, and pigs. Since Native American plants had not evolved to live with these new grazing animals, the landscape never recovered. The ecological impact on Australia, New Zealand, and Oceania was comparable. Indigenous flora was largely replaced by plants from the Old World that evolved over thousands of years with grazing animals. To this day, most of the weed species in the United States are of European origin.[31]

Moreover, the reintroduction of the horse signaled the beginning of a profound transformation of Amerindian life. Certain tribes such as the Cheyenne had been agriculturist village dwellers at one time. But when the horse came along, they quit farming. Horses and guns made Amerindians much more efficient hunters of the surviving megafauna, particularly the North American bison. Today, many people believe that horses and Amerindians have always belonged together. But this naïve conception of the Amerindian on horseback constitutes only a very recent phenomenon. For example, the heyday of the buffalo-hunting Plains Indians lasted only about half a century, roughly from 1780 to 1830.[32]

Without the Columbian Exchange and its social and ecological consequences, the Industrial Revolution would have been impossible. Industrialization provided a greatly diversified and expanded food base, laying the requisite basis of staple foods for an unprecedentedly rapid worldwide demographic expansion.

THE ENSLAVEMENT OF LAND AND NATURE

Slavery in the Americas complemented the early consolidation of capitalism as an increasingly globalizing force and mode of production. Between 1500 and 1600, some 275,000 African slaves were sent to America and Europe. In the seventeenth century, the number rose to an estimated 1,341,000, largely in response to the demand of sugar plantations in the Caribbean. It was the eighteenth century, however, that was to be the golden age of slaving, with the forcible export of more than 6 million people from Africa to the Americas between 1701 and 1810.[33]

The introduction of slavery to support the plantation economies in the Americas had its cultural correlate in the treatment of land. The land became a "slave" of the new system of export crop production. Planters cleared it of trees, making it more prone to drought and erosion. In 1690, trees still covered more than two-thirds of Antigua; by 1751, every acre suitable for cultivation had been stripped of forest cover.[34] Intensive cultivation of sugar cane mined the soil, robbing it of its nutrients. What Uruguayan writer Eduardo Galeano wrote of the northeast of Brazil was true of most of the Caribbean islands as well:

Sugar ... destroyed the [Brazilian] Northeast.... This region of tropical rainforests was turned into a region of savannas. Naturally fitted to produce food, it became a place of hunger. Where everything had bloomed exuberantly, the destructive and all-dominating latifundia left sterile rock, washed-out soil, eroded lands. At first there had been orange and mango plantations, but these were left to their fate, or reduced to small orchards surrounding the sugarmill-owner's house, reserved exclusively for the family of the white planter. Fire was used to clear land for canefields, devastating the fauna along with the flora: deer, wild boar, tapir, rabbit, pacas, and armadillo disappeared. All was sacrificed on the altar of sugarcane monoculture.[35]

The creation of sugar monoculture left these colonies dependent on Europe, North America, and the South American interior for their food. "To feed a colony in America," Abbé Raynal ironically observed in 1775, "it is necessary to cultivate a province in Europe."[36] At the end of the sixteenth century, reports Galeano, "Brazil had no less than 120 sugarmills worth some £2 million, but their masters, owners of the best lands, grew no food. They imported it, just as they imported an array of luxury articles which came from overseas with the slaves and bags of salt."[37] The export of sugar grew rapidly. After 1660, England's sugar imports exceeded its combined imports of all other colonial produce; by 1800, the English population consumed almost 15 times as much as it had in 1700.

Despite its importance, however, sugar was only one pillar in a triangular trade that linked Europe, Africa, and the Americas. The first leg in the triangle connected European ports to Africa. European ships carried a cargo of salt, textiles, firearms, hardware, beads, and rum. In Africa these products were bartered for slaves, who were packed into the American-bound vessels with each individual having a space as small as 5 feet 6 inches long and 16 inches wide. In the New World, the surviving slaves were auctioned off to plantation owners, and, in the last leg of the triangle, sugar, silver, molasses, tobacco, and cotton – all of which had been produced with the help of slave labor – were purchased and shipped back for sale in Europe. In Britain, such important seaports as Liverpool, Bristol, and Glasgow owed their rapid growth in the eighteenth century primarily to this triangular trade.[38] In short, in the early modern search for wealth, the newly colonized native territories were plundered to meet the need for new land, relying on slaves and indentured work systems for cheap labor. The expansion of capitalism and the growth of associated forms of commerce greatly accelerated the pace of ecocide, resulting in the death of hundreds of millions of large animals at the hands of hunters and traders.

In the following three sections, I sketch three major examples of ecocide in modernity: the commercial assault on species associated with the early modern global fur trade, the mass slaughter and near extermination of the North American buffalo in the nineteenth century, and the rise of commercial whaling.

EARLY MODERN FUR TRADE

Fur trade-based predation upon species already had a long and remunerative history in Europe and Asia at the time that the first European fur traders began their activities on the North American continent. Scandinavia had provided ancient Rome with furs, along with amber, sea ivory, and slaves, receiving gold, silver, and other treasures in return.[39] In the late ninth century CE, seigniorial traders such as Ottar, from the Norwegian fjords near modern Tromsoe, took marten, reindeer, bear, and otter furs in tribute from Lapp hunters and sold them in Norway, Denmark, and England.[40] In the early tenth century, the Viking Rus delivered sable, squirrel, ermine, black and white fox, marten, beaver, and slaves to Bulgar on the bend of the Volga. In 922 CE the Arab Ibn Fadan described graphically the voyage of Rus merchants down the Volga with sables and slave girls for the markets of the Islamic Levant. After the Vikings, the North German Hanseatic League captured the fur trade in the northland. From a trading post at Bergen they mercilessly exploited the Norwegians, forcing them to deliver and clean large quantities of fur and fish in return for payments advanced, thus operating a kind of "international debt peonage."[41]

In what today is Russia, the operations of the Viking Rus prompted the development of the polities of Kiev and Novograd in the ninth and tenth centuries. For these states, as for their successors, furs became the single most valuable item of trade from the earliest beginnings to the eighteenth century and beyond.[42] Indeed, the quest for domination and expansion has been portrayed as one "extended quest for domination of successive river basins by the control of portage between them, the speed of expansion being determined by the exhaustion (or local extinction) of fur-bearing animals in each successive basin." The Russians, like Ottar before them, collected furs through tribute (iasak) imposed on local populations as a body, and through a tithe[43] on all furs obtained by individuals. Indeed, furs so obtained later constituted a major item in the income of the Russian states, rising from 3.8 per cent of state revenues in 1589 to 10 per cent in 1644.[44]

The fur trade, and with it the earliest proximate modern rehearsal for the modern global commercial war on species, began in earnest in medieval times in Europe, when it involved the hunting of European animals to stock the wardrobes of the nobility and royalty. It involved mainly small animals, such as squirrels, martens, ermine (the white phase of the weasel), sables, and foxes, and they were usually trapped alive so that their furs could be collected undamaged. Several hundred squirrel pelts were needed to make one cloak, so the numbers killed were enormous. Eventually the population of fur-bearing animals in Western Europe was almost exhausted, leading to the exploration of the northern forests of Russia and the development of an international trading system. This trade became a major driving force behind the early modern Russian expansion into Siberia, and the fur trade became Russia's economic foundation.

It is estimated that, at the height of the squirrel trade in the fourteenth to sixteenth century, the region of Novgorod was exporting half a million squirrel skins a year. The fur-bearing animals of the vast Siberian forests were already virtually eliminated by the end of the eighteenth century.[45] When Russian traders had exhausted the terrestrial fur-bearing animals, they turned their attention to sea otters in the north Pacific. Between 1750 and 1790 about 250,000 sea otters were killed. Then otters became too scarce to be worth hunting and the trade collapsed.[46] Only when Czar Peter the Great launched Russia on its road to industrialization did the fur trade decline in importance. Even so, the "fur war" waged against animals for commercial ends remained the main contribution of Siberia to the Russian economy until the nineteenth century.[47]

From the earliest days of European settlement in North America, the fur trade was one of the main reasons for westward expansion. For a long time, the colonists simply traded their goods for furs collected by Amerindians. As skilled hunters and suppliers of pelts, the Amerindians were sought after as trading partners and thus were exposed to white culture. In exchange for their goods, the Amerindians received European products, both practical, such as iron tools and utensils, and decorative, such as bright-colored cloth and beads. They also received firearms and liquor, both of which had an enormous impact on Indian lifeways. A second and devastating effect of the fur trade with white settlers was the outbreak of European diseases among the Indian population. A third effect was the long-term ecological disruption of the food chain by the depletion of fur-bearing mammals. And finally, the fur trade brought European traders, trappers, and hunters on to Indian lands. Then came the trading and military posts, the miners,[48] and soon thereafter, the settlers. Although there is little comparison between the depredations imposed by these opportunistic individuals on the Amerindians and those imposed by the majority of the Spanish conquistadors, who sought to conquer, plunder, and enslave the Indian population, nevertheless fur traders were often the harbingers of an insensitive and exploitative culture that had emerged within the framework of early capitalism. However, as Eric Wolf notes, the fur trade was not a North American but an international phenomenon, inseparable from the socioeconomic and cultural dynamics of the early modern phase of capitalist expansion.[49]

As Native American societies prospered, they elaborated new cultural configurations that combined Native and European artifacts and patterns. Such expressions were made possible by the flow of new and valued European goods into a still self-regulating Native economy. As long as the Amerindians were able to direct most of the social labor available through kin-ordered relations to the task of guaranteeing their subsistence, the goods attained by part-time fur hunting supplemented rather than replaced their own means of production.[50] But as European traders consolidated their economic and political position, the balanced relation between Native trappers and the Europeans gave way to imbalance. Amerindians themselves came to rely increasingly on the trading post not only for the tools of the fur trade but also for the means of their own subsistence. This growing dependence pressured the native fur hunters to commit even more labor to the fur trade in order to pay for the goods advanced to them by the trader. Abandoning their own subsistence activities, they became specialized laborers in a putting-out system, in which entrepreneurs advanced both production goods and consumption goods against commodities to be delivered in the future. Such specialization tied the Native Americans more firmly into continent-wide and international networks of exchange, as subordinate producers rather than as partners.[51]

At the beginning of the nineteenth century, the fur trade in North America moved on to its last frontier, the land west of the Mississippi. In 1805, when Lewis and Clark, the first explorers of the area, crossed the Rocky Mountains and continued on to the Pacific coast, they reported that the area was richer in beaver and otter than any other region on the planet.[52] Once these animals were trapped, the trappers had nowhere else to go, but they could switch to less desirable species. For a few years the trade was sustained by muskrat and marten furs, but these, too, were soon depleted.[53]

As the traders demanded furs from one group after another, paying for them with European artifacts, each group adapted its way of life to the needs of the European manufacturers. At the same time, the demands of the Europeans for fur increased competition among the Native American groups. Competition for new hunting grounds and competition for access to the European goods soon became essential components of native technology as markers of differential status. The fur trade thus changed the character of warfare among Amerindian populations and increased its intensity and scope. It led to the loss of whole populations and the displacement of others from their previous habitats. Nor were furs the only item furnished by the Amerindians. The growing trade also required supplies, and as the commerce in furs expanded westward it altered and intensified the patterns by which food was produced for hunters and traders alike.

One of the favorite targets in North America was the beaver, the largest of the surviving rodents of the continent. Once extremely abundant throughout most of North America, it had gone into decline as early as the 1630s, when King Charles I of England decreed the compulsory use of beaver fur in the manufacture of hats to be worn by all members of high society. By 1720, over 2 million beavers had been killed in eastern North America. Beaver hats were fashionable until the early nineteenth century, by which time beavers had been virtually wiped out east of the Mississippi.[54]

In the nineteenth century, as beaver grew less important, it was replaced by sea otter and seal, exported mainly from North America to markets in China. Russia, too, lost its dominant role in the European fur market by the end of the seventeenth century, and sought outlets for its furs in China and elsewhere in Asia.[55] What the Europeans sought on the northwest coast of the New World was, above all, sea-otter pelts. Between 1785 and 1825, some 330 recorded vessels visited the coast, nearly two-thirds of them trading for two seasons or more.[56] Sea-otter skins were obtained at first in return for iron and other metals, later for clothing and blankets, and still later for rum, tobacco, molasses, and muskets. The Native American traders were mostly "chiefs" who mobilized their followers and personal contacts to deliver the otter skins, and whose power grew concomitantly with the development of the trade.[57]

For more than three centuries, the fur trade thrived and expanded in North America, drawing ever new Native American groups into the widening circuits of commodity exchange that opened up between the incoming Europeans and their native partners in trade. The trade first touched the food collectors and horticulturists of the eastern woodlands and sub-arctic. Then, with the expulsion of the French and the partition of the north between British Canada and the United States, it reached beyond the Great Lakes into the western sub-arctic, creating at the same time a new zone of supply in the area of the Plains. Finally, at the conclusion of the eighteenth century, the trade established a beachhead in the Pacific Northwest, eventually linking up, across the coastal mountains, with the advancing inland trading posts.[58]

Wherever it went, the fur trade brought with it contagious illness and increased warfare. Many native groups were destroyed and disappeared entirely; others were decimated, broken up, or driven from their original habitats. Remnant populations sought refuge with allies or grouped together with other populations, often under new names and ethnic identities. A few, like the Iroquois, expanded at the expense of their neighbors.[59] Some groups, located strategically or strong militarily, became the primary beneficiaries of the trade in furs.

The Hudson's Bay Company bore major responsibility for promoting the hunting of hundreds of thousands of fur-bearing animals every year in North America and exporting the hides and furs to Europe. The most valuable animals were the various members of the weasel family, including the short-tailed weasel in its white or "ermine" phase, otter, mink, pine marten, fisher, and wolverine. Of these animals, only weasels, otters, and mink remain today, and the weasel is the only one that is still abundant. In addition, these species also suffered greatly from reduction of their forest habitat.[60]

The loss of furs from other sources was a major incentive for the massive hunts for various types of seal.[61] The animals were usually clubbed to death when they came ashore to breed. The pattern was a familiar one: the discovery of large populations of a target species led to the development of intensive hunting, culminating in the extermination or regional depletion of the species. Then trappers moved to new areas and repeated the cycle. The first phase of the seal hunts (1780–1820) took place in many areas of the southern hemisphere and was carried out by sealers from Europe, Russia, Canada, and the United States. Massive seal hunts also developed in the North Atlantic, where hunters took advantage of the huge harp seal population that breeds on the pack ice around Labrador and Newfoundland. The sealers, mostly from Canada, focused on the newborn seals, whose pure white fur yielded high profits. Started in the early nineteenth century, the Newfoundland sealing industry peaked in the 1850s at about 600,000 animals killed. Ultimately, it reduced the size of the herds by about 80 per cent, causing the decline of the industry in the early twentieth century.

In the Bering Sea, Russian hunters stalked the northern fur seal off the Pribilof Islands after having wiped out the sea otters. The number of seals killed fell from 127,000 in 1791 to 7,000 a year in the 1820s. In this short period 2.5 million animals had been killed. The population recovered when the Russian hunters moved to other areas, but after Alaska was sold to the United States in 1867, the total killed went back up to 250,000 per year. By the turn of the century, the seal population had again fallen dramatically.[62]

THE MASS SLAUGHTER OF THE NORTH AMERICAN BISON

In North America, the only herbivores to survive the late Pleistocene megafauna extinction were bears, elks, moose, and bison. However, all these species underwent further rapid decline due to subsequent human transformations of habitat and predation. Like the war on fur animals, the mass slaughter and near-extermination of the North American bison is a particularly striking example of the momentous changes in society–nature relations brought on by capitalism in the early modern era.

Bison belong to the same family as modern cattle. They are ruminants with cloven hoofs and hollow, unbranched horns. A typical bull stands 6 feet high and is 10 feet long, weighing over a ton. The average life span is about 30 years. Migrating seasonally, often following the same routes year after year, bison always sought the easiest paths around obstacles and across terrain. Their trails were later used as the basis for most of our railroads and modern highways. Prized for their meat and hides, as well as for their symbolic value as trophies, bison were hunted almost to extinction. By 1891 the bison population in the United States had been reduced to a mere 541 animals.

When the Europeans first arrived, some 40 million to 75 million bison roamed over a third of North America. Commercial hunting of bison for meat began in the 1830s and soon reached 2 million animals a year. After 1870, when bison hides began to be made into commercial leather, it rose to 3 million. The Union Pacific Railroad, completed in 1869, divided the bison into northern and southern herds, making them easier to hunt. The southern herd was largely exterminated in the early 1870s. After completion of the Northern Pacific Railroad in 1880, the slaughter of the northern herd proceeded at a rapid pace. As the environmental historian William Cronon notes, the bison met their end "because their ecosystem had become attached to an urban marketplace in a new way."[63]

Moreover, the mass slaughter of bison was "a calculated military strategy designed to force the Native Americans on to reservations."[64] Professional hunters like Buffalo Bill Cody shot the animals for their "entertainment" and often left the carcasses to rot. About 2.5 million buffalo were killed annually between 1870 and 1875. Amerindians quickly perceived the arrival of Europeans in North America not just in terms of conquest, brutality, and enslavement, but as a threat to their very way of life. Many Plains Indians, for example, understood that killing off the bison herds constituted a serious threat to their survival. At the end of the nineteenth century, both the free-roaming Amerindians and their animal counterparts were no more, and the destruction of the North American environment continued into the next century.

THE RISE OF COMMERCIAL WHALING

Commercial whaling is one of the worst examples of wildlife over-exploitation in the early modern history of capitalism, comparable to the near-extermination of the American bison and the assault on fur species. Several species of whale have gone entirely extinct because of whaling, and other species have been reduced to herds too rare to be worth hunting.[65] The whale species that are commercially hunted are of two major types. First, there are the toothed whales, represented mainly by the sperm whale, which lives in many of the world's oceans and feeds mainly on squid. The sperm whale was hunted for both its meat and its oil, which was used as fuel for lighting. Another product was spermaceti, a liquid, waxy substance found in the huge head, which was used in the manufacture of smokeless candles and as a lubricant for machines. The second major type of whale that was subjected to human commercial assault was the baleen whale. Baleen whales feed on swarms of shrimp-like crustaceans called krill by straining sea water through long, fringed baleen plates that extend from the roof of a cavernous mouth. These whales were hunted not only for their meat, which was either eaten or made into oil, but also for their baleen, a strong flexible material that was used for corset stays,[66] buggy whips, and other applications.

Subsistence whaling has been part of human history for thousands of years; evidence suggests that people engaged in whaling as far back as 3000 BCE.[67] The age of global commercial whaling began in Japan and Southeast Asia in the first few centuries CE.[68] From 800 to 1000 CE, Norwegians and Basques living on the north coast of present-day France and Spain began commercial whaling in Europe. This early whaling was done from small boats using hand-thrown harpoons attached to a coiled rope. This rope allowed the whalers to manipulate the whale until it was exhausted. The whale was then pulled alongside the boat and killed with a hand lance. During this early period of commercial whaling, the hunting vessel was a small boat discharged from a mother ship and propelled by a six-man crew using oars.[69]

Inuits, Amerindians, and Vikings also used to hunt whales, but their activities did not threaten entire stocks or species. Technical innovations, growing markets, and the economic imperatives of early capitalism, however, soon greatly accelerated the predation on these majestic animals. In the late eighteenth century, commercial whaling experienced its so-called golden age. Particularly desired and sought after originally were whales with high oil content. A sub-arctic species of Greenland whales fulfilled this condition best; indeed that is why they were called "right whales."

Technological improvements in the eighteenth century led to the development of fast ships, allowing the commercial hunting of whales to begin in earnest. Whaling entrepreneurs pursued these animals to such an extent that northern right whale stocks were on the edge of extinction within a few decades. Still, the whaling industry continued full throttle, enticed by rising prices for whale products. Industrial-style whaling reached its apex in 1868, when the explosive harpoon gun was invented. These guns were mounted on steam-driven vessels, making it possible to catch the fast-swimming blue, fin, sei, and minke whales. The construction of huge "factory ships" made it possible for whalers to stay at sea for long periods, increasing dramatically the number of whales they could hunt and process. As a result of excessive hunting, commercial whaling declined sharply around 1860. The British whaling fleet, for example, declined due to over-harvesting and the introduction of vegetable oil, steel-boned corsets, and gas-fired lamps. By 1908, the whale population in the Arctic Ocean had dropped to the point where whaling was no longer a viable major industry – even in the formerly whale-rich waters of Alaska. Still, the slaughter of whales continued with increased efficiency. By 1912 the United States Whaling Corporation, for example, used what were referred to as "killing boats."[70] A muzzle-loading whale gun with a 3-inch bore was used. Part of the harpoon contained an explosive, timed to detonate inside the whale. By 1925, the invention of the stern slipaway allowed whalers to haul whole carcasses aboard a factory ship to be processed. In the decades to follow, the slaughter expanded, with several tens of thousand of whales being killed for profit every year yielding millions of barrels of oil. During the winter of 1930–31 alone, some 29,000 blue whales were slaughtered.

Between 1946 and 1985, an estimated 2 million large whales fell victim to the unequal contest between the species and the commercial interests of the largest whaling nations, Norway, the former Soviet Union, and Japan.[71] Commercial whaling was stopped in 1986 when the members of the International Whaling Commission (IWC) came to an agreement to forgo the hunt on these gigantic sea mammals (weighing up to 130 tons). But the decision to forgo or reduce the hunt on large cetacean species was not based on "biophilia" or on an ethical revolution of inter-species sentiments on the part of the board of IWC.[72] Instead, there were two more immediate causes. On the one hand, the numbers of the great whales were reduced so drastically that it was no longer commercially lucrative to hunt them; on the other, the IWC was forced to yield to the worldwide campaign of environmentalists who protested the ecocidal mass killings.

At present, only about 300 right whales survive in the North Atlantic and 250 in the North Pacific, and the species is showing no signs of recovery.[73] The survival of the few remaining blue whales in the Antarctic is now imperiled by global warming. A species related to the right whale, the bowhead whale, was hunted to extinction in the Atlantic Ocean but still exists in the North Pacific. Although its numbers are minuscule, these whales are still hunted by Alaskan Inuit peoples.[74] American whalers also hunted the sperm whale, first in the Atlantic from bases in New England, later in the Pacific from bases in Hawai'i.[75] They also hunted the California gray whale in the lagoons of Baja California, where they go to breed, and from 16 shore stations along the coast of California. The California gray whale was hunted almost to extinction in the late 1800s, then recovered; it was hunted almost to extinction again by factory ships in the 1930s and 1940s, and recovered again.[76]

The scale of the early modern commercial assault on nature has been unprecedented, characteristically involving a pattern of overexploitation of species. Whereas early and classical modern commercial annihilation of the planet's species occurred primarily because of over-exploitation, in the late modern era, the commercial war on species expanded to include the outright destruction of entire ecosystems and habitats.

4 THE PLANET AS SACRIFICE ZONE

Progress, under whose feet the grass mourns and the forest turns into paper from which newspaper plants grow, has subordinated the purpose of life to the means of subsistence and turned us into the nuts and bolts for our tools. (Karl Kraus, "In These Great Times")[1]

We have created an industrial monster, which, being easily aroused by the smell of money, continues at will to devour our rapidly vanishing virgin landscapes, excreting progress in the process. (Peter Marks, A Vision of Environment: Is Life Worth Living Here?)[2]

THE ENCLOSURE OF THE COMMONS: A GLOBAL PHENOMENON

From the seventeenth century to the present, political and legal maneuvers were initiated throughout the world to enclose publicly held land, thus fundamentally altering the economic relationships between people and their natural environment and paving the way for the industrial and urban revolutions.[3] Throughout medieval Europe collective forms of landholdings coexisted with individualized holdings. Generation after generation, people farmed the same lands, trod the same paths, and organized themselves communally in order to sustain their existence. The novel social practice of enclosed public lands – the "enclosure of the commons" – emerged first in Tudor England. The rising capitalist class joined aristocrats in their efforts to remove millions of people from the commons in order to make space for sheep. After all, wool became a crucial commodity in the growing textile markets of the early Industrial Revolution. Peasants were dislodged from their lands and forced to migrate to the cities and work in factories, a process that has continued until today. The enclosure movement, sometimes referred to as "the revolution by the rich against the poor," caused considerable hardship to the smallest landholders and the landless squatters who possessed only a tiny cottage and a small vegetable garden.[4]

In the eighteenth and nineteenth centuries, the enclosure movement developed into an increasingly global undertaking. From Australasia and Oceania to the Americas and Africa, indigenous peoples were being moved off their land by legal and illegal subterfuge. People's resistance was frequently met with mass killings. But the dominant social classes were not content with just enclosing the land. As environmental thinker Jeremy Rifkin observes:

Nature, once an independent force, both revered and feared, has been reduced to an assortment of exploitable resources, all negotiable in the open marketplace. The privatization and commodification of the Earth has elevated humanity from servant to sovereign, and made nature an object of pure commercial exchange. The great landmasses, the vast oceans, the atmosphere and electromagnetic spectrums, and now the gene pool have all been desacralized and increasingly rationalized, their worth measured almost exclusively in monetary terms.[5]

The effects of these changes on human life, not to mention that of the rest of the biosphere, are pervasive and essentially incalculable. All our notions of security in the modern age, both personal and national, flow from the privatization of the world. The passage from the medieval world of sacred, communal arrangements to the industrial world of secular, market forces brought with it the fall of public man and the meteoric rise of the private individual. Alienated human life, itself now enclosed, becomes a struggle for individual autonomy, where life retreats behind walls and where personal bank accounts and private property come to define human worth. Psychologically, this has meant a "systematic withdrawal from the external world of group participation and its enthusiastic retreat into a new psychic world of self-reflection and self-absorption."[6]

The destruction of the commons was essential for the Industrial Revolution, to provide a supply of natural resources as raw material for industry. But the enclosure movement should not be seen merely as a historical episode that occurred in early modern England. Rather, it is a global phenomenon – the guiding metaphor for understanding conflicts and contradictions being generated by the expansion of human colonization of the planet. Thus, the enclosure of the commons represents the modern mechanism that has produced increasingly violent and progressively ecocidal relationships between modern industrial societies and nature.

THE INDUSTRIAL REVOLUTION

The full impact of the Industrial Revolution in the mid-nineteenth century accelerated the pace of global ecological destruction. The Industrial Revolution represents a milestone in the history of ecocide and environmental degradation. Machines, not land, became the central means of production. Sociologically, the process involved the proletarianization of large segments of the population, who lost their direct control over the means of life and had no other means of livelihood but to sell their labor power. Roads, railroads, factories, and smokestacks appeared everywhere. Urban sprawl became a common phenomenon. The environment near the new factories was transformed into a wasteland. The standard of living for most people in the industrial workforce was far below that of a yeoman farmer. But work in a factory workforce was better than starving in the crowded countryside.[7] Historian Donald Worster describes the ethos of industrialism in the following way:

The capitalists ... promised that, through the technological domination of the Earth, they could deliver a more fair, rational, efficient and productive life for everyone.... Their method was to free individual enterprise from the bonds of traditional hierarchy and community, whether the bondage derived from other humans or the Earth. That meant teaching everyone to treat the Earth, as well as each other, with a frank, energetic self-assertiveness.... People must ... think constantly in terms of making money. They must regard everything around them – the land, its natural resources, and their own labor – as potential commodities that might fetch profit on the market. They must demand the right to produce, buy, and sell those commodities without outside regulation and interference.... As wants multiplied, as markets grew more and more far-flung, the bond between humans and the rest of nature was reduced to the barest instrumentalism.[8]

This "bare instrumentalism" led to great material productivity as well as to unprecedented environmental exploitation. With the invention of the steam engine and as timber became scarce, coal mining increased dramatically. The use of coal raised immediate practical problems of mine construction: how to pump water, transport the coal, and control its combustion. It required greater concentrations of labor around the mines and mills, and it lifted science and technology to prominent positions in human society.

The factory system shaped the modern city, as we know it, along with creating local, regional, and global environmental hazards.[9] States emerged as regulators of the economy and managers of social conflict – and, to the rest of the world, the high modern era is characterized by the consolidation of colonialism into a full-blown assemblage of competing imperialists, with European empires scrabbling for "territories" and markets all over the globe.

Colonialism and imperialism pillaged the ecologies and societies of the conquered territories, while contributing relatively little to their economic progress. Colonization in the industrial age meant the extension of the division between town and country to the periphery of the world economy; the transformation of the ecology of the periphery, which was consequently tailored to meet the requirements of the colonists. The global assault on the planet's species and environment is the logical extension of the violence inherent in colonialism and imperialism.

ECOLOGY AND MODERN WARFARE

With the Industrial Revolution, the causal connection between the modern war economy – notably the industrial arms race, culminating in the twentieth century – and progressive global ecocide becomes obvious. The industrialization of warfare emerged as one of the most ecologically and socially damaging institutional features of modernity, described by the great Spanish painter Francisco Goya as the "most evil and dangerous of human traditions."[10] From the outset, mechanized warfare was put in the service of commercial interests. Capitalism involves, indeed is predicated upon, the separation of large sectors of the populations from control over the means of life. This disenfranchisement of the laboring population and primary producers from direct control over conditions of their life, in other words, becomes a critical causal variable and determinant in the increasing deadliness and brutality of modern industrial war.[11]

The ecological and social violence contained in modern warfare, further, is inseparable from the associated modern geopolitical constellation of nation states.[12] Modern individuals make history not as individuals or classes but as unified wholes, as nations. Modern history, therefore, is made through the interaction of nations that compete for global dominance in the modern universe of perpetual warfare.[13] Vast economic inequalities spawned by global capitalism combined with nationalist conflicts have rapidly assumed planetary proportions, threatening the survival of all sentient beings. As philosopher Walter Benjamin points out:

Instead of using technology to make the Earth inhabitable, imperialistic warfare uses it for destruction. Technology made it possible to enact this immense wooing of the cosmos on a planetary scale. But because the lust for profit of the ruling classes sought satisfaction through it, technology betrayed man and turned the bridal bed into a blood bath. Man's greed leads to a one-sided mastery of nature; instead of imbuing nature with the power to look at him in return, he turns it into an object ready for consumption. Mankind's self-alienation has reached such a degree that it can experience its own destruction as an aesthetic pleasure of the first order.[14]

The history of modern industrial warfare is the history of a movement from limited to unlimited, or "total," war – a war without mercy. This holds true also for relations between society and nature. For most people today, the two world wars seem a long time ago. Still, these massive conflicts were the first international wars in which the ecological and social resources of nations were mobilized.[15] The two world wars set ominous precedents for the remainder of the twentieth century. Among other developments, they reflected the brutal face of modernity in the tacit acceptance of biological and chemical warfare, not to speak of nuclear weapons.[16] The Cold War represented the logical next step of a capitalist modernity that produced a military-industrial complex and an arms race of previously inconceivable proportions.[17] According to a US army medical doctor who oversaw the physical examinations of the irradiated indigenous people of Rongelap Atoll, a nuclear test site in Micronesia: "Those Cold War days were strange times, for neutron bombs were regarded with almost spiritual reverence, at least in Washington where they had been ordained the device that would forever establish peace trumpets from heaven proclaiming this Truth. So I volunteered ... "[18]

The second half of the twentieth century witnessed a global assault on the environment of unprecedented magnitude. In ecological terms, with the post-world war era we enter a juggernaut world that is truly ecocidal.[19] The first uneasy acknowledgment of the predicament appeared in the midst of the Cold War with the publication of the Club of Rome's *The Limits of Growth*.[20] Since then, it has become even more difficult to ignore the fact that global political economic developments have pushed humanity into a socially and ecologically unsustainable direction, thus amplifying existing ecocidal tendencies.[21] In addition to exacting an exorbitant toll on human lives, industrial warfare and the arms race of the twentieth century inflicted severe damage on the environment. The modern war system greatly accelerated the destruction of wildlife and pristine ecosystems worldwide. In the following section, I will discuss some concrete examples of modern ecocidal activities as a deliberate strategy of warfare.

ECOCIDE AND MODERN WARFARE

As mentioned in previous chapters, the earliest Neolithic settled communities defended their territory against other human groups. The establishment of sedentary agricultural societies undoubtedly increased the potential for warfare by establishing exclusive ownership of land and resources. Early military conflicts have been documented to have had a variety of effects on ecosystems and biodiversity. For example, when a New Guinea highland tribe defeats another in a war, it does not immediately take over the territory of the vanquished. Instead, the winners cut down the fruit trees raised by them, perhaps to reduce the chances of the defeated people attempting to reclaim their territory.[22] As conflicts intensified and the means of warfare became increasingly sophisticated, so-called scorched-earth policies became more common.

Perhaps the earliest documented example of systematic destruction of environment by warring armies is the destruction of the North African city of Carthage by the Romans. After Roman troops razed the city they covered the surrounding land with salt in order to destroy their enemy's means of subsistence. There exists no archaeological evidence that the site of ancient Carthage was resettled after the Roman destruction on any significant scale until the end of the first century BCE.[23] The modern record of industrialized warfare, however, presents a more serious picture as far as scopes of ecological devastation are concerned.

Although modern industrial warfare has immensely raised the social and ecological stakes, the leitmotiv of warfare has stayed the same for millennia: whatever is militarily attractive remains an option. Twentieth-century conflicts extended warfare to large-scale battles over habitat – that is, the expansion of violence through the destruction of environment. In short, the social practice of deliberate large-scale ecocidal devastation by warring armies is an entirely late modern phenomenon. Indeed, the notion of "ecocide" was originally developed in the 1950s and 1960s as an analytical term in the context of the devastating imperial wars in Southeast Asia to describe the practice of scorched earth policies and environmental terrorism by warring armies.

As used in this study, "ecocide" refers to certain acts that intend to disrupt or destroy species development and an entire ecosystem. Acts of war associated with ecocide include the use of weapons of mass destruction, whether nuclear, biological, or chemical, and attempts to provoke natural disasters such as volcanoes, earthquakes, or floods. In addition, ecocidal acts of warfare include the military use of defoliants, the use of explosives to impair soil quality and to enhance the prospect of disease; the bulldozing of forest or croplands for military purposes; attempts to modify weather or climate; and the forcible and permanent removal of humans or animals from their places of habitation in the pursuit of military or other objectives.

A nineteenth-century antecedent of ecocide by a warring army is exemplified in the systematic destruction of buffalo herds by the US army in order to obliterate the subsistence base of the resisting indigenous inhabitants of the region, the native North American Plains Indians. Defoliation in Vietnam, damage to marine life in the 1991 Gulf War, and destruction of agricultural land in the Horn of Africa during the Cold War, are the most prominent twentieth-century examples of the impact of the depredations of modern international industrial warfare-based conflicts with nature.[24]

The first major well-documented modern example of environmental warfare occurred earlier in the beginning of the twentieth century, in 1938 during the Second Sino-Japanese War when the Chinese dynamited the Huayuankou dike of the Huang He (Yellow) River in an attempt to halt the marching Japanese forces.[25] This military tactic succeeded in drowning several thousand Japanese soldiers and halting their advance into China along this front. In addition, the resulting flooding ecologically ravaged three provinces and inundated several million hectares of farmland. The human costs were staggering: eleven cities and 4,000 villages were flooded, killing several hundred thousand civilians and leaving millions homeless. This little-known act of environmental warfare, performed by a defending army, is perhaps the single most devastating act of environmental warfare in history in terms of the number of human lives claimed.[26]

World War II contains further examples. In addition to the two Japanese cities obliterated by atomic weapons, scores of pristine Pacific atolls were blasted, burned, and pulverized under intensive air and naval bombardments.[27] More than 450,000 acres of Libyan farmland were riddled with 5 million land mines. Nazi troops flooded 17 per cent of Dutch farmlands – 200,000 hectares (494,000 acres) – with sea water. European bison were slaughtered to near-extinction to supply the mess kitchens of German and Soviet troops in eastern Poland.[28] German civilian administrators with the occupying forces in Poland excessively exploited the Polish forests for timber, greatly diminishing the resource base of Poland.[29] Soviet armed forces carried out retaliatory deforestation in the wake of World War II in occupied parts of western Europe, harming the region's ecology and crippling post-war social development.

It was not until the US–Vietnam conflict, however, that an offensive army utilized deliberate large-scale ecologically destructive technologies.[30] Carrying 20 tons of bombs into the stratosphere, a US B-52 bomber could strike from 30,000 feet without warning, turning entire villages into sudden eruptions of flaming sticks, human limbs, and thatch. A formation of B-52s could obliterate a "box" approximately five-eighths of a mile wide by 2 miles long. These flying behemoths dropped 13 million tons of bombs on North and South Vietnam, Cambodia, and Laos – triple the total tonnage dropped in World War II. Such ferocious carpet-bombing, as historian William Thompson notes, left at least 25 million craters – each averaging 60 square yards – in a country nearly the size of Washington state. When the tropical rainforest canopy – up to 50 feet thick – resisted the onslaught of bombs, shells, and bullets, US forces developed the 15,000-pound Daisycutter bomb, which exploded with a shock-wave that killed earthworms 100 meters (330 feet) from the impact crater. The aerial and ground bombardment detonated the equivalent of an 8-kiloton bomb over Vietnam every 24 hours.[31]

Heavy bombing and herbicide spraying contributed to the precipitous decline of the red-shanked duoc langur – one of eleven mammals found only in Southeast Asia. Air-dropped poisons and high explosives also brought the lemur, the pileated gibbon, the Ouston's civet, and the wild forest ox to the brink of extinction. South Vietnam's lobster industry was wrecked by over-production to satisfy members of the occupying imperial army. The tiger population was similarly devastated for the souvenir trade. Elephants and water buffalo used by the Vietcong to move supplies were attacked and slaughtered by US pilots and ground troops, just as the Romans had targeted Hannibal's elephants centuries before.[32]

Encouraged by state official fixations on technological solutions, deliberate, large-scale spraying of eco-toxins in Vietnam had commenced soon after the beginning of the war in the early 1960s. According to Thompson, a total of 18.8 million gallons of pesticides were sprayed over 20 per cent of the forests of South Vietnam. In one decade, 990,000 acres of prime agricultural lands were poisoned. "Agent Orange," the most commonly employed "jungle-eating" defoliant in Vietnam, spread DNA-damaging mutagens throughout Vietnam's war-torn biological environment. As a result, the rate of miscarriages and birth defects began to increase among Vietnamese women. Precious ancient tropical forests were eliminated by the blades of giant bulldozers weighing almost 3 tons. Dubbed "Roman plows" by their historically minded operators, these Earth-wrecking jungle eaters plowed under the entire village of Ben Suc and scraped clean 1,400 acres of fertile rice paddies tilled by the community's 3,000 inhabitants.[33] South of Saigon, in the Plain of Reeds, the 5 foot tall eastern sarus crane came under attack as US forces dug hundreds of drainage ditches across 39,000 acres of sedge marshes. Once the coastal mangroves were dry, the soldiers sprayed the shrubbery with flame-throwers. By the war's end, more than half of the mangrove swamps in South Vietnam had been destroyed by chemical poisoning and napalm. Overall, an estimated 5 million acres of inland tropical forests had been heavily damaged by bombs, shells, bulldozers, and toxic defoliants.[34]

The displacement resulting from this environmental holocaust brought suffering to entire populations of animals and humans. In an ecological domino effect, starving hill tribes were forced to turn from contaminated rice fields to the forests for survival. Logging for cash and land-clearing accelerated together with subsistence hunting. In Ba Be National Park, threatened leaf monkeys were shot by villagers to provide meat for their families. Before the United States entered the fray, southern Vietnam had been predominantly rural, with 85 per cent of its population living simple lives in the lush countryside. By the war's end, 3 million of Vietnam's 17 million inhabitants had become refugees living in cities.[35]

Deforestation, erosion, dried-up water sources, and flooding have increased drastically since the war ended. The primary cause of this water-related havoc is the decrease in Vietnam's forest cover from 44 per cent of the total land area in 1943 to only 24 per cent 40 years later. Between 100,000 and 200,000 tons of topsoil per hectare wash down swollen rivers to the sea each year. Deforestation is continuing in post-war Vietnam as surviving forests are felled to rebuild 10 million homes, schools, hospitals, roads, and irrigation systems. This inexorable pressure is shrinking the forests the country needs for long-term sustainability at a rate of 494,000 acres a year. With more than two-fifths of southern Vietnam's once-verdant countryside a post-war wasteland, unusable for either agriculture or forestry, a report by the International Union for Conservation of Nature and Natural Resources argues that much of this ecological damage can never be repaired. Even more ominous, a report by Asia-Pacific's Environment Network of Malaysia concluded that Vietnam is a country facing "gradual extinction."[36]

Following Vietnam, the recent civil wars in former Yugoslavia and Rwanda further illustrate the devastating environmental effects of late modern war and its capacity of causing serious ecological damage. Almost all of the Yugoslav national parks in the war zones were destroyed, including the Plitcic Lakes, Biokovo, Trsteno Arboretum, Krka River, Kopack Rit Bird Reserve, and the Osijek Zoo. Deer, game, and domestic animals starved, sickened, or were shot by machine-guns. Energy and chemical plants were destroyed and chemicals are leaking into the ecosystem.[37]

THE PLANET AS NATIONAL SACRIFICE ZONE

No epoch in human history has demonstrated as blatantly and grotesquely the fundamental incompatibility of warfare and nature as the hot and cold national wars of the late modern era. The devastating, often irreparable, effects of warfare on global ecosystems, as the sections above have chronicled, clearly illustrate the incompatibility of modern industrial warfare and nature. Ecological systems are fragile. In order to continue to support subsystems of living things, ecosystems must maintain a number of processes such as integrity of species habitat, biodiversity, photosynthesis, and nutrient replenishment.[38] Industrialized armed conflicts disrupt these processes with unprecedented severity. Late modern warfare's ability to destroy nature, as environmental researcher Ruth Sivard concedes, "has become increasingly formidable."[39] In addition, modern industrial warfare is producing direct and indirect threats that are no longer limited to the actual conflict. Also the intensity, scope, and technological means of wars have increased near exponentially. Before the Persian Gulf War, there were 227 other wars in the past century alone, wreaking varying degrees of environmental damage.

Even in "peacetime," as indicated above, modern military industrial activities are particularly dangerous to species and the environment. For example, the process of creating and maintaining the world's stockpile of over 50,000 nuclear weapons is, as one US General Accounting Office (GAO) report put it, one of the more potentially dangerous industrial operations in the world.[40] Not only does nuclear weapons production involve the intricate manipulation and transportation of enormous quantities of radioactive materials; it also creates great volumes of non-radioactive hazardous wastes. And because all operations are carried out under strict secrecy, civilian environmental agencies and citizen watchdog groups are kept in the dark.[41] Moreover, the military enterprises are also the least regulated hazardous industries in the world. Because of the extensive military use of electronics and fire extinguishers, the ozone damage of military endeavors is extensive. The US Defense Department, towards the end of the Cold War, accounted for 76 per cent of emissions of a type of halon called halon-2111, and nearly half the emissions of the form of CFC called CFC-113.[42] Halons in most civilian fire extinguishers are never released to the atmosphere because they are never used. But US military regulations require that the fire-fighting equipment of every tank be tested with halons; no substitutes are allowed. Other nations' armies undoubtedly have similar procedures. The modern arms race and military-industrial complex get a black mark for their greenhouse gas record, too. In 1988, the military consumed an estimated 1,589 trillion BTUs of energy – 86 per cent of all energy used by the US government and about 14 times the energy used by all urban public and private mass transit in America.[43] The total carbon emissions of the world's combined military forces is probably on the order of 140 million tons, nearly equal to the annual emissions of the United Kingdom.[44]

The world's armed forces, according to environmental analyst Ruth Leger Sivard, "are the single largest polluter on Earth."[45] A Canadian Peace Report study found that today's armed forces are responsible for 10 to 30 per cent of global environmental damage, 6 to 10 per cent of worldwide air pollution, and 20 per cent of all ozone-destroying chlorofluorocarbon use.[46] The GAO reports that the Department of Defense currently generates 500,000 tons of toxic waste annually – more than the top five chemical companies combined.

Even under the strictest regulations, the production, testing, maintenance, and deployment of conventional, chemical, biological, electromagnetic, and nuclear arms would generate enormous quantities of toxic and radioactive waste.[47] Every step of war preparation involves significant ecological damage. Excavating the Earth to extract uranium and rare metals for weapons production poisons large tracts of land and precious ground water. Multinationals' strip mines also strip rights and customs from the indigenous peoples whose sacred lands are often expropriated by war-makers.[48]

Until recently, many ecologists have tended to underestimate or neglect the impacts of warfare and arms production on natural history. Yet, as Mike Davis argues, the Cold War has been not only an unmitigated modern social disaster, but also the "Earth's worst ecodisaster in the last ten thousand years."[49] There is now incontrovertible evidence that huge areas of Eurasia and North America, particularly the militarized deserts of Central Asia and the Great Basin in North America, have become unfit for human habitation, perhaps for thousands of years, as a direct result of weapons testing by the Soviet Union, China, and the United States. In the United States, these "national sacrifice zones," now barely recognizable as parts of the biosphere, are also the homelands of indigenous cultures who themselves may have suffered irreparable genetic damage.[50]

Unraveling the hidden history of national sacrifice zones – from the "secret holocausts" of Siberia to the pulverized and irradiated coral atolls of the Pacific islands to the millions of irradiation casualties and genetically damaged people of former Cold Warring nations – has been largely the result of grassroots resistance efforts by the new social movements. Mike Davis has charted the devastating impact of militarism on much of the American West, and compares it to the ecological disasters afflicting large parts of the former Soviet Union. There, the hidden history of the Cold War came to light most dramatically when environmental and anti-nuclear activism, first stimulated by Chernobyl in 1986, emerged massively during the crisis of 1990–1. Grassroots protests by miners, schoolchildren, health-care workers, and indigenous peoples forced disclosures such as the chilling accounts of the 1957 nuclear catastrophe in the secret military city of Chelyabinsk-40, as well as the poisoning of Lake Baikal by a military factory complex. Soon also the wall of silence around radiation accidents at the Semipalatinsk "Polygon," the chief Soviet nuclear test range in Kazakhstan, came down.[51] The relationship between ecological disasters and the disintegration of the USSR is more than metaphorical. As political historian Murray Felsbach notes, "When historians finally conduct an autopsy on the Soviet Union and Soviet Communism, they may reach the verdict of 'death by ecocide.'"[52]

The ecocidal legacy of the Cold War in the United States has been amply documented by the photojournalistic investigative work of the so-called Atomic Photography Guild.[53] Their work represents politically engaged exposés of the Cold War's impact upon the American West since the mid-1980s, providing "not only vital clues for the reconstruction of a major disaster-zone but also echoes of the utopian hopes which inspired the pioneer surveyors of the west."[54] The photographer Richard Misrach has repeatedly penetrated some of the most secret spaces of the so-called Pentagon Desert in California, Nevada, and Utah. His documentary work depicts a Bosch-like landscape, including dead-animal disposal sites located near reputed plutonium "hotspots" and military toxic dumps in Nevada.[55] The Great Basin of eastern California, Nevada, and western Utah and its "plutonium periphery" – the Columbia River-Snake Plateau, the Wyoming Basin, and the Colorado Plateau – constitute the Pentagon's national sacrifice zone.[56] It has few landscape analogues anywhere else on Earth.[57]

Few Americans are aware of the role of the Pentagon in turning the Great Basin into a silent, toxic desert. Nor, until now, have we had cause to reflect on how "demilitarization" may just be a new and perverse dispensation for continuing ecocide and internal colonialism.[58] The modern arms race, and the rise of industrial warfare, as the above discussion illustrates, represents an exceedingly damaging political ecological configuration. Any attempt toward a comprehensive study of the modern mass-extinction event must be considered gravely incomplete without an accounting of the staggering social and ecological costs of the modern arms race and twentieth-century industrial warfare. What it clearly illustrates is that, from an ecological perspective, any division of the global ecosystem into nation-states is ultimately ecocidal. The picture that emerges here is that of a stupendous and epochal disaster.[59] Private ownership and profit-oriented economies, embedded in a system of corporate nations, are clearly not conducive to maintaining the natural heritage of the planet as a common resource for all humanity. Common resources are not shared "in common," in the traditional sense of land and resources belonging to a community, as a source of wealth for all and the responsibility of all.

The lessons to be learned from the social evolution of civilizations in the Holocene period is that the Neolithic institutional invention of warfare is tremendously costly, not merely in immediate social terms but also in long-term, and perhaps irreversible, ecological terms. The contemporary late modern scale of worldwide social and military expenditures, as the economist John Kenneth Galbraith recognized, is not simply "foolish and cruel," but is a "highly conditioned social form of insanity."[60] Jacob Uexkuell and Bernd Jost, for example, have calculated that "all known programs for the saving of the environment and for the worldwide satisfaction of the needs of the poor could easily be taken care of with the global military budget of only one year."[61] During the height of the Cold War, the trillion dollars a year the world spent on arms would have wiped out nearly the entire Third World debt.

Back in the midst of the Cold War, it would have taken only $9 billion a year – or a fraction of the annual world military expenditures – to secure the world's topsoils, only $3 billion to restore the forests, $4 billion to halt desertification, $18 billion to provide readily available contraceptives worldwide, and $30 billion for clean water.

These inverted priorities, as Emmanuel Wallerstein noted, are not the neutral decisions of a market, they are the priorities of powerful people in powerful nations, mostly men whose gender, race, and class interests drive the capitalist political economic system and its worldwide system of accumulation and deprivation.[62]

The modern arms race that emerged in tandem with the rise of modern nation-states and capitalism over the past five centuries, and which has been particularly ruinous in its late modern manifestation, has been essentially a process, as Alan Durning suggests,

... by which we have pillaged our houses to build walls around them. We are left, sadly, with impressive walls and an impoverished home – a planet with poisoned air, water, and soil, with worn farms, denuded hillsides, and with fewer species living each hour.[63]

Demilitarization presents a particularly obvious opportunity to eliminate a significant waste of financial and physical resources while simultaneously eliminating a great, perhaps the greatest, single cause of ecological destruction and human suffering in our modern world. An estimated 10 to 30 per cent of all global environmental degradation is due to military-related activities.[64] But, in an increasingly polarized world with increasing inequities, injustices and blowbacks, a process rendered acute by recent neo-liberal forms of economic globalization, the dismantling of our permanent global war economy looks ever more like a utopian dream.[65] Throughout the world, environmental policies remain a low priority. This is illustrated by the fact that the UN Environment Programme (UNEP) has been struggling to keep its meager annual budget of $100 million during the decade following the Rio Earth Summit, while global military spending is more than $2 billion a day.[66] The total cost to save what remains of the world's 25 biodiversity hotspots over the next ten years has been estimated at some $5 billion (some $5 million annually over ten years). Yet worldwide annual military expenditures are more than $900 billion. Without military and economic disarmament, there can be no lasting social and ecological peace. "On the contrary," as Albert Einstein noted, "the continuation of military armaments in their present extent will with certainty lead to new catastrophes."[67]

THE PLANET AS DEMOGRAPHIC SACRIFICE ZONE

Scholars of ecocide have identified at least a half-dozen major underlying causes for current declines in species and devastation of natural ecosystems. Most of them agree that population growth – which includes both global and local natural increase and migration – is one of these primary causes of ecocide.[68] In short, gaining people means losing species. This truism has never been more consequential than in the modern era. Since farming economies first came into existence 480 generations ago, the human population has increased a thousand-fold, to more than 6 billion. Half of this increase has occurred in the last 30 years.[69] The enormous increase in the planet's population is causing severe pressures on its ecosystems, resulting especially from activities associated with the production of food and the use of timber and fibers. Vast areas of the Earth's surface, especially in arid and semi-arid regions, have nearly ceased to be biologically productive. According to the United Nations Food and Agricultural Organization, if present rates of land degradation continue, there will not be a single fully productive hectare of arable land on this planet in less than 200 years.[70] Perhaps two of the best illustrations of the demographic threats to biodiversity are the worldwide expansion of human and livestock biomass, which continues to increase at essentially exponential rates in a world of finite size, and the related human appropriation of Net Primary Production of Photosynthesis (NPP) on land. In 1850, humans and their livestock represented perhaps 5 per cent of total terrestrial animal biomass, a century later this value represented just over 10 per cent and currently is somewhat more than 25 per cent.[71] Ten years from now it is sure to be in the neighborhood of 30 per cent. This increase in human and livestock biomass occurs at the expense of wildlife biomass, a loss that is measurable in both quantitative and qualitative terms – that is, both in loss of numbers of individuals within a species and in loss of numbers of species.[72] In other words, these losses in biodiversity result largely from an arrogation of nature by the ever-expanding human population, an expansion that has been variously likened to a biospheric pathology or cancer.[73] Indeed human demands on the environment have been growing even more rapidly than population increases suggest, as indicated by the even more rapid increases of productive and consumptive activities.[74] By the late 1980s, humans worldwide were already consuming, diverting, or putting into reserve more than 40 per cent of all Net Primary Production of Photosynthesis generated on land.[75]

Traditional concerns about the relationship between population growth, environmental degradation, and ecocide have largely focused on aggregate population levels. However, the impact of humans on the world environment is as much a function of *per capita* consumption as overall population size.[76] The exhaustion of biological diversity and natural resources is overwhelmingly due to over-consumption and technological application, not simply increased population growth. The US, for example, comprises only 5 to 6 per cent of the world's population but consumes 30 to 40 per cent of the world's resources. The vast majority of US over consumption is directed by and benefits only a small percentage of the US population.[77] A significant proportion of consumption of natural resources in the global North, further, is sustained by resource flows from the southern to the northern hemisphere.[78]

Some indicators suggest that ecosystem and resource limits have already been reached. World fish harvests peaked at 100 million tons in 1989. By 1993, they had declined 7 per cent from 1989 levels. Growth in grain production has slowed since 1984, with *per capita* output falling 11 per cent by 1993. World economic growth has slowed from over 3 per cent annually in the decade 1950–60 to just over 1 per cent in the decade 1980–90 and less than 1 per cent from 1990 to 1993.[79] The Worldwatch Institute, extrapolating from historical data, forecasts that if current trends in resource use continue and if world population grows as projected, by 2010 *per capita* availability of rangelands will drop by 22 per cent and the fish catch by 10 per cent. The *per capita* area of irrigated land, which now yields about a third of the global harvest, will drop by 12 per cent. And cropland area and forestland per person will shrink by 21 per cent and 30 per cent respectively.[80]

Rapid population growth, combined with unsustainable consumption patterns in a world where a small minority of 20 per cent of the world population consume over 80 per cent of its resources, have massively increased pressures on biodiversity habitats. Recent research suggests that species extinction during the past century have occurred at least 1,000 times more frequently than in pre-human eras. From projected habitat losses based on current trends, some biologists project that 2 to 13 per cent of the world's species could go extinct in the period between 1990 and 2015. More could disappear as a result of other causes, such as invasions of exotic species and diseases, pollution, over-harvesting, and human-induced climate change.[81]

Conversion of natural habitat to human use will further reduce the value of remaining wild areas for most wildlife. When development chops wild lands into fragments, native species often decline simply because the small remnants cannot meet their biological needs. For example, studies of US forest birds indicate that species that prefer to nest on forest interiors are more subject to predation and lay fewer eggs when habitat fragmentation forces them to nest along forest edges. A study in southern California indicated that most canyons lose about half the native bird species depending on chaparral habitat within 20 to 40 years after the canyons become isolated by development, even though the chaparral brush remains. Biologist William Newmark's 1987 study of 14 Canadian and US national parks showed that 13 of the parks had lost some of their mammal species, at least in part because the animals could not adapt to confinement within parks surrounded by developed land. The Breeding Bird Survey, a volunteer group that tabulates nesting birds each June, found that 70 per cent of neo-tropical migrant species monitored in the eastern United States declined from 1978 to 1987. So did 69 per cent of monitored neo-tropical migrants that nest in prairie regions. Declining species include such familiar songbirds as veeries, wood thrushes, blackpoll warblers, and rose-breasted grosbeaks. As human population growth continues to push development into wild areas, fragmentation will increase, and its overall negative effect on wildlife survival will intensify.[82]

The pressures on these rich natural resources and environmental systems, particularly on biodiversity-rich regions of the Asia-Pacific, have been continuously increasing over the past few decades. The world's current population of 6.1 billion is projected to hit 8 billion by 2025, with 97 per cent of that growth occurring in the global South.[83] Perhaps most worrisome to conservation biologists is that some of the most rapid human population growth is taking place in the vicinity of some of the world's biologically richest yet most vulnerable habitats. High population growth rates in 25 "biodiversity hotspots" – identified by Conservation International as especially rich in endemic species – have already experienced dramatic reductions in the amount of original vegetation remaining within their boundaries.[84]

Nearly one-fifth of humanity lives within these already severely degraded 25 hotspots, despite the fact they enclose only one-eighth of the habitable land area of the planet. In addition, more than 75 million people, or 1.3 per cent of the world's population, now live within the remnants of the world's three major tropical wilderness areas: Upper Amazonia and the Guyana Shield in South America, the Congo River basin of central Africa, and New Guinea and adjacent Melanesia. Areas of rich biodiversity facing the greatest risk include south India's Western Ghats and Sri Lanka, the Philippines, the Caribbean, the Tropical Andes, and Madagascar.[85]

Unlike other natural resources, biodiversity is especially affected by both extensive means of acquiring food and shelter (farm expansion and suburban sprawl), and intensive means (intensive agriculture and urban concentration). Farm expansion and sprawl play an important role in the clearing of terrestrial and wetland habitat. At the same time, intensive solutions to food and shelter needs tend to overload aquatic and marine ecosystems with pollutants. Clearly, the additions to human population projected for at least the next half-century will require further appropriation of the Earth's ecosystems. Such growth, coupled with an expected growth of consumption, further globalization of trade, and much-needed improvements in the living standards of the world's poor, is likely to put at further risk much of the remaining biodiversity in the bioregions.

The twentieth century was marked by a profound historical development: an unwitting evolution of the power to seriously damage global ecosystems. Warfare represents one source of this power. Even the complexities of global arms control, however, are now dwarfed by the changes inherent in runaway population growth, a further source of modern ecocide. Diminishing the ecological threat posed by warfare involves relatively few parties, well-established international protocols, alternative strategies that carry easily assessed costs and benefits, and widespread recognition of the severity of the threat. In contrast, curbing the devastating global impact of population growth is more difficult, since it involves coordination of the most personal life decisions of every inhabitant of the planet, in a context in which socioeconomic incentives for sacrificing the future for the present are often overwhelming.[86]

Population growth seems to affect everything, but for a number of reasons, changes in population trends will come about only slowly.[87] First, demographic change is inherently a gradual process, operating not in terms of months or years, but generations. In a world where policy makers are faced with short-term crises that demand immediate responses, tackling the thorny issues of population growth involves enormous practical obstacles. Second, the topic of population growth does not generate the continuous news coverage that might attract wider public attention. Third, international meetings on population and women's issues have met with staunch religious opposition, most notably, from the Vatican and some Muslim communities.[88] Political and religious groups in many countries may seek to block the implementation of publicly supported programs that they see as eroding morals or promoting promiscuity. Even so, as little as $20 billion a year could provide contraceptives to every woman who wants them, allowing families throughout the globe to reduce births voluntarily.[89] Third, tensions will inevitably arise over resource allocation, because the best strategy for addressing population growth calls for simultaneous investments in health, education, and the empowerment of women, in addition to contraceptive and reproductive health services. Some social scientists have expressed disappointment that the new focus on human development downplays the importance of lowering fertility.[90]

The moral of the story here is that globally we are procreating ourselves into a future of accelerating forest loss, fresh water depletion, and poverty. Global social and ecological deprivation has increased in absolute numbers. By 2025, most of the population of developing countries will face water shortages, two out of every three persons on Earth will live in "water-stressed" conditions, and rising seas could inundate large areas, displacing 70 million people in China alone.[91] Clearly there are multiple causes, but efforts at alternative social development and global ecological restoration are, without a population program, like "mopping the floor with the water turned on."[92] Zero population growth within the next generation is one of the critical prerequisites for reducing the progressive degradation of the global environment and the annihilation of species.

5   ECOCIDE AND GLOBALIZATION

To attract companies like yours ... we have felled mountains, razed jungles, filled swamps, moved rivers, relocated towns ... all to make it easier for you and your business to do business here. (Advertisement by the Government of the Philippines, in *Fortune*)[1]

Environmental degradation is caused by the interaction of economic, political and cultural power with demographic change. The driving force of that process in capitalist societies, which are now approaching something like universality, are economic forces, institutions and actions. No social theory of the environment and environmental degradation can adequately capture the origins of that degradation or provide a basis for considering its control without attending to the dynamics of capitalist production and consumption. Acknowledging that other forces are at work, or that traditional socialist economic alternatives and assumptions are flawed, does not diminish the need to critically engage with those dynamics. (David Goldblatt, *Social Theory and the Environment*)[2]

THE IMPACT OF GLOBALISM

This most recent historical phase of ecocide corresponds to the formal ending of the imperial era of capitalism. The rich countries of the global North have embarked on the neo-liberal project of global deregulation and marketization. This gigantic ideological effort at "liberalizing" global markets has been termed by political theorist Manfred B. Steger "globalism."[3] It coincides with the social process of "neo-liberal globalization" – a phenomenon characterized by transnationalization of production, output fostering, the permeability of national boundaries, the compression of time and space fueled by the revolution in communications and transport technologies, and the appearance of transnational corporations (TNCs) as the central engines of economic power.[4]

Global markets are now dominated by global mega-corporations which are among the most undemocratic and unaccountable of human institutions. By its nature, the corporation creates a legal concentration of power while shielding those who wield that power from accountability for the consequences of its use. Many mega-corporations command more economic power than do the majority of states, and they dominate the political processes of nearly all states. Their growing power, along with their lack of accountability, poses a serious threat to the basic economic and political rights of people everywhere.[5] Their international sales often dwarf the gross domestic product (GDP) of entire nations. Of the world's 100 largest economic systems, 47 are corporations, each with more wealth than any of 130 countries. Indeed, only 17 countries can boast a higher GDP than General Motors.[6] The GDP of Israel in 1992 was US $69.8 billion; the sales of Exxon during the same year were US $103.5 billion. The GDP of Egypt in 1992 was US $33.6 billion; the sales of Philip Morris during the same year were US $50.2 billion.[7] Some 200 companies that own over a quarter of the world's productive assets exert enormous political pressure on relatively weak states.

Corporations clearly are an integral part of the late modern ecocidal juggernaut. In many ways, TNCs define our progressively ecocidal world, and they do so by effectively silencing, trivializing, or legitimizing their exceedingly damaging social and ecological practices. The deeply anti-democratic organizational nature of TNCs plays a key role in the contemporary course of action and policy of global capitalism that has brought our planet to the brink of social and ecological collapse.

TNCs today thrive within today's philosophical and economic framework of neo-liberalism. Neo-liberalism is a variation on the classical liberalism of the nineteenth century, when Great Britain and other imperialist powers relied on the ideology of market competition and "free trade" to justify both capitalism at home and colonialism abroad.[8] The labor movements in the global North and the anti-imperialist movements in the global South ended classical liberalism and colonialism in the 1950s. Keynesianism – a form of "controlled capitalism" named after economist John Maynard Keynes – emerged as the dominant post-war social arrangement. Its main features included the construction of the welfare state, state subsidies to industry, and the state management of many collective bargaining processes. In the 1980s, however, Keynesianism was replaced by neo-liberal arrangements championed by conservative politicians like British Prime Minister Margaret Thatcher and US President Ronald Reagan. Corporate globalization is an extension of this neo-liberal revolution known as the "Washington Consensus." Its principal spokespeople are the CEOs and management personnel of huge corporations that control much of the international economy and have the means to dominate policy formation as well as to structure thought and opinion.[9]

These corporations not only pursue profits in low-wage markets but also seek to escape the tighter regulatory frameworks of the global North, thus greatly accelerating the destruction of ecosystems and biodiversity in the global South.[10] In addition, twenty-first century agribusiness has opted for unprecedentedly manipulative techniques of genetic food engineering and development of new synthetic fertilizers, pesticides, and herbicides.[11] Ever larger areas of the global landscape are drawn into the exclusive orbit of corporate globalization, accelerating 500 years of ecological degradation and progressive ecocide.[12] In short, neo-liberal globalization constitutes the last and most destructive phase of global industrialization, an era that the economist Ernest Mandel calls "late capitalism," or "global capitalism."[13] A striking illustration of the detrimental social and ecological consequences of neo-liberalism since the 1980s is the experience of the majority of people in the global South, who have been subjected to the neo-liberal structural adjustment programs imposed on them by the International Monetary Fund (IMF) and the World Bank. The long-term social and ecological consequences of these programs appear to be irreparably damaging. Most people in the global South remember the 1980s not as a decade of progress but as a decade of regression. By 2000, *per capita* income in Africa was down to the level of the 1960s, when many African countries achieved their independence. In Latin America, as well, *per capita* income in 2000 had not exceeded its 1980 level. In addition, the total Third World debt increased from US $500 billion in 1980 to US $965 billion in 1985, and then exploded to almost US $1.3 trillion by the end of the decade. By 2000, the debt burden of developing countries surpassed US $2 trillion.[14] While foreign aid fell from US $69 billion in 1992 to US $53 billion in 2000, the developing world's debt has risen by 34 per cent since the Rio Earth Summit.[15] In order to earn the money necessary to service this enormous debt, developing countries have had to increase their export revenues. Since their natural resources constitute the bulk of their export revenues, Third World governments from Brazil to Bangladesh to Cameroon have been forced to mine for even more minerals, harvest more trees, and drill for more oil in the remotest corners of their respective regions.[16]

Since the late 1970s, the top 15 Third World debtor nations have tripled the rate of exploitation of their forests – a phenomenon undoubtedly related to their pressing need to gain foreign exchange to make interest payments. Indonesia and Brazil, two heavily indebted countries of the world that also happened to contain much of the planet's remaining virgin tropical forests, saw their rates of deforestation increase by 82 per cent and 245 per cent respectively.[17] Hence, it should come as no surprise that the speed of destruction of the world's centers of biodiversity has greatly accelerated since the onslaught of neo-liberal forces starting in the 1980s.

POVERTY AND ECOCIDE

Social inequalities generated by neo-liberal globalization have kept large segments of the population in the global South in poverty. In 1990, 2 billion people subsisted on less than US $2 a day.[18] Indeed, impoverishment is one of the main contributors to ecocide and environmental degradation in the global South. Without jobs and without productive land, poor people are forced on to marginal lands in search of subsistence food production and firewood, or they move to the cities. Those who stay on the land are forced to graze livestock herds in places where vegetation is sparse or soil and shrubs are easily damaged, and to create agricultural plots on arid or semi-arid lands. In tropical forests and ecologically sensitive areas, more and more people exploit open access resources in a desperate struggle to provide for themselves and their families. The toll on natural resources takes many forms – soil erosion, loss of soil fertility, desertification, depleted game and fish stocks, massive loss of species and their natural habitats, depletion of groundwater resources, and pollution of rivers and other bodies of water.[19] As a result, the carrying capacity of land and its biological resources is reduced. This degradation further exacerbates poverty and threatens not only the economic prospects of future generations but also the livelihood, health, and well-being of current populations. The aforementioned debt crisis and structural adjustment programs deepen the correlation between poverty and environmental degradation.

Ghana, the Philippines, and Indonesia serve as warning examples of the damaging environmental consequences of structural adjustment programs that mandate intensified export production to gain foreign exchange. Ghana increased its production of cocoa to deal with its debt, but unfortunately the terms of trade deteriorated because the rise in cocoa production in Ghana was accompanied by a 48 per cent decline in the world cocoa price between 1986 and 1989. Burdened with deteriorating terms of exchange, Ghana was forced into even greater indebtedness to cover its burgeoning trade deficit, with its external debt rising from US $1.1 billion in 1988 to US $3.4 billion in 1988.[20] To make up for declining foreign exchange earnings from cocoa, the Ghanaian government with World Bank support revived commercial forestry. Timber production rose from 147,000 cubic meters to 413,300 cubic meters per annum from 1984 to 1987, accelerating the destruction of Ghana's already reduced forest cover. At the 1990s rate of deforestation, predicted political economist Fantu Cheru, Ghana would be stripped of its forests by the year 2000.[21] The same forces that, in the 1980s, accelerated the devastation of Ghana's forest resources, have since worsened degradation of the country's forests, wildlife, water, biodiversity, and health of the people by pursuing aggressive gold mining operations which involved the massive conversion of indigenous lands into mining areas and industrial estates.

Like Ghana, the Philippines has been a faithful implementer of the neo-liberal structural adjustment formula. The country has been paying as much as 25 to 30 per cent of its foreign exchange earnings to service its debt. Out of the almost US $50 billion worth of products exported by the country between 1981 and 1989, traditional resource-based exports accounted for almost US $23 billion, or over 45 per cent.[22] The portion of the Philippines covered by forests declined from 50 per cent in the 1950s to less than 18 per cent by the end of the 1990s, with most of the wood being exported to Japan. Its coastal fish resources were already depleted by the late 1980s. Of its original 500,000 hectares of mangroves, the coastal breeding grounds of fish, less than 30,000 hectares remained by the end of the century. Most of those important environments have been converted into fish or prawn farms geared mainly to producing for foreign markets.[23] Indeed, the "blue revolution" of aquaculture, and in particular prawn farming in countries such as the Philippines, Malaysia, Thailand, Vietnam, Bangladesh, Ecuador, and Mexico, reveals the devastating environmental impact of debt-driven, export-oriented production.

Not only has the creation of prawn farms to service the Japanese, US, and European markets entailed the destruction of mangroves and associated coastal breeding grounds for fish, it has also disrupted traditional agriculture. The inflow of salt water due to the elimination of mangroves threatens to lower productivity of adjacent rice fields. The high demand for fresh water leaves little of this most precious resource for rice farming. In some areas, water supplies have dropped precipitously, prompting local authorities to ration it.[24]

A final striking example is provided by Indonesia, perhaps the most richly endowed center of biodiversity in Southeast Asia. In this country widespread poverty exists in spite of its immense natural resources. Ruthless partnerships of foreign investors and local elites have implemented economic liberalization to acquire personal wealth at the expense of Indonesia's indigenous population and environment.[25] During the last two decades of the twentieth century, more than 1 million hectares of Indonesia's tropical forests – one of the world's richest genetic storehouses – were cut down. Former Indonesian President Suharto articulated the relationship between Indonesia's debt and deforestation in the late 1970s when he noted: "We do not have to worry our heads about debts, for we still have forests to repay those debts." Two decades later, deforestation rates had risen threefold, and Indonesia produced about 70 per cent of the world's hardwood supply. Overall, wood products have become Indonesia's main non-fossil fuel commodities, earning more than US $3 billion annually.[26] A large proportion of Indonesia's pristine environments was developed into new industrial plantations of rubber, oil palm, and pulpwood. These activities required the clearing of hundreds of thousands of hectares of land, and setting fires was the cheapest option.

Hence, since the 1980s, Indonesian forests have been subjected to the largest artificial forest fires in human history, irreparably destroying much of the evolutionary vestiges of the most biologically diverse patchworks of ecosystems and habitats of the planet. These apocalyptic fires exposed some 100 million people to a thick smoky haze (which could be viewed through satellite photographic transmission on the Internet). The poor visibility due to smoke caused fatal airplane crashes and ship collisions in a region ranging from Borneo to Singapore. The air quality became so poor that the governments in the region were forced to declare a temporary state of emergency. At one point, Malaysian Prime Minister Mahathir Mohamad even wore a surgical mask in public – and urged his compatriots to do the same.[27] Mike Davis offered an insightful comment: "Billionaire arsonists set almost the entirety of [the] Malay Archipelago ablaze with their greed."[28]

The ecological damage is largely irreversible. For example, some 80 per cent of Indonesia's orangutan habitats were destroyed, only 2 per cent of the original habitat of orangutans in Indonesia were left intact.[29] Overall, the world is now losing forest cover at a rate without historical precedent: during the last 15 years of the twentieth century, total global forest cover dropped by about 180 million hectares, an area nearly as large as Mexico.[30]

The New World Order created by neo-liberal globalization is perhaps manifested most starkly through the chilling fact that more forest fires burned in any single year of the last decade of the twentieth century than in all of human history. In the process, these fires irreparably destroyed precious biodiversity resulting from millions of years of evolution.[31]

A TERMINAL GRAND BUFFET?

Among critical voices in the field of social ecology, there is an overwhelming consensus that the present situation is fundamentally unsustainable. Various commentators have coined different terms for this predicament; some call it "ecocide" or "terracide," others refer to it as "planetocide." Unfortunately, the gap between this insight and existing social and ecological practice has even widened in recent years. Population growth during the 1990s alone exceeded the growth experienced in the previous 10,000 years. Given the population growth of 40 per cent in the last 30 years, and a quadrupling of consumption, how can we reverse the loss of biodiversity, the damage to the global atmosphere, and the degradation of the environment?[32] It is clear that the prevailing mode of global development cannot be "sustainable," that is, we are in the process of compromising the ability of the future generations to meet their needs.[33]

William Catton was the first environmental sociologist who diagnosed the late modern global trajectory of human social and ecological relations in progressive ecocidal or speciescidal terms of what he called "overshoot." "It is becoming apparent," he noted already in the early 1980s, that nature must, in the not far distant future, "institute bankruptcy proceedings against industrial civilization, and perhaps against the standing crop of human flesh," just as nature had done many times in response to previous episodes of overshoot.[34] "Overshoot" simply means that we have exceeded the carrying capacity of planet Earth.[35] If the present world population of 6.1 billion people were to live at current North American ecological standards, a reasonable first approximation of the total productive land requirement would be more than 10 billion square miles (assuming present technology). However, there are only just over 5 billion square miles of land on Earth, of which only 3.4 billion are ecologically productive cropland, pasture, or forest. In short, we would need at least two more planets of Earth's size to accommodate the increased ecological demands[36] as there are obvious limits to the regenerative capacities of nature. The loss of species and the associated reduction of biodiversity are, for all practical purposes, irreversible and final.

Overshoot lowers carrying capacity. Transgressing the carrying capacity starts an ecocidal downward spiral toward zero. Biologist David Klein's classic study of the reindeer on St Matthew Island in Alaska illustrates the point. In 1944 a population of 29 animals was moved to the island, without concern for its impact on the local ecosystem. Within two decades, the reindeer population swelled to 6,000, only to "crash" within three years to a total of 41 females and one male, all in miserable condition. Klein estimates that the carrying capacity of the island was about five deer per square kilometer. At the population peak, there were 18 reindeer per square kilometer. After the crash, there remained only 0.126 animals per square kilometer. The recovery of depleted food resources would take decades; indeed, with a continuing resident population of reindeer, it may never occur.[37]

The example shows that overshoot is a temporary condition, to be followed by a drastic decline in population. A possible human crash in the twenty-first century is a distinct possibility. So far, the world's governments have done very little to avoid such a possible crash. For example: the 1992 UN Environment Conference in Rio de Janeiro, Brazil, failed largely because of corporate resistance. The world's only remaining superpower, the United States of America, has failed to ratify several important treaties on biodiversity and climate change drafted during the 1990s.[38]

In the era of neo-liberal globalization, human beings have turned into "Future Eaters," or *Homo esophagus colossus*. Our species engages in what is the largest – and perhaps the terminal – Grand Buffet in the history of our planet. Everything people consume has an impact on the environment – taking a single branch from the forest leaves some mark on the ecosystem. Still, not all consumption is necessarily bad. For one, our intervention in nature is essential to human survival, but many of our activities, particularly in the late twentieth century, constitute wasteful luxuries. Indeed, the existence of widespread poverty on Earth shows that many consume too little of the essentials of life – food, fuel, and shelter. According to the UN Human Development Report, 3 billion humans, or half of the world's population, are now malnourished, suffering from micronutrient deficiencies brought on by a combination of low income and inadequate distribution of food.[39] Some forms of consumption, such as the excessive burning of fossil fuels, are inherently harmful, whereas others, such as the use of forest products and the growing of food crops can be sustained virtually indefinitely – if done wisely – without causing damage to the environment.

It is the nature and scale of consumption that matter, and much of the consumption that is taking place in the global North is extremely damaging to the environment. For example, the coal we are burning to generate electricity produces particulates, acidic compounds, mercury, and other toxic materials that pollute the air, soil, and water. The gasoline we use to keep our cars on our congested highways creates smog and harmful gases. To supply the late-capitalist industrial global demand for wood products, the timber industry thins and clearcuts millions of acres of publicly and privately owned forests annually. Even our appetite for meat has become a serious problem, since the amount of grain needed to feed livestock multiplies the impact of intensive methods of agriculture on air, soil, and water. Hence, reducing fossil fuel consumption, changing our agricultural practices, and distributing environmental risks more evenly are critical steps toward the collective survival of our species.[40]

The people who claim the lion's share of the Grand Buffet disproportionately reside in the rich countries of the northern hemisphere, particularly in the United States. Compared to people living in the poorer countries of the global South, the members of this group consume enormous quantities of energy, metals, minerals, forest products, fresh water, fish, grains, and meat. According to the Worldwatch Institute, a typical citizen of an advanced industrial country uses 3 times as much fresh water, 10 times as much energy, and 19 times as much aluminum as a typical citizen of a developing country. The average American citizen uses twice as much fossil fuel as the average resident of Great Britain and two-and-a-half times as much as the average Japanese. The United States produces and consumes one third of the world's paper, despite having just 5 per cent of the world's population and 6 per cent of its forest cover.[41] The sheer waste of materials by this "planetary consumer class" is astounding: the average American discards nearly a ton of trash per year, two to three times as much as the average European, not to speak of less privileged citizens in the global South.[42] Of course, not all Americans fall into the same consumer category, given the tremendous social inequalities existing in the richest country on Earth. Obviously, affluent people tend to consume far more. They tend to travel farther and more frequently, ride in gas-guzzling cars like sports-utility vehicles. Likewise, there exists enormous wealth even in the poorest developing countries. Indigenous elites are eager to spend their money the same ecocidal way as many affluent Americans do. Consumerism is not just a facet of American life, but a burgeoning and highly differentiated worldwide trend. The term *Homo esophagus colossus* fits this global consumer class, given their enormous negative impact on the planet's species and biodiversity.

ECOCIDE AND THE GLOBAL TREADMILL OF PRODUCTION

The concept of the global "treadmill of production" is a term coined by Galbraith to demonstrate how our late modern materialist and "consumer-oriented" society operates.[43] The global treadmill system, largely responsible for the accelerated pace of ecocide, constitutes "a kind of giant squirrel cage."[44] Everyone is part of this gigantic treadmill and is unable or unwilling to get off. Investors and managers are driven by the need to accumulate wealth and to expand the scale of their operations in order to prosper within a globally competitive milieu. For the vast majority of the world's people, the commitment to the treadmill is more limited and indirect: they simply need to obtain jobs at livable wages. But to retain these jobs and to maintain an acceptable standard of living it is necessary, like the Red Queen in *Through the*

Looking Glass, to run faster and faster in order to stay in the same place.[45] An increasingly large proportion of people within this global treadmill system – currently estimated at more than 850 million people – are either underemployed or unemployed.

Considering these large, structural forces, it is not merely individuals acting in accord with their perceived needs and acquired desires, but the global treadmill of production itself that has become the main culprit in the ecocidal endgame. As discussed in previous chapters, this treadmill has been churning for some time, creating a predicament that is at odds with the basic ecological health of the planet. As John Bellamy Foster points out, a continuous 3 per cent average annual rate of growth in industrial production, such as obtained from 1970 to 1990, would mean that world industry would double in size every 25 years, grow sixteenfold approximately every century, increase by 250 times every two centuries, 4,000 times every three centuries, and so on.[46]

Further, the tendency of the present global treadmill of production is to expand consumption of raw materials and energy in order to generate higher profits. The treadmill relies heavily on energy-intensive, capital-intensive technology, leading to a more rapid depletion of high-quality energy sources and other natural resources, and to ever larger amounts of waste being dumped into the environment.[47]

The global landscape is increasingly littered and suffused with microtoxic and radiological time bombs. The degree of toxicity in the environment has risen steadily over the last half century. Some of the 100,000 synthetic chemicals introduced in the last century are affecting the reproductive systems of animals and humans – even generations after exposure. For example, by the end of the twentieth century, over 1,000 tons of plutonium had been produced worldwide. The annual radiation of the plutonium used in the world's 424 nuclear power plants alone would be capable of destroying all living creatures on earth.[48] In short, the global treadmill of production has produced an exceedingly damaging global social configuration. "It would seem," writes Foster, "that from an environmental perspective we have no choice but to resist the treadmill of production."[49]

The most vocal environmental activists have long argued that resistance to ecocide must take the form of a far-reaching moral revolution.[50] In order to carry out such a "moral transformation," however, we are unlikely to succeed unless we confront what sociologist C. Wright Mills called "the higher immorality," that is, forms of "structural immorality" built on the institutions of power and the treadmill of production.[51] Structural immorality produces societies characterized by the loss of the capacity for moral indignation, the growth of cynicism, falling levels of political participation, and the emergence of an atomized, commercially centered existence.[52]

Under the conditions of a global corporate culture with industry geared toward profitable production and exchange, we can expect people to be more interested in the value of commodities than in the increasingly precarious state of the planetary environment and the progressively ecocidal scope of the contemporary mass extinction crisis.

Resistance to the depredations of the global treadmill must be based on the repudiation of the process of commodification of living beings and the environment. A respectful coexistence of diverse life forms – human and otherwise – must be pursued on the basis of relinquishing the myth of the rational subordination of nature as well as its related dogma of self-interested accumulation, both of which arose during the Enlightenment. Resistance to the global treadmill of production has come mainly from social movements representing the underprivileged and marginalized. As the late German Green Party leader Petra Kelly emphasized, ecological concerns are always tied to issues of economic justice – the exploitation of the poor by the rich.[53]

Every environmental struggle of today is also a struggle fought over the expansion of the global treadmill, as in the case of landless workers or villagers who are compelled to destroy nature in order to survive, or large corporations that seek to expand profits with little concern for the ecocidal and social devastation that they leave in their wake. To be sympathetic towards the powerless means to embrace a common morality that constitutes the foundation from which to combat the immorality of the treadmill. Above all, we must recognize that increasing production will not eliminate poverty. As the historical record of the twentieth century shows, economic expansion and growth merely raise the ecocidal stakes.

THE FAILURE OF ENVIRONMENTAL EDUCATION

Most modern institutions of formal education and schooling are an integral part of the global treadmill of production.[54] The educational analogy to the global "treadmill of production" is the "degree-mill" of ideological repro-duction. Modern schooling has played an instrumental part in ideologically reproducing the progressively ecocidal global predicament. After all, as social critic and linguist Noam Chomsky notes:

... the universities are not independent institutions. They are dependent on outside sources of support and those sources of support, such as private wealth, big corpora-tions with grants, and the government (which is so closely interlinked with corporate power you can barely distinguish them).[55]

Let me make two general observations about the relationship between ecocide and education. Environmental education historically emerges at the point when, first, ecology becomes a profitable branch of secondary industries within the framework of global capitalism, and when, second, modern societies are for the first time confronted with the possibility of their self-annihilation.[56] School-based environmental education over the past few decades has been slowly developing. Relatively little attention has been paid to community-based and other practical forms of education.

But even school-based environmental education requires further improvement. Allan Schnaiberg, one of the leading US environmental sociologists, was one of the first academics to raise concerns about the poor state of environmental education in the institutions of higher learning in the United States and elsewhere.[57] Schnaiberg argues that "few of our undergraduates really are exposed to much systematic thinking about environmental issues in their experiences." What passes for "environmental education," in Schnaiberg's words, "is deeply flawed at every level of the educational system." He concludes on a pessimistic note: "I have repeatedly found, in teaching and in meetings (including professional meetings), that students and even colleagues lack any really systematic perspective on ecological systems, on social systems, and especially on the systematic relationship between the two."[58] In short, the dominant institutions – the culture industry, schooling, and the media – have failed to develop a serious educational initiative because they are too deeply rooted in the existing political-economic structures of the global treadmill of production.

THE IDEOLOGICAL TURN

The tendency to conceptualize environmental problems in ideological terms is one of the symptomatic responses to the problems engendered by the progressively speciescidal global treadmill of production. By "ideology" I understand a system of widely shared beliefs and values that simplify and distort social reality in order to protect specific power interests. Thus, dominant ideological processes produce political and cognitive distortions of the species-survival situation. Corporate media reporting on environmental affairs typically focus on the horrific extent of a given environmental calamity, but usually they ignore causality by emphasizing the immediate rather than underlying causes. This often finds expression in the journalistic predilection for using passive language wherever possible, leaving the audience ill-equipped to imagine themselves as active agents combating an environmental crisis. Statements such as "we are faced with the loss of large numbers of species by the end of the century," or "the holes in the ozone layer are growing," or "the world's rainforests are rapidly receding," or "global warming is producing extreme weather events such as superhurricanes and century floods," may provoke an awareness of environmental problems, but they conveniently leave the sources of the global ecological crisis unexamined.[59]

Questions relating to human agency, that is, to the social and economic processes by which we arrive at a state of scorched trees and dead otters and poisoned whales, are rarely raised in public discourse. Neither educational training nor popular media coverage encourage us to ask historical questions about the actors, institutions, and processes behind the oil-slicked beaches, destroyed rainforests, or the toxic substances in our communities. Critical theorists and grassroots activists who insist that progressive ecocide and other so-called "environmental problems" represent collective existential issues that are not reducible to technical matters are frequently portrayed as "troublemakers" or "wild-eyed prophets of doom." To the contrary, they merely suggest that our "environmental problems" are deeply rooted in the foundations of late modern society itself.

Critical social theorists have variously called for a radical expansion and extension of democracy in the direction of a new "ecological democracy."[60] Producing new institutions, social relations, and culture would make possible more life-affirming relations among humans and between humans and other species. An emancipatory political ecology, then, would have to begin with a relentless critique of ecocide, loss of biodiversity, and the globalization of environmental degradation.[61] The remaining part of this chapter elaborates in more detail on some of the essential elements of this emancipatory vision of species emancipation.

THE CURRENTS OF ECOLOGICAL DEMOCRACY

What do grassroots movements for social and environmental justice think of the relationship between capitalism and the ecological crisis? Critical social ecologists have generally argued that since capitalism is based upon the principle of "growth or death," a "green" capitalism is unsustainable and therefore impossible.[62] Given its institutional logic, capitalism must continually expand, in the process creating new markets, increasing production and consumption, invading more ecosystems, and using more resources. Sociologist Takis Fotopoulos has argued that the main reason why the project of "greening" capitalism is just a "utopian dream" lies in "a fundamental contradiction that exists between the logic and dynamic of the growth economy, on the one hand, and the attempt to condition this dynamic with qualitative interests on the other."[63]

Moreover, proponents of ecological democracy argue that global competition between nation-states is another element responsible for ecocide. As international competition becomes more intense and weapons of mass destruction spread, the seeds are being sown for catastrophic global warfare involving nuclear, chemical, and biological weapons. Because such warfare would be the ultimate ecological disaster, the green and peace movements are but two aspects of the same basic project. Similarly, ecological democrats recognize that domination of nature and male domination of women have historically gone hand in hand. Hence, so-called "eco-feminism" is yet another aspect of ecological democracy.

Since feminism, ecology, and peace are key issues of the new social movements more broadly, radical environmentalists believe that mainstream social movements for social and environmental justice should adopt more radical democratic principles of direct political action rather than choosing the gradual road of trying to elect environmentally conscious people to state offices. Radicals criticize mainstream greens for confining their attack to what they consider to be the "wrong ideas" of modern society, that is, its "materialistic values" and individualistic tendencies. For the proponents of a more pragmatic approach to environmental issues, the radical critique misses the point that ideas and values do not "just happen," but are the product of a given set of social relationships. This means that it is not just a matter of changing our values in a way that places humanity in harmony with nature, but also a matter of understanding the social and structural origins of the ecological crisis. While ideas and values need to be challenged, real change will not occur if our hierarchical relationships and social inequalities remain in place. In short, the social and institutional context that reproduces ecocidal practices must be transformed in order to arrive at an ecologically sensitive society. Our present ecocidal predicament did not develop in a social vacuum and is, therefore, not reducible to the biological deficiency of our species or some inherent feature of so-called "human nature."

A key argument for a more direct form of global democracy put forward by a rainbow coalition of progressive social movements since the 1960s is that the effective protection of our planet's species and their habitats requires that ordinary citizens be able to take part at the grassroots level in decision-making that affects their environment. That way, they would be more likely to take on special corporate interests that tend to dominate the so-called "representative" system of government. Thus, a constructive global resolution to the social and ecological crisis presupposes inclusive forms of ecological democracy in both the political and the economic sphere – a transformation that, in the contemporary cultural context, would amount to a social and ethical revolution.

THE IMPERATIVES OF ECOLOGICAL DEMOCRACY

The challenge of an ecologically sustainable form of global social development is to safeguard what remains of the biological heritage of the planet. In addition, the task is to provide people all over the world with a broad mix of stable jobs, goods, and services that meet human needs in ways that promote equity, efficiency, and environmental protection. This goes well beyond recycling "green" products, building ecological business parks, conserving rainforests, controlling greenhouse gas emissions, and so on. The current proliferation of mass extinction indicates that the contemporary global model of development is socially and ecologically unsustainable. As the 1987 Brundtland Report notes, the conventional model of development cannot but "compromise the ability of the future generations to meet their needs."[64] The dominant geoculture is out of synch with ecological reality.

Experts continue to debate whether there are limits to the supply of natural resources. In either case, the global reach of Western TV, films, video, and advertising means that unprecedented numbers of people are now constantly aware of all the commodities they do not have. To assume that the poor will accept their subordinate position indefinitely would be naïve. Nationalist, fundamentalist, and paramilitary movements are increasing in most countries, and increasingly their leaders will have access to nuclear, chemical, and biological weaponry. Hence, providing sustainable development for all is not merely a matter of protecting the environment; it is essential to regional and global security.

Despite this bleak outlook, people committed to ecological democracy refuse to accept ecocide as a *fait accompli*. William Greider has proposed a number of intermediate steps governments should take in order to avert the looming catastrophe:[65]

- Moderate the flow of goods by imposing emergency tariffs to rectify trade deficits, change labor practices in developing countries, and allow labor to share in the ownership of capital
- Restore national and regional controls over global capital
- Restore a progressive tax system
- Stimulate an ecologically responsible form of global growth by boosting consumer demand from the bottom up
- Compel trading nations to accept more balanced trade relations and absorb more surplus production
- Forgive the debt of the poorest countries in the global South
- Reorganize monetary policy to confront the realities of a globalized money supply both to achieve greater stability and to open the way to greater growth
- Defend labor rights in all markets and prohibit sweatshops
- Reformulate the idea of economic growth to escape the wasteful nature of consumption
- Defend social policies against free-market fundamentalism

Wangari Maathai, a feminist human-rights campaigner and founder of the Kenyan Greenbelt Movement, also sketched out some principles of ecological democracy.[66] Emphasizing "issues vital to building environmentally sound and socially equitable societies," she challenged her audience to implement the following tasks:

- eliminating poverty
- establishing fair and environmentally sound trade
- reversal of the net flow of resources from South to North
- recognition of the responsibilities of business and industry
- changes in wasteful patterns of consumption
- internalization of the environmental and social costs of natural resources use
- assuring equitable access to environmentally sound technology and its benefits
- redirection of military expenditures to environmental and social goals
- democratization of local, national, and international political institutions and decision-making structures

In similar fashion, the following list of broadly construed guidelines drawn up by the rainbow coalition-based International Green Movement may further serve as a useful vision for global social movements intent on realizing global ecological democracy.

- Ecological Wisdom
- Personal and Social Responsibility
- Post-Patriarchal Values
- Decentralization
- Future Focus
- Grassroots Democracy
- Respect for Diversity
- Community-Based Economics
- Non-Violence
- Global Responsibility

There is a growing recognition that a democratization of the economy and the state is a necessary precondition for solving the worldwide social and environmental crisis of the late modern era. A feminist, green, and social justice-oriented vision would be sensitive to the needs of the planet and all its species, including humans. It would champion the perspective of those who are already suffering through racism, sexism, poverty, and exploitation. Such a commitment would be "green" because of its vision of creating an ecologically sustainable society; it would be democratic in its support of a more egalitarian society; it would be feminist in its realization that most human beings who lack basic needs are women. The imperatives contained in ecological democracy seek to preserve people's right actively to participate in decisions that affect their lives. The right to participate and deliberate in political matters resides only in the individual; it should *not* extend to corporations.[67] The minimum standard of dignified human life should not emerge as an appendix of economics; politics must be restored to the center of human interaction. Indeed, basic needs are not mere physical; they include emotional and intellectual dimensions as well. Along those lines, social thinker Manfred Max-Neef has identified nine basic needs:

- Subsistence
- Affection
- Understanding
- Participation
- Leisure
- Creation
- Identity
- Meaning
- Freedom

The continued viability of our planet's biodiversity, including that fragile species known as humans, will critically be predicated upon the emancipatory project I call "ecological democracy."

ENVISIONING AN EQUITABLE GLOBAL COMMONS

Even from a purely pragmatic perspective, there are several reasons why it is in the best interest of developed nations to radically narrow the gap between rich and poor. First, it will help the global South to protect what remains of its vast reservoirs of biodiversity, whose destruction affects at least two major elements of carrying capacity. The need for wild plants and microorganisms, which already supply the active ingredients in more than 25 per cent of modern pharmaceuticals, may become acute, as the human population grows more susceptible to disease.[68] Biodiversity is also critical to maintaining crop resistance to pests and drought, supplying the raw materials for genetic engineering, and thus hopefully permitting a future phenomenal boost in agricultural yields required to feed an exponentially growing population.

Second, developing nations have advanced far in demonstrating their power to severely degrade the entire planet's life support systems simply by following development paths taken by the rich. Elementary calculations indicate that the mobilization of coal reserves to fuel even a modest increment of development could overwhelm any efforts by industrialized nations to compensate by reducing their own greenhouse gas emissions. Similarly, a further large increase in methane and nitrous oxide releases would accompany the currently planned expansion of agriculture and the continued destruction of tropical forest. It has long been recognized that the rapid deployment of less-damaging technologies, such as solar-hydrogen energy technologies, in developed nations and their transfer to the rest of the world is required to secure just this atmospheric element of the global commons.

Third, the ever-growing disparity between rich and poor carries severe implications for social carrying capacity, including intensifying economic dislocation and social strife as the transfer of capital, labor, and refugees across steepening gradients of social and economic difference accelerates. Political challenges also loom large as the ranks of those with little to lose increase, nuclear capability proliferates in the developing world, and vulnerability to terrorism increases.

In short, the lesson and moral of the story here is that there is no escape by lifeboat possible, even for the rich. All nations will have yet to come to grips with the planet's limits to carrying capacity, acknowledging that there are not merely socially created scarcities or "social limits to growth," but also absolute scarcities or ecological limits to growth.[69] Unless measures are taken by the rich to facilitate sustainable development, the continued destruction of humanity's life support systems is virtually guaranteed. However, it is the premise of this book that civilizational and ecological collapse is *not* a *fait accompli*; a world catastrophe is not inevitable, and a sustainable and socially just society is both technologically and economically possible. As sociologist Anthony Giddens proposes, humanity ought to be "looking for a theory of society which is a globalizing society, where markets (are) very important, but can be reconciled with social cohesion and a measure of social justice as well as with an open, cosmopolitan community."[70]

For environmentalists, one crucial task should be to examine the ways in which institutions define and foster different conceptions of interests. Individuals' preferences and conceptions of their interests need to be the end point of analysis, not its starting point.[71] Economics needs to move away from concern about commensuration and prices – either real or "shadow" – and "towards an inquiry into the institutional conditions under which individuals are enabled to nurture a concern for the environment and treat it in a rational and sensitive way."[72]

Some central questions to be asked are: what institutional frameworks develop a concern for future generations and the non-human world? What frameworks encourage rational argument and debate about environmental matters? What are the institutional conditions of sustainable economic practices? What institutions and power relationships undermine such conceptions? Inquiries of this type, while they are ignored by neo-classical economic traditions, are a crucial part of an older, Aristotelian tradition.[73] Environmental philosopher John O'Neill notes that one task of this tradition is:

... to craft political and social associations which enable every person to act virtuously and live happily, while limiting the power of institutions of the market, which encourages unlimited acquisitiveness and thus the vice of pleonexia, the desire to have more than is proper.[74]

Despite the claims of orthodox economists, such associations would treat individual wants with a great deal more respect than bureaucracies based on cost-benefit thinking. Ecologically sound institutions would acknowledge, for example, that problems of mass extinction, flooded wetlands, or polluted oceans can be properly understood or dealt with only by taking into consideration the economic history and the irreducible plurality of social practices and locally rooted communities. The next few decades present humanity with a window of opportunity for laying the institutional foundations for an equitable global commons. Crucial here is the "freedom to make public use of one's reason in all matters," as Immanuel Kant put it.[75]

EPILOGUE

LIVING IN THE AGE OF ECOCIDE

At the dawn of the twenty-first century, it has become apparent that, for the first time since the extinction of the dinosaurs 65 million years ago, changes of enormous ecological significance are occurring on our planet. These changes are the result of the actions of a single species of animal, *Homo sapiens sapiens*. The ozone layer in the stratosphere, which has protected terrestrial life for hundreds of millions of years from the ultraviolet radiation from the sun, is beginning to disintegrate. Progressive changes in the climate of the planet resulting from the release of greenhouse gases are only now reluctantly being acknowledged.[1] Other significant developments include important ecological changes in the oceans, severe damage of the forests of the Northern Hemisphere due to acid rain, and the rapid disappearance of tropical forests. Since 1970, the world's forests have declined from 4.4 square miles per 1,000 people to 2.8 square miles per 1,000 people. A quarter of the world's fish stocks have been depleted, and another 44 percent are being fished to their biological limits.[2]

"Without hyperbole," notes biologist Stephen Hubbell in one of the most important recent research contributions to ecology and biogeography, "we can truthfully say that we are almost out of time to save much of the diversity of life on Earth."[3] Humans already sequester an astonishing 40 percent of the entire terrestrial primary production of the Earth for our selfish use. Capturing such an enormous fraction of the Earth's natural productive capacity comes at a huge cost in terms of loss of natural habitat or reduction in the viability or outright mass extinction of species.

More than any other ecological predicament, the modern mass extinction crisis is an indicator that life on our planet is out of synch.[4] Species extinction is irreversible, particularly if measured on a human evolutionary time scale. Its accelerating pace ought to be considered as an environmental problem of more importance than even the depletion of the ozone layer, global warming, or pollution and contamination. The synergism and combined input of contemporary military, demographic, and socioeconomic depredations suggests that the juggernaut of late modernity has entered an increasingly ecocidal phase.

As the Nobel Laureate, novelist, and philosopher Elias Canetti suggests, "the planet's survival has become so uncertain that any effort, any thought that presupposes an assured future amounts to a mad gamble."[5] To reiterate, however, historical outcomes are not predetermined. None of the social tendencies sketched above are "inevitable" in a fatalistic sense. Instead, these are the historically contingent outcomes of human social and cultural evolution – the aggregate result of human agency operating under varying sets of enabling and constraining conditions historically imposed by social institutions and the environment. Human beings occupy neither a central nor a trivial place in the universe. We may well be the only species of its kind in the galaxy, but we represent only one among myriad life forms that evolved on that planet we call Earth during the past 4 billion years. Although we share 98.3 per cent of our genes with chimpanzees, our species evolved into something quite different. Less than 2 per cent of our genes have enabled us, for better and worse, to found civilizations and religions, to develop intricate languages, create art, develop scientific principles. The same potential, however, has also afforded us the capacity to destroy all of our achievements overnight.

The social evolution of the modern human species has progressed by unprecedented, fantastic, leaps and bounds. Even so, we have barely begun to understand that humans evolved in an evolutionary context of extraordinary biodiversity. We have barely begun to grasp the momentous implications of the precarious nature and fragile state of the planet's ecological systems. We have barely begun to acknowledge the historical implications of the fact that our species has socially evolved into a colonizing, polarized, class-divided, and conflict-ridden assembly of walking ecological disasters.

The bitter irony of this ecocidal predicament is that our species constitutes the most adaptable of all known creatures that have ever existed on Earth. As science writer Colin Tudge put it, humans are an "all-purpose animal that in principle can solve any problem."[6] The acquisition of language – enabling our genus to negotiate our environment in ways unlike those of any other species – was perhaps the most decisive factor.[7] Reason and insight, the great human features, have given us the power to forge a world to fit our own comfort. Both divided and united, we carve the planet's surface into fields and streets, shopping malls and parking lots, with little regard for what was there before. We replace "wilderness" with structures that offer a more immediate, short-term benefit.[8]

If history teaches us anything, it is that our global impact on other species and habitats can be ignored only at our peril. Humans represent an intricate part of biodiversity, and the comparative environmental history and sociology of civilization clearly show that by destroying our environment we are destroying ourselves. The late Quaternary mass extinction and the introduction of sedentary agriculture set into motion a historical roller coaster oscillating between economic boom and ecological bust cycles. It led to the meteoric rise and often violent collapse of civilizations. Modernity has raised the global social and ecological stakes to a monumental level by massively expanding the scale of ecocide. Humans have an amazing capability to believe that economic plenty will last forever. But it never does. The late modern world resembles a kind of suspended treadmill on which people busy themselves with everything except with those things that are destroying them. Repression and denial do not just take the psychological form of evading an authentic inner life. As I noted in previous chapters, the widespread denial of the scale of global environmental problems has deeper social institutional and ideological roots.

Whether the world becomes an ecological wasteland of exterminated species, evicted forest people, swollen urban slums, and millions of acres of degraded pastures and poisoned rivers will ultimately be decided by the historical outcome of emancipatory human struggles. The ongoing contest over the conservation of the remaining ecosystems will be waged together with the battle for social and environmental justice and distribution. But the future outcome of these emancipatory struggles will not be determined in the circles of the established political institutions. More likely, those who determine it will be an umbrella of burgeoning coalitions of consumers, government agencies, and non-governmental organizations.

I have argued in this study that the lack of democratic participation in the economic sphere lies at the root of the global crisis. Our inability to come up with a meaningful form of ecological democracy has fueled the process of mass extinctions of species. Accelerated by neo-liberal ideology, globalization has led to the concentration of economic resources in fewer and fewer hands, thus structuring decision-making processes over the use and applications of social wealth in accordance with the instrumental imperatives of capital accumulation. The related demographic explosion of the late modern era has also greatly amplified the power of humans to displace and annihilate other species. The rise of the modern arms race and industrialization of warfare occurring within the geopolitical context of competitive modern nation-states has caused further ecological damage to our planet.[9] As a consequence, many socially committed and politically active people around the world have joined together in a growing progressive coalition dedicated to the issues of ecology, peace, labor, gender rights, and human rights. For these activists, the fate of our planet has never seemed as frightening and insecure as it does today.[10]

Thus we live in an age of ecocide, caught somewhere between an unparalleled destructive industrial past and an uncertain future that holds out either the specter of annihilation or the promise of ecological democracy. The challenge posed by ecocide is enormous. If we fail in our collective responsibilities vis-à-vis our increasingly species-impoverished planet, we will have failed to live up to the noble claim of wisdom contained in the name of our species: "*Homo sapiens sapiens*." Then we have only ourselves to blame. Stephen Jay Gould once remarked that "dinosaurs should be a term of praise, not of opprobrium. They reigned supreme for more than 120 million years and died through no fault of their own."[11] Unless we act soon to drastically reverse our current ecocidal course, we will have graced this planet for a far shorter time than our mighty reptile forebears.

GLOSSARY

NB: Glossaries are not neutral and always involve a point of view.

Agency: The ability of people to change the institutions in which they live. People make their own history; however, they do not make it just as they please, but under circumstances directly encountered, given, and transmitted from the past.

Agrodiversity: Agrodiversity, or agricultural biodiversity, refers to the part of genetic resources that feeds and nurtures people – whether derived from plants, animals, fish, or forests. We are losing genetic resources for food and agriculture at an unprecedented rate, with three-quarters of the worldwide genetic diversity in agricultural crop cultivars and animal breeds already lost since 1900.

Alienation: The domination of humans by their own products – material, political, and ideological – the separation of humans from their humanity, the interference with the production of authentic culture, the fragmentation of social bonds and community. The solution to alienation is social change rather than psychological counseling.

Anthropocentrism: Sometimes also referred to as "human-centrism" or "speciesism," not unlike "racism," "ageism," or "sexism"; it is contrasted to "ecocentrism" or "biocentrism." The practice of treating the human species as if it were the center of all values and the measure of all things.

Anthropogenic: Caused or produced by humans.

Australopithecus: Meaning "southern ape": the genus to which the very earliest hominids, who lived around 2 million to 4 million years ago in Africa, belong. (The "Lucy" fossil is an example of Australopithecus.)

Background extinction: The rate of extinction typical of most of the fossil record. Before humans existed, the species extinction rate was (very roughly) one species per million species per year (0.0001 per cent). Estimates for current species extinction rates range from 100 to 10,000 times that, but most hover close to 1,000 times pre-human levels (0.1 per cent per year), with the rate projected to rise, and very likely sharply.

BCE and CE: The notations BCE (for "Before the Common Era") and CE (for "Common Era"), which are arbitrarily modeled on the Western calendar, represent an attempt by world historians to establish a trans-parochial time frame.

Biodiversity: The variety of living organisms of all kinds – animals, plants, fungi, and micro-organisms – that inhabit an area. Synonymous with species richness and relative species abundance in space and time, or "life on Earth." The diversity of life today in all corners of the Earth is the result of over 3 billion years of evolution, and when it is threatened the consequences are far-reaching, but not always understood.

Bioinvasion: The spread of non-native, or "exotic," species, bioinvasion may be the least visible and least predictable of all the major dimensions of global ecological decline. Next to habitat loss, it is also one of the most dangerous, because exotics often create pressures for which there is no local evolutionary precedent: native species simply may not be adapted to live with the invaders.

Bioregion: The term is derived from the Greek terms for "life" and "territory," and thus it means a place defined by its life forms and the carrying capacity of the land. Bioregionalism implies an understanding of the land, its geographical features, its resource inventory, and its carrying capacity as a self-sufficient human and wild habitat. The term is considered liberating in the way it opens up to communitarian values of cooperation, participation, and reciprocity.

Biosphere: That part of Earth within which life exists, including (1) the lithosphere, the uppermost layer of Earth approximately 2 miles deep; (2) the hydrosphere, the oceans; and (3) the troposphere, the lower atmosphere. All living matter is the product of the biosphere.

Bourgeois society: A type of society in which exchange relationships replace social relationships in which cultural items (e.g. sex, drugs, foods, loyalty, sports) and nature (air, water, biodiversity, etc.) become commodities exchanged for profit, and in which private profit is the central test of production. Sociologists also use the term "post-bourgeois industrial society" to describe social-cultural conditions in the late modern era.

Cambrian period: The earliest period of the Paleozoic era, extending from 500 million to 550 million years ago.

Carrying capacity: Defined by ecologists as the population of a given species that can be supported indefinitely in a defined habitat without permanently damaging the ecosystem upon which it is dependent. It is usually defined as the average maximum number of individuals of a given species that can occupy a particular habitat without permanently impairing the productive capacity of that habitat.

Class: Class is one of five great systems of social domination which affect patterns of health, housing, self-esteem, religion, education, recreation, and politics. The critical definition of class is different from that used by many sociologists who use terms like middle-class to refer to level of income rather than relationship to the process of production. Critics of class societies point out that such systems do not allow the rational control of economic life, but rather distort society/nature relations into progressively speciescidal or ecocidal directions. (See *Systems of social domination.*)

Colonization: A type of exchange relation between societies and their physiological and biological natural environments. This exchange relation is a prerequisite of metabolism, the flows of materials and energy between society and nature; it cannot be described within the logic of input-output models, but rather within the logic of domination.

Commodification: The practice of converting use value into exchange value; a process of turning goods and services, even land, labor, and biodiversity, into products for sale in the market. Food, for example, has a use value, but its exchange value may be set so high that people starve even when there is a lot of food; the same is true for any essential goods or services once they have been commodified.

Corporation: A group of people joined in a common purpose to hold property, make contracts, and share profits according to the terms of a formal agreement or contract (charter) recognized by the state.

Critical theory: An approach to the study of society holding that human interests shape and guide the research enterprise from the formation of analytic categories to the quest for accurate, relevant, timely, and sensible information. Critical theory has an overt political goal: that of a rational and decent society.

Culture: The human species' most notable anthropological characteristic. Humans make themselves by widening and deepening their culture. Whether termed material, social, or spiritual, culture includes the multitude of relations between humans and nature: the procuring and preservation of food; the securing of shelter; the utilization of the objects of nature as implements or utensils; and all the various ways in which humanity utilizes or controls, or is controlled by, the natural environment.

Democracy: Greek: *demos,* the people; *kratein,* to rule: rule of the people. Not to be confused with republican forms of governance. The elements of a strong democracy include open discussion, direct voting on significant issues, policy formation in all realms of social life: economics, education, religion, and public life. (See also *Ecological democracy.*)

Depoliticization: The process of reducing the range of a question that is to be settled by collective and public discourse; thus (a) treating questions of foreign policy, employment policy, crime, environment, education, and science as settled, or (b) turning them over to technicians to manage. Most major news networks treat public issues as if they were depoliticized, that is, as if they were spectacles to be watched rather than problems to be solved by the public.

Ecocide: Acts undertaken with the intention of disrupting or destroying, in whole or in part, a human ecosystem. Ecocide includes the use of weapons of mass destruction, whether nuclear, bacteriological, or chemical; attempts to provoke natural disasters such as volcanoes, earthquakes, or floods; the military use of defoliants; the use of bombs to impair soil quality or to enhance the prospect of disease; the bulldozing of forests or croplands for military purposes; the attempt to modify weather or climate as a hostile act; and, finally, the forcible and permanent removal of humans or animals from their habitual place of habitation on a large scale to expedite the pursuit of military or other objectives. The concept of ecocide is analytically expanded here to describe contemporary holocaustic patterns of global environmental degradation and anthropogenic mass extinction of species. (See also *Overshoot.*)

Ecological democracy: To give a voice and a vote to mute nature in all human deliberations. Here, representative democracy becomes essentially that: humans re-present – make present again – the other creatures in all that we do. Ecological democracy cannot be achieved apart from grassroots democracy and economic democracy, and vice versa.

Ecological footprint: In the early 1990s, researchers at the University of British Columbia began to calculate the amount of land needed to sustainably supply national populations with resources (including imported ones) and to absorb their wastes. They dubbed this combined area the "ecological footprint" of a population, which can be used to measure the "load" imposed by a given population on nature and to determine the land area necessary to sustain current levels of resource consumption and waste discharge by that population.

Ecological sustainability: That which is needed to maintain indefinitely the bioproductivity (production of organic matter through photosynthesis) of the ecosystem of the biosphere, in which prevailing conditions satisfy the universal health needs of the human population.

Ecology: The word "ecology" is ancient in origin, derived from the Greek term *oikos*, from which "economy" is also derived. Until relatively recently, ecology referred either purely to social organization (sociology) or to natural relations (biology). Used in an interdisciplinary way, as in this book, ecological thought raises problems that are unlike any that human beings have ever faced before.

Ecosystem: A recognizable interrelated whole consisting of both living organisms and the non-living environment, defined over a particular area. For example, a tropical forest, grassland, or lake, including the dynamic complex of plant, animal, fungal, and micro-organism communities in it and their associated non-living environment interacting as an ecological unit. Three principles characterize an ecosystem: complexity, uncertainty, and interconnectedness.

Egalitarian society: A society based on the principle that all are entitled to equal treatment and rights in the society. The point of an egalitarian society is not that everyone is treated exactly alike (as in a massified bureaucratic system) but rather that everyone is accorded full status as a human being to produce culture. People can play very different roles and earn different rewards in such societies, but no one is excluded by reason of birth.

Evolution, natural: According to Darwin, what forms of life evolve, persist and continue to evolve or go extinct depend on the biological interplay between mutation, selection, and adaptation – or, if you will, on trial (and contingency) and error. There are many skips, jumps, twists, and reversals in plant, animal, and human evolution, which lead some to suppose a God created each species and continues to create new species. But a revision of Darwinian thought called "punctuated equilibrium" explains these jumps empirically rather than theologically.

Evolution, social: Generally, a view that society is changing for the better as a consequence of the struggle for survival in which the best (fittest) social forms survive. Most such theories celebrate whatever benefits their sponsors, but there is little evidence that things are getting better and certainly no assurance that things get better all by themselves.

Extinction: The disappearance of any lineage of organisms, from populations to species to higher taxonomic categories (genera, families, phyla). Extinctions can be local or global (total), and they strike both on the land and in the sea. Catastrophic exogenous causes can include meteorite impacts and comet or neutrino showers; catastrophic earth agents include volcanism, glaciation, variations in sea level, global climatic changes, and changes in ocean levels of oxygen or salinity, and the actions of human societies.

Future Eaters: A term coined by Tim Flannery in his paleohistorical work of the same name, in which he demonstrates that humans dominate rather than live as part of their environment, eating into the "capital resource base," exhausting it rather than using it sustainably, and eating away their own. The habit of "future eating" has recently become almost universal for humans. We are perhaps the first generation of future eaters who have looked over our shoulders at the past, but we have done so quite late in the process of environmental destruction.

Genera: The plural form of *genus*, referring to a taxonomic group of related species.

Global climate change: Current and predicted changes in global temperature, rainfall, and other aspects of weather due to increased human production of carbon dioxide and other greenhouse gases. Rapid global climate change and increase in frequency and intensity of extreme weather events are expected to accelerate modern mass extinction of species.

Globalization: A set of social processes, defined by various commentators in different and often contradictory ways depending upon their vantage points. Some see it as a polite term to describe the disastrous global expansion and universalization of capitalism, while others believe that the associated compression of time and space and the effective erasure of national boundaries for economic purposes herald unprecedented progress.

Habitat fragmentation: The process by which a continuous area or habitat is divided into two or more fragments by roads, farms, fences, logging, and other human activities. Habitat fragmentation is one of several mechanisms of biodiversity loss.

Holocene: Of, belonging to, or designating the geologic time of the two epochs of the Quaternary period, extending from the end of the Pleistocene epoch to the present.

Hominid: Refers to all human-like primates, that is, members of the genus *Homo*. Archaeologists have produced convincing evidence that over 15 different species of human-like primates have existed over the 6 million-year sojourn of the hominid family, and that many of these species existed simultaneously.

Homo esophagus colossus: A creature with a gigantic esophagus, capable of irreversibly devouring entire ecosystems. (Related or equivalent terms include *Homo ecocidus* and *Homo terricidus*.)

Homo sapiens sapiens: The modern-day human, a subspecies of *Homo sapiens* who appeared approximately 40,000 years ago in the middle of the last ice age, whose cultural practices included rituals associated with hunting, birth, and death. Cro-Magnon man, one of the best-known early populations of *Homo sapiens sapiens*, was an advanced hunter who used the bow and arrow to hunt for food, and whose remains have been found in quite a few late Stone Age sites in Eurasia.

Hotspots: Areas that (a) feature exceptional concentrations of endemic species and (b) face imminent threat of habitat destruction. Identification of the world's hotspots – there are roughly 18 to 25 in number, depending on the criteria employed – provides a means by which to focus on areas where threats to biodiversity are most extreme and where conservation efforts can be potentially most effective. Forests and other habitats in these remaining biodiversity hotspot areas have been reduced to a small fraction of their pre-human levels, and most are at immediate risk of disappearing.

Human load: Total "human load" imposed on the "environment" by a specified population is the product of population size times the average *per capita* resource consumption and waste production. The concept of load recognizes that human carrying capacity is a function not only of population size but also of aggregate material and energy throughput. Thus, the human carrying capacity of a defined habitat is its maximum sustainably supportable load. (See *Ecological footprint.*)

Ice age: A period of time when the Earth's climate is cold, resulting in glaciation, or the advancing of ice sheets. The last great ice age began about 115,000 years ago and ended only 10,000 years ago.

Ideology: A set of beliefs is ideology if: (1) it is false, (2) if it is believed by most people, and (3) if it is in the interest of the ruling class. Ideology represents an attempt on the part of all ruling classes to universalize their own beliefs, values, morality, and opinions as part of the "natural order of things" and indicates that humans are capable of (re)producing phantoms (unrealities), typically involving cognitive and political distortions of the survival situation.

International Monetary Fund: The financial agency used by rich countries to force debtor nations to institute state policy in order to return both principal and interest to the banks that loan money to them. Higher taxes and fewer programs of social justice ensue as a result of its work, and a great share of gross national income in poor nations goes to debt servicing.

Internationalization: Refers to the increasing importance of international trade, international relations, treaties, alliances, and the like. The basic unit remains the nation, even as relations among nations become increasingly necessary and important. Globalization, by contrast, refers to global economic integration of many formerly national economies into one global economy, mainly by free trade and free capital mobility, but also by easy or uncontrolled migration.

Introduced species: A species found in an area outside its historically known natural range as a result of intentional or accidental dispersal by human activities (also known as exotic species or alien species).

Juggernaut: Something, such as a belief or an institution, that elicits blind and destructive devotion or to which people are ruthlessly sacrificed; an over-whelming, advancing force that crushes or seems to crush everything in its path. The *American Heritage Dictionary* definition is adopted here as a metaphor to describe the progressively ecocidal and self-destructive, "runaway" quality of the late modern world economy and its associated culture.

Late modern: From 1945 onward; a period in which the types of environmental degradation include global warming, ozone depletion, marine pollution, deforestation, desertification, soil exhaustion, overspill and collective resource problems, acid deposition, nuclear risks, global biodiversity decline, and hazardous wastes. The key forces of environmental degradation include Western growth and consumption, socialist industrialization, industrialization of the global South and demographic explosion, and new high-consequence risks from nuclear, biological, and chemical technologies.

Late Quaternary mass extinction event: An ongoing series of selective prehistoric extinctions, typically catastrophic, eliminating within the past 40,000 years two-thirds or more of large land mammals of America, Australia, and Madagascar, and at least half the species of land birds on the remote islands of the Pacific. Humans are present, or suspected to be present, in virtually all cases of extinction. (See *Quaternary*.)

Liberalism: Refers to those who advocate absolute freedom in the marketplace; the unrestricted right to own, use, abuse, or sell; the right to turn anything into a commodity if there is a demand; the right to move capital and jobs anywhere in the world where profits are higher or costs lower.

Market economy: A network of buying and selling usually based upon use value, supply, and demand. Neoliberal economists argue that a free market works best in the long run; most socialists/Marxists hold that it should be replaced by collective planning such that production and distribution should be based on needs rather than profit.

Mass extinction: An extinction occurring over a relatively short period that is of large magnitude, wide biogeographic impact, and involves the extinction of many taxonomically and ecologically distant groups. Five major mass extinction events took place in Earth's history, the most dramatic of which occurred some 245 million years ago and destroyed 90 per cent of species on land and sea. Perhaps the most commonly known mass extinction marked the close of the Cretaceous period, around 65 million years ago, with the disappearance of the dinosaurs.

Megafauna: Refers mainly to large herbivores such as mammoths, mastodons, huge ground sloths, cave bears, and woolly rhinoceros, as well as the carnivores that fed on them, such as dire wolves and saber-toothed cats. Large terrestrial vertebrates are variously defined as greater than 1, greater than 10, and greater than 44 kg adult body weight; the latter category is equivalent to 100 pounds and similar to the average weight of adult humans.

Meng Tze: A Chinese philosopher, also known as Mencius, who lived during the fourth century BCE. He was acutely aware of environmental degradation in his time, warning the rulers of imperial China in vain of the unsustainable use of resources and land.

Mesozoic era: The age of dinosaurs, and dragonflies with 5-foot wingspans. The geologic era occurring between 230 million and 65 million years ago that included the Triassic, the Jurassic, and the Cretaceous periods, characterized by the development of flying reptiles, birds, and flowering plants, and both the appearance and the extinction of dinosaurs.

Metabolism: Here refers to the physical processes of input, transformation, and output that occur between societies and their natural environment. Natural resources are "ingested," processed internally, and released into the environment, and history may be written as an enormous increase in this metabolic process. A person in an industrial society consumes 15 to 20 times the amount of biomass, 20 times the amount of water, and about 10 times the amount of air that his or her individual metabolism alone would require; this expansion, of course, puts an enormous pressure upon the environment. (See *Colonization*.)

Modernization: An economic theory holding that science, technology, art, and all essential goods and services must be mass produced and mass marketed in order to maximize social well-being. Much mischief is done in "underdeveloped" countries by replacing community and agrarian/craft work with low-wage work in capitalist markets; this displaces people from land and kin to become the surplus labor in large ghettos, *barrios*, *favelas*, and cities around the world. Young people, dispossessed of land and cut off from their family, must find work at low wages or turn to begging, prostitution, theft, or worse.

Nationalism: Giving one's overriding loyalty to one's own nation and putting the interests of that nation above those of all other nations. Nation-states have been around for some 300 years and are one of the many sources of war, injustice, social-ecological destruction, and exploitation; they are just now beginning to merge into blocs, or dissolve into ethnic or regional segments.

Nature: From Latin *natura*, meaning birth, change, growth; that is, things and processes of a kind that existed on Earth before human culture became a force in the biosphere. Early use of the term in Plato and Aristotle referred to that which changed, in contrast to the laws of the gods, which were eternal and unchanging.

Neo-liberalism: A tenacious movement based on populist ideology, arguing for the reduction of bureaucracy and state control. Neo-liberalism advocates the need for a weak state, "free market"-based solutions, and the separation of economic and political spheres. When confronted with environmental issues, neo-liberal discourse tends to stress that their seriousness is exaggerated, and it criticizes environmentalists for downplaying the remarkable resilience and recovery power of nature.

Neoteny: Defined as retention of juvenile characteristics in the adults of species. Neoteny explains many of the differences between humans and other apes. Many of the central features of our anatomy link us with fetal and juvenile stages of primates: small face; vaulted cranium and large brain in relation to body size; unrotated big toe; foramen magnum under the skull for correct orientation of the head in upright posture; primary distribution of hair on head, armpits, and pubic areas. We retain not only the anatomical stamp of childhood, but its mental flexibility as well; thus, albeit nearly indistinguishable from chimpanzees in terms of DNA, humans are lifelong learners.

Order: A term in biology referring to the taxonomic category of organisms ranking above a family and below a class. (See *Taxonomy.*)

Over-exploitation: Harvesting of a natural resource, such as fish or timber, at a more rapid rate than can be naturally replenished. Much biodiversity loss in the early and pre-modern era was due to local and regional over-exploitation; in the late modern era, however, habitat destruction on an increasingly global scale becomes a prime culprit in mass extinction of species.

Over-extension, social and ecological: A condition that often afflicts complex systems during periods of expansion. The success that occurs early in a period of expansion may lead to the construction of systems that are dependent upon continual growth or, put another way, upon continual infusion of capital. (See *Overshoot.*)

Overkill: The destruction of native fauna by humans, either by gradual attrition over many thousands of years, or suddenly in a few hundred years or less. Sudden extinction following initial colonization of a landmass inhabited by animals especially vulnerable to the new human predator represents, in effect, a prehistoric faunal Blitzkrieg. (Overkill also accurately describes the effects of recent human cultures on many surviving species of large mammals.)

Overshoot, ecological: The condition of a population when it exceeds its available carrying capacity or maximum persistently supportable load. The population may survive temporarily but will eventually crash as it depletes vital natural capital (resource) stocks. A population in overshoot may permanently impair the long-term productive potential of its habitat, reducing the habitat's future carrying capacity.

Phanerozoic: The major division of geological time from 550 million years ago to the present, the time of the planet's greatest biodiversity.

Pleistocene: An epoch in Earth's history from about 2–5 million years to 10,000 years ago, when the most recent glaciations occurred. The geological time that ended with the last glacial period, the appearance of humans, and megafauna extinctions on all major continents.

Prehistory: The first of the three stages that human societies pass through, according to Enlightenment historiographical thought. In prehistory, humans are at the mercy of the blind forces of nature; in the second, history, science, and theory begin to offer human beings some control over their future; in the third, post-history, knowledge and politics come together in democratic forms to allow human beings to build social institutions that are supportive of ecologically sustainable practice and the continuance of species.

Primary production: The amount of energy produced by photosynthetic organisms in a community; also known as "net primary production of photosynthesis" (NPP).

Primate: Placental mammals of the order Primates, typically with flexible hands and feet, hands with opposable first digits, and good eyesight. The order includes lemurs, lorises, monkeys, apes, and humans. There are three suborders of primates: *Anthropoidea* (humans, apes, Old World monkeys, and New World monkeys), *Prosimii* (lemurs, lorises, and bush babies), and *Tarsioidea* (tarsiers).

Private property: The set of rights that the owner of something has in relation to others who do not own it. The word "private" originates from the Latin *privare*, which means to deprive, showing the widespread original view that property was first and foremost communal.

Quaternary period: The ice ages of at least the past 1.81 million years, including the Pleistocene and the Holocene. (See *Late Quaternary mass extinction event*.)

Social change: A product of human beings' continuing attempts to realize their innate rationality in the context of a social ecological lifeworld that both enables and constrains. Thus social change is a product of the inborn, special capacity of humans to create knowledge, to interpret it, to communicate with one another, and to learn from the past.

Social Darwinism: A theory of social change originated by Herbert Spencer which holds that progress is inevitable if people only cease interfering with nature. This has been taken to mean that if others stop interfering with the plans of private business, there will be progress; thus, it represents a more formal version of *laissez-faire* ("let it be") cloaked in the language of science.

Socialization: The process by which young people are taught to honor the values and embody the norms of a society. The term first appeared in 1828 and was used to explain the way in which human behavior is patterned by interaction within primary groups such as family, school, and play groups. Socialization includes the rights and obligations to reproduce existing social relationships or to work within the system to change it.

Social justice: Refers to a set of policies and programs in which housing, health care, education, transportation, recreation are distributed on the basis of perceived social need rather than, or in addition to, profit. Note that "justice" varies with the mode of production; what is fair and right depends upon the social relationships that are considered normal. (If justice is blind, social justice is not.)

Social stratification: The structured inequality of entire categories of people, who have different access to social rewards as a result of their status in a social hierarchy. A process by which some people in a society are channeled into inferior or superior social positions. There is usually class, race, and gender inequality; such inferiority affects one's capacity to create culture and to enter into social relationships, thus diminishing the human potential of those both at the bottom and at the top.

Specialization: The performance of a narrowly defined task, usually relating to technical work; the rationale is that one can do something efficiently if one does it all the time. Specialization often subdivides labor so much that the worker loses sight of the purpose of work, and control over his or her work; specialists can be useful in capitalism because, since they know little of the social meaning of their labor, they tend not to experience guilt or shame at the results of their work. (See *Technocracy.*)

Sustainable development: A pattern and path of economic and social development compatible with the long-term stability of environmental systems, particularly those essential to human well-being.

Systems of social domination: There are five major systems of domination which variously make up all recent stratified societies. They include stratification patterns based on class (elitism), gender (sexism), ethnicity (racism), age (ageism), and territory (tribalism and nationalism). The domination of human societies over non-human species and nature and their accompanying ideologies (speciesism, anthropocentrism) could be added as additional analytical categories. (See also *Class; Social stratification.*)

Taxonomy: The classification of organisms in an ordered system that indicates natural relationships. The science, laws, or principles of classification; systematics; division into ordered groups or categories.

Technocracy: Political rule by engineers, scientists, and other specialists, the rationale being that there is a natural division of labor and that the experts should make decisions since they alone know what is right and natural. In a well-designed society, knowledge would be widely available, such that professionals and lay persons would share the research process as well as decisions about how to use knowledge gained from it. (See *Specialization*.)

Threatened species: Species that are, often, genetically impoverished, of low fecundity, dependent on patchy or unpredictable resources, extremely variable in population densities, persecuted, or otherwise prone to extinction in human-dominated landscapes.

Treadmill of production: A term derived from the economist J.K. Galbraith's view of how our present materialist and "consumer-oriented" society operates. The methods and aims of production of this society have a profound influence on how people view themselves and nature.

Tributary societies: Societies in which commoners owe the rulers tribute (in the form of taxes, labor, loans that need not be repaid, or even gifts); in which production is organized politically rather than through direct control of the means of production. Some tributary systems have been relatively loosely organized, such as feudal Europe, medieval Japan, and pre-colonial Bali; others have been exceptionally tightly organized, such as dynastic Egypt, the pre-Colombian Inca Empire, and imperial China.

Trophic: Pertaining to food or nutrition.

Water pollution: Lowering of water quality due to input of sewage, pesticides, agricultural run-off, and industrial wastes that can result in harm to aquatic plants and animals. Two-thirds of the world's population lacks adequate access to clean drinking water and sanitary facilities, and by 2025 half of the world's population will experience water shortages.

TABLES

Table 1: Species remaining to be described out of an estimated total of 30 million

■ 1.7 million described species

□
2.83 million
species remaining to be described

SOURCES: World Resources Institute, the World Conservation Union, and the United Nations Environment Program, in consultation with the Food and Agriculture Organization and the United Nations Education, Scientific and Cultural Organization, *Global Biodiversity Strategy* (World Resources Institute, Washington, DC, 1992), p. 156.
NOTE: The number of described species in 1992 is 1.4 million. The estimated number of described species in 1997 is 1.7 million. Estimates of total species diversity range between 5 million and 100 million species. Most estimates fall between 30 million and 50 million species.

Table 2: Four categories of the instrumental value of biodiversity

Category	Example
Goods	Food, fuel, fiber, medicine
Services	Pollination, recycling, nitrogen fixation, homeostatic regulation
Information	Genetic engineering, applied biology, pure science
Psycho-spiritual	Aesthetic beauty, religious awe, scientific knowledge

SOURCE: Gary K. Meffe and C. Ronald Carroll et al., "Conservation Values and Ethics," *Principles of Conservation Biology* (Sunderland, MA: Sinauer Associates, Inc. Publishers, 1994), p. 25.

Table 3: Ecosystem functions and their uses

Regulation functions	Production functions	Carrier functions	Information functions
Providing support for economic activity and human welfare through: – protecting against harmful cosmic influences – climate regulation – watershed protection and catchment – erosion prevention and soil protection – storage and recycling of industrial and human waste – storage and recycling of organic matter and mineral nutrients – maintenance of biological and genetic diversity – biological control – providing a migratory nursery and feeding habitat	Providing basic resources, such as: – oxygen – food, drinking water, and nutrition – water for industry, households, etc. – clothing and fabrics – building, construction, and manufacturing materials – energy and fuel – minerals – medicinal resources – biochemical resources – genetic resources – ornamental resources	Providing space and a suitable environment inter alia for: – habitation – agriculture, forestry, fishery, aquaculture – industry – engineering projects such as dams and roads – recreation – nature conservation – etc.	Providing aesthetic, cultural and scientific benefits through: – aesthetic information – spiritual and religious information – cultural and artistic inspiration – educational and scientific information – etc.

SOURCE: Adapted from V.H. Heywood, R.T. Watson, and United Nations Environmental Programme, *Global Biodiversity Assessment* (Cambridge and New York: University of Cambridge Press, 1995), p. 879.

Table 4: Degree of extinction[i] (%) in the five major mass extinctions in the fossil records

Mass extinction	Families Observed extinction	Calculated species-level extinction	Genera Observed extinction	Calculated species-level extinction
1. End-Ordovician 439 Ma[ii]	26	84	60	85
2. End Devonian 367 Ma	22	79	57	83
3. End Permian 243 Ma	51	95	82	95
4. End Triassic (Norian) 208 Ma	22	79	53	80
5. End-Cretaceous 65 Ma	16	70	47	76

SOURCE: Jeffrey S. Levinton, "Extinction, Rates of," *Encyclopedia of Biodiversity* (San Diego, CA: Academic Press, 2001), 2:715–729 [719].
NOTES: (i) Extinctions/standing taxonomic richness ×100.
(ii) Ma = Million years.

Table 5: Milestones in hominid cultural evolution

6 million to 2 million years BCE
- *Aridipithecus ramidus*, the oldest known possibly bipedal ape represented by fossils from sites in Ethiopia. These first chimp-sized prehumans with an upright posture appearing in the East African Rift Valley are followed approximately 4 million years ago by the better-known *Australopithecus africanus*, a small-brained upright walker from the sites in northern Kenya; and *Australopithecus afarensis*, a big-faced apelike species to which the famous "Lucy" belonged.

2 million years BCE
- *Homo erectus* had a brain of 1,100 cc (three-quarters the size of anatomically modern humans), suggesting that having a large brain helped in acquisition of skills like tool using, which is not unique to humans (used by finches, chimps), tool making, and the use of fire, which is unique to humans (making possible artifacts ranging from flint axes to, more recently, computers). 98% of hominid history is defined by hunting/gathering and foraging/scavenging modes of life.

130,000 BCE
- Modern anatomy is first recognized for early *Homo sapiens* (the earliest fossils are documented in Africa with an estimated founding population of c. 10,000 people).

Table 5: *continued*

30,000 BCE
- Worldwide range of fully modern humans, *Homo sapiens sapiens*; theories suggest that both the ability to use language and the ability to think objectively about oneself ("self-consciousness") depended on brain growth and may have had a crucial role in ensuing human success.
- 15,000 BCE => Oldest grinding stones (with world population at c. 8 million)
- 9000 BCE => Domestication of sheep
- 8500 BCE => First semi-permanent settlements
- 8000 BCE => Barley domesticated
- 6500 BCE => Towns of a few thousand (e.g. Jericho)
- 6000 BCE => Pottery
- 5500 BCE => Irrigation
- 4500 BCE => The (pottery-making) wheel
- 3500 BCE => Uruk, Sumer, with 50,000 inhabitants

Fifteenth–twenty-first century CE
- Modernity (Early, High, Late, Post), industrial-capitalist revolution, colonialism, imperialism; 80 years from Darwin's *Origin of Species* to Hiroshima and Nagasaki; Cold War and colonization of space (Sputnik vs satellite, moon landing); population bomb and population explosion (1,000% world population increase between 1600 and 2000); globalization (revolution in transport and communications technologies, compression of space and time); biotechnology and genetic engineering; more than 6 billion humans use almost 50% of net productivity of photosynthesis (NPP) of land ecosystems and 30% overall; destruction of rain forests and globalization of environmental degradation, destruction of ozone layer; doubling of CO_2, global warming; climate change; widespread pollution (nuclear, chemical, biological), acceleration of soil erosion, desertification; mass extinction of species and the genuine possibility of a global collapse of biodiversity in the near future (ecological overshoot); global ecological restoration?

SOURCE: Adapted from Clive Ponting, *A Green History of the World: The Environment and the Collapse of Civilizations* (London: Penguin Books, 1991), p. 53.

Table 6: Human forces driving changes in biological diversity (before 1500; 1500 to 1800; since 1800)

Before 1500 (world conquest, terrestrial colonization, military expansion of empires)
- Fire (e.g. burning of land and cooking)
- Hunting gathering, and scavenging (e.g. megafauna overkill)
- Domestication of plants and animals; intensification of agriculture and trade
- Intensification of agriculture by plowing
- Offshore traffic and trade
- Building up of large empires (e.g. Persian, Roman, and Mongol), with considerable expansion of communication and transportation systems
- Long-range wars and military expansion; Establishment of "market economies" (e.g. Venice)

1500 to 1800 (early orthodox modernity: mercantile capitalism, early colonialism)
- Exploration, discovery, and colonization by Europeans of other territories and continents (e.g. the "Columbian Exchange")
- Establishment of new market economies and trading centers (e.g. Amsterdam, London) favoring the globalization of trade exchange
- Revolution in food customs (e.g. increased use of tea, coffee, chocolate, rice, sugar, potatoes, corn, beef, and lamb)
- International introductions of exotic spices through activities of acclimatization societies, botanical gardens and zoos, and for agricultural, forestry, fishery, or ornamental purposes
- Large-scale labor migration

Since 1800 (high, late, and post-modernity: Industrial Revolution, high colonialism, imperialism, arms race, economic liberalism, global rift, demographic explosion)
- Rapid improvement of transportation systems (roads, railways, navigation canals)
- Large-scale industrial production and emergence of transnational corporations (TNCs)
- Construction of large engineering works for irrigation and hydropower
- High-input, chemicalized agriculture; mechanized fisheries and forestry
- World wars and displacement of human populations
- Tropical deforestation and resettlement schemes
- Afforestation of arid lands with exotic species
- Increased urbanization and creation of habitats characterized by cosmopolitan species
- Release of genetically engineered organisms and synthetic ecotoxins, bioaccumulation
- Anthropogenic climate change and destruction of atmosphere ozone layer

Table 6: *continued*

SOURCES: Modified after V.H. Heywood, R.T. Watson, United Nations Environment Programme, *Global Biodiversity Assessment* (Cambridge and New York: Cambridge University Press, 1995), p. 719. And F. di Castri, "History of biological invasions with special emphasis on the Old World," in J.A. Drake, H.A. Mooney, F. di Castri, R.H. Groves, F.J. Kruger, M. Rejmanek, and M. Williamson (eds), *Biological Invasions: A Global Perspective*, SCOPE 37 (Chichester and New York: John Wiley, 1989, on behalf of the Scientific Committee on Problems of the Environment [SCOPE] of the International Council of Scientific Unions), pp. 1–26.

Table 7: Late Pleistocene megafauna extinction – (percentages and weights in kg)

All herbivores	1,000 (kg)
75% of herbivores	100–1,000 (kg)
41% of herbivores	5–100 (kg)
<2% of herbivores	< 5 (kg)

SOURCE: Adapted from Peter J. Bryant, "Extinction and Depletion from Over-Exploitation," *The Origin, Nature and Value of Biological Diversity, the Threats to Its Continued Existence, and Approaches to Preserving What Is Left* [A Hypertext Book] (Irvine, CA: School of Biological Sciences University of California, Irvine, 1997).
NOTE: The Late Pleistocene and Late Quaternary megafauna extinctions occurred at different times on different landmasses and oceanic islands. The timing of this recent mass extinction spasm coincides with arrival of the first anatomically modern humans.

Table 8: Onset dates of major extinction episodes

	Years before present
Africa and SE Asia	50,000
Australia	45,000
North Eurasia	13,000
North America	11,000
South America	10,000
West Indies	4,000
Aotearoa (NZ)	900
Madagascar	800

SOURCES: Adapted from Peter J. Bryant, "Extinction and Depletion from Over-Exploita-tion," *The Origin, Nature and Value of Biological Diversity, the Threats to its Continued Existence, and Approaches to Preserving what is Left* [A Hypertext Book] (Irvine, CA: School of Biological Sciences University of California, Irvine, 1997). Timothy Flannery, *The Future Eaters: An Ecological History of the Australian Lands and People* (Melbourne: Reed Books, 1995).

Table 9: Causes of biodiversity loss

- Unsustainably high rates of human population growth and natural resource consumption (increasing world population means that more and more consumers are making more and more demands for an infinite variety of wildlife and wildlife products)
- Steadily narrowing spectrum of traded products from agriculture and forestry, and the introduction of exotic species associated with agriculture, forestry, and fisheries
- Economic systems and policies that fail to value the environment and its resources
- Inequity in ownership and access to natural resources, including the benefits from use and conservation of biodiversity
- Inadequate knowledge and inefficient use of information (deficiencies in knowledge and its application)
- Legal and institutional systems that promote unsustainable exploitation

---

SOURCE: United Nations Environmental Programme (UNEP), "Six Fundamental Causes of Biodiversity Loss," *Global Biodiversity Assessment* (Cambridge: UNEP, 1995), p. 924.

Table 10: Mechanisms of biodiversity loss

- Large-scale habitat destruction (which now extends to even the remotest corners of the Earth)
- Introduced species (bioinvasions)
- Over-exploitation of plant and animal species (with sophisticated weaponry, over-efficient harvesting technologies, and modern transportation systems to ensure the supply, many wildlife populations are simply collapsing under the pressure)
- Pollution of soil, water, and atmosphere
- Industrialized agriculture[i] and forestry
- Global climate change

SOURCES: Adapted from WRI, IUCN, UNEP, FAO, UNESCO, *Global Biodiversity Strategy: Guidelines for Action to Save, Study, and Use Earth's Biotic Wealth Sustainably and Equitably* (Washington, DC: WRI, 1992), pp. vi, 244.
NOTE: (i) "Industrial agriculture" here means the entire food system, including packaging and delivery.

Table 11: Projection of species loss for 2100 CE

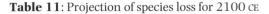

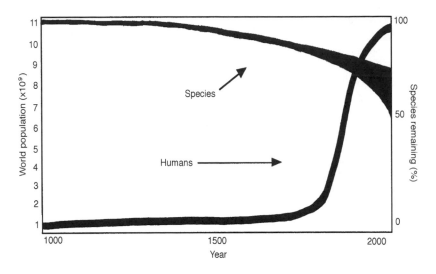

SOURCE: Francesca Grifo and Joshua Rosenthal, "Causes and Consequences of Biodiversity Loss," *Biodiversity and Human Health* (Washington, DC: Island Press, 1997), p. 40.

Table 12: Exhaustion of fur seal hunting in the Southern Hemisphere, 1780–1820

1790–91	Tristan da Cunha
1790–91	Falkland Islands
1790–91	Tierra del Fuego
1797–1803	Mas Afuera (Juan Fernandez Islands)
1800–25	South Georgia
?	South Shetland Islands
1800–25	Kerguelen Island
?	Australian coast
1810–20	Macquarie Island

SOURCE: Peter J. Bryant, *Extinction and Depletion from Over-exploitation. Biodiversity and Conservation* [A Hypertext Book] (Irvine, CA: School of Biological Sciences University of California, Irvine, 1998).

Table 13: Wars and war deaths,[i] 1500 to 2000

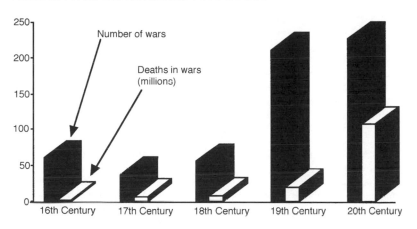

SOURCE: Ruth Leger Sivard, *World Military and Social Expenditures* 1993, 15th edn (Washington, DC: World Priorities Press, 1993), p. 3.
NOTE: (i) Covers only wars with estimated annual deaths of 1,000 or more. NB: The estimated share of war-related deaths that were civilian in 1970 was 60 per cent. By 1990 the estimated share of war-related deaths that were civilian had reached 90 per cent (see Michael Renner, *Fighting for Survival* [New York: Norton, 1996]).

Table 14: The world's priorities? (Annual expenditures, in US $)

Saving the world's 25 biodiversity hotspots throughout the world over the next ten years (estimate)[i]	$5 billion
Combating land degradation [ii]	$6 billion
Basic education for all [iii]	$6 billion
Cosmetics in the United States [iii]	$8 billion
Ice cream in Europe [iii]	$11 billion
Perfume in Europe and United States [iii]	$12 billion
Reproductive health for all women [iii]	$12 billion
Basic health and nutrition [iii]	$13 billion
Pet foods in Europe and the United States [iii]	$17 billion
Water and sanitation for all [iii]	$35 billion
Universal access to basic education, health care, reproductive health care, adequate food, clean water, and sewers [ii]	$40 billion
Cigarettes in Europe [iii]	$50 billion
Alcoholic drinks in Europe [iii]	$105 billion
Illegal drugs [iv]	$400 billion
Oil [v]	$450 billion
Military spending [vi]	$900 billion

Table 14: *continued*

SOURCES: (i) Biodiversity Hotspots ("We could go far towards safeguarding the hotspots and thus a large proportion of all species at risk for an average of $20 m per hotspot per year over the next five years, or $500 m annually…. The scale of spending needed is peanuts relative to space probes and military spending – just twice the cost of a single Pathfinder mission to Mars…. And even if the sum needed were a hundred times larger, it would be worth paying to prevent the planet being impoverished" – Norman Myers, cited in Alex Kirby, "Islands of hope to challenge extinction," *BBC News Online*, Wednesday, February 23 2000, 19:17 GMT. Available: http://news6.thdo.bbc.co.uk/hi/english/sci/tech/newsid%5F653000/653894.stm, reviewed May 2002. Paul Rogers, "A $5 billion plan to save world's forests," *San Jose Mercury News*, August 20 2000, posted at 12:37 a.m. PDT, at http://www.mercurycenter.com/local/center/brazil082000.htm, reviewed November 2000.)

(ii) Djauhari Oratmangun and I. Gede Ngurah Swajaya, "Reality and ambitions of world summit on sustainability," *Jakarta Post*, April 14 2001 ("An estimated average of US$6 billion will be needed annually to ensure that the program to combat land degradation is implemented").

(iii) Estimated additional annual cost to achieve universal access to basic social services in all developing countries, in United Nations Development Programme (UNDP), "The World's Priorities?" *Human Development Report, 1998* (New York: Oxford University Press, 1998). Reprint, Multinational Monitor, and September 1998 edition, p. 37.

(iv) Illegal drugs: UN Research Institute, *States of Disarray: The Social Effects of Globalization* (London: UNRISD, 1995).

(v) Crude oil sales: Based on shipments reported in *BP Statistical Review of World Energy* (London: British Petroleum, 1995).

(vi) Military spending: Bonn International Center for Conversion, *Conversion Survey 1996: Global Disarmament, Demilitarization and Demobilization* (Oxford: Oxford University Press, 1996). ($780 bn orig. fig. cited in 1995; $900 bn is adjusted estimate for 2000.)

Table 15: Population density and habitat loss, countries of major importance for biodiversity

	Population density		Habitat loss historically associated with projected 2050 population density (%)
	1995	2050	
	(no. per sq. km)		
Brazil	188	288	41
Madagascar	256	874	67
Mexico	478	807	67
Zaire	200	726	67
Colombia	345	600	78
Indonesia	1,090	1,757	85

SOURCE: Lester R. Brown, Gary Gardner, and Brian Halweil, *Beyond Malthus: Sixteen Dimensions of the Population Problem, Worldwatch Paper 143* (Washington, DC: Worldwatch Institute, September 1998), p. 21. NB: Habitat loss tends to accelerate with an increase in the country's population density. This is bad news for the world's biodiversity hotspots –

species rich ccosystems at greatest risk of destruction. Twenty-four of these hotspots containing half of the planet's species have been identified globally. Some of the most important hotspot countries will reach population densities that have been linked with very high rates of habitat loss. Five of the six most biologically rich countries (listed above) could see more than two-thirds of their original habitats destroyed by 2050 if this historical relationship holds (Brown et al. 1998: 19–20).

Table 16: Percentage of species worldwide classified as threatened

| | Share of species that is ... | | |
	in immediate danger of extinction	vulnerable to extinction	Total share of species threatened with extinction
Birds	4	7	11
Mammals	11	14	25
Reptiles	8	12	20
Amphibians	10	15	25
Fish	13	21	34

SOURCE. Lester R. Brown, Gary Gardner, and Brian Halweil, *Beyond Malthus: Sixteen Dimensions of the Population Problem*, *Worldwatch Paper 143* (Washington, DC: Worldwatch Institute, September 1998), p. 20.

Table 17: Number of species considered "threatened" by the World Conservation Monitoring Centre[i]

Group	Endangered	Vulnerable	Rare	Indeterminate	Total
Mammals	177	199	89	68	533
Birds	188	241	257	176	862
Reptiles	47	88	79	43	257
Amphibians	32	32	55	14	133
Fishes	158	226	246	304	934
Invertebrates	582	702	422	941	2,647
Plants	3,632	5,687	14,485	5,302	26,107

SOURCE: Robert Barbault, "Loss of Biodiversity, Overview," *Encyclopedia of Biodiversity*, vol. 3 (San Diego, CA: Academic Press, 2001), p. 765.
NOTE: (i) The WCMC considers all species classified as "endangered," "vulnerable," "rare," or "indeterminate" as threatened.

Table 18: Factors responsible for some extinctions and threatened extinctions

	Percentage due to each cause[i]					
Group	Habitat loss	Over-exploitation	Species introduction	Predators	Other	Unknown
EXTINCTIONS						
Mammals	19	23	20	1	1	36
Birds	20	11	22	0	2	37
Reptiles	5	32	42	0	0	21
Fishes	35	4	30	0	4	48
THREATENED EXTINCTIONS						
Mammals	68	54	6	8	12	–
Birds	58	30	28	1	1	–
Reptiles	53	63	17	3	6	–
Amphibians	77	29	14	–	3	–
Fishes	78	12	28	–	2	–

SOURCE: From W.V. Reid and K.R. Miller, *Keeping Options Alive: The Scientific Basis for Conservation Biology* (Washington, DC: World Resources Institute, 1989). SECONDARY SOURCE: Robert Barbault, "Loss of Biodiversity, Overview," *Encyclopedia of Biodiversity*, vol. 3 (San Diego, CA: Academic Press, 2001), pp. 765.
NOTE: (i) Some species may be influenced by more than one factor; thus some rows may exceed 100 per cent.

Table 19: Rate of human population increase at different periods in history

Period in history	Additional number of people per year
Primeval (hunter-gatherer) phase	50
Early farming and early urban phase	50,000
From 1650 to 1960	7,000,000
From 1960 to 2000	90,000,000

SOURCE: Stephen Vickers Boyden, *Biohistory: The Interplay between Human Society and the Biosphere* (Paris: UNESCO; Carnforth, Lancs., UK; Park Ridge, NJ, USA: Pantheon Pub. Group, 1992), p. 107.

Table 20: World population milestones and projections

World population	Reached in
1 billion	1804 (all of human history)
2 billion	1927 (123 years later)
3 billion	1960 (33 years later)
4 billion	1974 (14 years later)
5 billion	1987 (13 years later)
6 billion	1999 (12 years later)
FUTURE POPULATION PROJECTIONS	
7 billion	2013 (14 years later)
8 billion	2028 (15 years later)
9 billion	2054 (26 years later)

SOURCE: Adapted from United Nations Population Division, *The World at Six Billion*. (ESA/P/WP.154).[1] NB: Population growth seems to affect everything but is seldom held responsible for anything. Some of the key reasons for this predicament are (1) growth is invisible from day to day; (2) there is "scale paralysis," a sense of powerlessness in response to the size of the problem; (3) many people are unable to comprehend such large numbers; (4) population growth is never an immediate political problem, but only a long-range one, and thus can be put off; and (5), last but not least, the subject is often controversial and divisive.
NOTE: 1 See United Nations Dept. of Economic and Social Affairs, Population Division, *World Population Prospects: The 1998 Revision* (New York: United Nations, 2000), United Nations Dept. of Economic and Social Affairs, Population Division, *World Population Projections to 2150* (New York: United Nations, 1998).

Table 21: Actual and projected changes in world population, food, energy, and economic output

	Actual – 1950 compared to 1993	Scenario projection – 1995 compared to 2050
Population	2.2×	1.6×
Food (grain)	2.7×	1.8×
Energy	4.4×	2.4×
Economy	5.1×	4.3×

SOURCE: National Research Council, *Our Common Journey*, report of the Board of Sustainable Development (Washington, DC: National Academies Press, 1999).

Table 22: Annual *per capita* consumption in selected nations

Country	Meat (kg)	Paper (kg)	Fossil fuels (kg of oil equivalent)	Passenger cars (per 1,000 people)	Total value of private consumption
United States	122	293	6,902	489	$21,680
Japan	42	239	3,277	373	$15,554
Poland	73	54	2,585	209	$5,087
China	47	30	700	3.2	$1,410
Zambia	12	1.6	77	17	$625

SOURCE: Bill Moyers, *Earth on the Edge*, see http://www.pbs.org/earthonedge/science/trends.html, reviewed May 2002.

Table 23: Share of the world's income held by income group, 1965–90

Population	Percentage of world total income			
	1965	1970	1980	1990
Poorest 20%	2.3	2.2	1.7	1.4
Second 20%	2.9	2.8	2.2	1.8
Third 20%	4.2	3.9	3.5	2.1
Fourth 20%	21.2	21.3	18.3	11.3
Richest 20%	69.5	70.0	75.4	83.4

SOURCE: Roberto Patricio Korzeniewitcz and Timothy Patrick Moran, "World-Economic Trends in the Distribution of Income, 1965–1992," *American Journal of Sociology* 102(4) (January 1997), pp. 1000–39. Note: Percentage figures refer to people living in poorest 20%, etc., of nations.

Table 24: Share of global income of the richest and poorest 20% of world's population

Year	Share of richest 20% %	Share of poorest 20% %	Ratio of richest to poorest
1820	–	–	03 to 1
1870	–	–	07 to 1
1913	–	–	11 to 1
1960	70.2	2.3	30 to 1
1970	73.9	2.3	32 to 1
1980	76.3	1.7	44 to 1
1989	82.7	1.4	59 to 1
1990	–	–	60 to 1

Table 24: *continued*

Year	Share of richest 20% %	Share of poorest 20% %	Ratio of richest to poorest
1995	–	–	61 to 1
1997	–	–	64 to 1
1998	86.0	1.3	66 to 1

SOURCE: Data collected from United Nations Development Program (UNDP), *Human Development Reports*, issues published from 1992–9 (New York: Oxford University Press, 1999).

NOTE: The increasing income gap between the fifth of the global population living in the richest countries, and the fifth living in the poorest countries, is clear in the table above. This trend resembles that experienced in the last three decades of the nineteenth century, when rapid global integration was also taking place; inequality defined by income between the top and bottom state increased from 3:1 in 1820, to 7:1 in 1870, to 11:1 in 1913. In addition to the gap in income, inequality is evident in other spheres, as Table 25 reveals.

Table 25: Concentration of global income, resources, and wealth, 1999

	20% global population in highest-income countries	20% global population in lowest-income countries
% of world GDP	86	1
% of world export markets	82	1
% of foreign direct investment	68	1
% of world telephone lines	74	1.5

SOURCE: United Nations Development Program (UNDP), *Human Development Report*, 1999 (New York: Oxford University Press, 1999), p. 3.

Further global wealth factoids:

- Organization of Economic Cooperation and Development (OECD) countries, with 19 per cent of the global population, represent 71 per cent of global trade in goods and services, 58 per cent of foreign direct investment, and 91 per cent of all Internet users.
- The world's richest 200 people more than doubled their net worth in the four years 1994 to 1998, to more than US $1 trillion. The assets of the top three billionaires are more than the combined GNP of all the least developed countries in the world and their 600 million people.
- The recent wave of mergers and acquisitions is concentrating industrial power in megacorporations – at the risk of eroding competition. By 1998 the top ten companies in pesticides controlled 85 per cent of a US $31 billion global market; the top ten in telecommunications, 86 per cent of a US $262 billion market.
- In 1993 just ten companies accounted for 84 per cent of global research and development expenditures and controlled 95 per cent of all US patents of the past two decades. Moreover, more than 80 per cent of the patents granted in developing countries went to residents of industrial countries. SOURCE: UNDP, as above.

Table 26: Gross National Product *per capita* in the species-rich states

Country	1988 (US$)	Country	1988 (US$)
Tanzania	160	Papua New Guinea	810
Zaire	170	Thailand	1,000
Uganda	280	Bolivia	1,099
Ecuador	284	Colombia	1,139
China/India	340	Peru	1,300
OECD Average	17,400		

SOURCE: World Bank, *World Development Report* (Oxford: Oxford University Press, 1989). SECONDARY SOURCE: Timothy Swanson, *Global Action for Biodiversity* (IUCN, WWF, and Earthscan Publications: London, 1997), p. 184.

Table 27: Seven 'I' solutions for conserving biodiversity

- Investigation: learning how natural systems function
- Information: ensuring that facts are available to inform decisions
- Innovation: finding new ways to use biological resources sustainably
- Incentive: using tools to help biodiversity
- Integration: promoting a cross-sectoral approach to conserving bio-diversity
- Indigenous communities: returning management responsibilities to those whose welfare depends on the resources managed
- International cooperation: building productive collaboration for conserving biodiversity

SOURCE: Jeffery A. Neely, "Biodiversity in the Global Community: Why it has Become Such an Important Social Economic and Political Issue," in *Proceedings of a Conference on Prospects of Cooperation on Biodiversity Activities, Chiang Rai, Thailand 15–19 January 1996*, edited by Jeffrey A. Neely, Chief Scientist, IUCN – The World Conservation Union. Gland, Switzerland and Suntha Somchevita. Office of Environmental Policy and Planning, Thailand. Published by Office of Environmental Policy and Planning. Ministry of Science, Technology and Environment. Bangkok, Thailand, pp. 10–17.

Table 28: Liquidating our assets

Amount of topsoil created by nature each year	0.4 billion tons
Amount lost to erosion	25.4 billion tons
Time it takes the global human economy to consume the equivalent of 22 million tons of oil	1 day
Time it took to the planet to create this energy	10,000 days
Number of species lost to extinction each year, on average, during the past 65 million years	1 to 10

Number lost in the past year (conservatively
  estimated)   1,000 to 10,000
Time it took for the world to lose 1 per cent of its forests,
  on average, during the 30 centuries prior to the
  Industrial Revolution   100 years
Time it is taking to lose 1 per cent now   1 year
Natural Resources: Since 1970, the world's forests have declined from 4.4
square miles per 1,000 people to 2.8 square miles per 1,000 people. In
addition, a quarter of the world's fish stocks have been depleted and another
44 per cent are being fished to their biological limits.

SOURCE: Worldwatch, "Matters of Scale: Liquidating our Assets," *World Watch* 10(5)
(September/ October) (1997), p. 39. "UNEP Human Development Report 1998," in *New
York Times*, September 27 1998.

Table 29: Arteriosclerosis of the Earth

Number of large dams (at least 15 meters high) that were blocking the world's rivers as of 1950	5,270
Number that had been built by 1985	36,562
Number of large dams in China as of 1950	2
Number that had been built by 1985	18,820
Kilometers of the world's once free-flowing rivers that had been artificially altered for navigation by 1900	8,750
Kilometers altered by 1980	498,000
Average frequency of major floods of the Rhine River in Karlsruhe, Germany, (7.6 meters or more above flood level) between 1900 and 1977	once every 19 years
Average frequency during the last 19 years, after extensive engineering which eliminated natural flood controls	once every 2 years
Number of salmon caught in the Rhine River (Germany and Holland) annually, 100 years ago	150,000
Number caught annually by the end of the 1950s	0
Millions of pounds of salmon and steelhead caught in the Columbia River by commercial fishermen in 1884	42.2
Millions of pounds caught in 1994	1.2

SOURCE: Janet N. Abramovitz, *Imperiled Waters, Impoverished Future: The Decline of
Freshwater Ecosystems, Worldwatch Paper 128* (Washington, DC: Worldwatch Institute,
1996).

Table 30: The social effects of globalism

Price of a jar of Avon "skin-renewal" product being advertised on Brazilian TV and then sold door-to-door in the Amazon Basin by an army of 80,000 Avon saleswomen	$40
Average household income per day of the women in the region, who are persuaded to forgo buying clothes or shoes in order to purchase the Avon product	$3
Average hourly wage of workers at 2,200 factories of General Electric, Ford, General Motors, GTE Sylvania, RCA, Westinghouse, and other US companies with plants in the free-trade zone of Mexico along the US border	$1.64
Average hourly wage of manufacturing workers in the "home" country of these companies	$16.17
Worldwide profits of Walt Disney Company in 1993	$300 million
Amount taken home by chairman Michael Eisner in the same year	$203 million
Number of the 100 largest economic units in the world that are nations	49
Number that are corporations (as measured by sales)	51
Number of elephants in Burundi in 1986	1
Number of elephant tusks, all certified as originating in Burundi, exported that year	23,000
Number of billionaires (people with the net worth of a thousand millionaires) in the world in 1989	157
Number of billionaires just five years later, in 1994	358
Number of the world's richest people whose collective wealth adds up to $762 billion	358
Number of the world's poorest people whose combined income adds up to $762 billion	2,400,000,000
Portion of global income going to the richest fifth of the population	83 per cent
Portion of global income going to the poorest fifth	1 per cent
Number of billionaires in Mexico in 1989	2
Number in 1996	24
Combined income of the poorest 17 million Mexicans in 1988	$6,600,000,000
Wealth of the richest *single* Mexican	$6,600,000,000
Ratio of income of the richest fifth to the poorest fifth of the US population in 1970	4 to 1
The same ratio in 1993	13 to 1
Life expectancy in the most developed countries in 2000	79
Life expectancy in the least developed countries in 2000	42

The Super Rich: The world's 225 richest individuals, of whom 60 are Americans, with total assets of $311 billion, have a combined income of wealth of over $1 trillion – equal to the income of the poorest 47 per cent of the entire world population.

The Ultra Rich: The three richest people in the world have assets that exceed the combined gross national product of the 48 least developed countries

SOURCES: United Nations Research Institute for Social Development (UNRISD), *States of Disarray: The Social Effects of Globalization* (London: UNRISD, 1995); *World Watch* 9(4) (July/August) (1996), p. 39. Worldwatch Institute, "Matters of Scale: The Global Economy," *World Watch* 10(3) (1997), p. 39. World Health Organization (WHO), *World Health Report 1995*, in *World Watch* 9(5) (September/October) (1996), p. 39. "UNEP Human Development Report 1998," in *New York Times*, September 27 1998.

Table 31: Who dominates the world?

Number of people employed by the UN	53,589
Number of people employed at Disneyland	50,000
Total budget of the UN in 1995–6 (two-year budget)	$18.2 billion
Revenue of a single US arms manufacturer (Lockheed Martin) in 1995	$19.4 billion
UN peacekeeping expenditures in 1995	$3.6 billion
World military spending in 1995	$767 billion
Number of UN peacekeepers for every 150,000 people in the world	1
Number of soldiers in national armies for every 150,000 people in the world	650
US contribution to the UN budget, *per capita*	$7
Norwegian contribution to the UN budget, *per capita*	$65
Number of US troops serving in UN peacekeeping operations in 1994	965
Number of US troops serving in international missions under US command in 1994	86,451
Cost of the 1992 Earth Summit	$10 million
Cost of the 1994 Paris Air Show and Weapons Exhibition (US portion)	$12 million
UN Environment Programme (UNEP) budget per year	$100 million
Global military spending per day	more than $2 billion

SOURCES: Compiled by Michael Renner, "Matters of Scale: Who Dominates the World," *World Watch* 9(6) (November/December) (1996), p. 39. Kofi A. Annan, Christopher Flavin and Linda Starke, *State of the World, 2002: A Worldwatch Institute Report on Progress Toward a Sustainable Society* (New York: W.W. Norton, 2002).

Table 32: Bioinvasions

Weight of the total world catch of fish and seafood in recent years	86 million tons
Weight of non-native jellyfish in the Black Sea in 1998	900 million tons
Percentage of the Great Lake fish catch that was native salmon and trout in 1900	82
Percentage that was native salmon and trout in 1966, after overfishing, chemical pollution, and bioinvasions including the spread of the exotic predatory sea lamprey killed off the native fish	0.2
Number of species of native birds in Hawai'i in prehistoric times	111
Number of native species left today, after mass extinctions caused by human-carried invasions of exotic diseases and predatory pigs, rats, and other mammals	60
Percentage of the crop harvest in medieval Europe that was destroyed by pests	30
Percentage of the crop harvest in the world today that is destroyed by pests	35 to 42
Profit per hectare gained by Australian ranchers from the introduction of exotic forage plants	$2
Costs per hectare to the Australian public of controlling those plants, which have no effective natural controls in that ecosystem	$30 to $120

SOURCE: Chris Bright (senior editor of World Watch), *Life Out of Bounds: Bioinvasions in a Borderless World* (New York: W.W. Norton, 1998).

Table 33: Monoculture impact

Varieties of asparagus grown in the United States in 1903	46
Number of turn-of-the-century varieties surviving by the 1980s, after the advent of large-scale monoculture led to a gradual suppression of genetic diversity[i]	1
Varieties of sweet corn grown in the United States in 1903	307
Turn-of-the-century varieties grown in the 1980s[i]	12
Number of jobs provided by 10,000 hectares of diversified farming in Hawai'i	1,800
Number of jobs provided by an equal amount of land used for a monoculture pulp plantation	60
Quantity of farmed oceanic fish and shrimp raised in 1996 by using ground-up ocean fish as feed	1 million tons
Quantity of wild ocean fish that had to be ground up to provide the feed	5 million tons
Amount of fish caught per person worldwide and sold for human consumption in 1996	16 kilograms

Amount of sea urchins, sponges, and other marine life that
was hauled up with the fish and discarded,
per person (approximate) — 200 kilograms
Amount spent to produce the food consumed in the
United States in 1996 (farm cost) — $126 billion
Amount spent on marketing it — $421 billion

SOURCES: Cary Fowler and Pat Mooney, *Shattering: Food, Politics, and the Loss of Genetic Diversity* (Tucson: University of Arizona Press, 1990). Worldwatch, "Matters of Scale – Monoculture: The Biological and Social Impacts," *World Watch* 11(2) (March/April) (1998), p. 39.
NOTE: (i) This number does not include the modern varieties that have largely displaced the older ones. Modern varieties are much higher yielding, but they are far less genetically diverse and they require far more pesticide and chemical fertilizer.

Table 34: Driving up CO_2

Amount General Motors and several other auto-oriented corporations were fined after being found guilty of conspiring to monopolize the transportation industry by buying up rail systems in 83 US cities and dismantling them	$5,000
Amount it would cost to rebuild these rail systems	$3,000,000,000
The combined 1995 population of Africa, Asia, Oceania, today and Central and South America, which that year had a total of 200 million motor vehicles	4.40 billion
The 1995 population of the United States, which also had a total of 200 million motor vehicles	0.27 billion
Area of the United States paved over by roads and parking lots	153,730 square kilometers
Combined area of all US national parks	191,501 square kilometers
Ratio of bicycles to cars in China	250 to 1
Ratio of bicycles to cars in the United States	0.7 to 1
Amount of carbon dioxide that a car running at 27.5 miles per gallon emits over 100,000 miles	31,752 kilograms
Amount of carbon dioxide that a human walking that same distance would produce	59 kilograms

SOURCES: Noelle Knox, *Detroit News*, March 2 1997. Jim Klein and Martha Olson, *Auto-Free Times*, winter 1996–7. American Automobile Association, *World Motor Vehicle Data* (Detroit, MI: 1997). Jane Holtz Kay, *Asphalt Nation* (New York: Crown Publishers, 1997). Steve Nadis and James MacKenzie, *Car Trouble* (Boston, MA: Beacon Press, 1993). Human CO_2 estimates: Jason Archibald, "Matters of Scale," *World Watch Magazine* 10(6) (November/December) (1997), p. 39. NB: By 2000, the Earth's atmospheric carbon level had been raised to about 360 parts per million (ppm) – a level not experienced in 420,000 years. Atmospheric CO_2 concentrations will likely be more than 700 ppm by 2100. Worldwatch, "Matters of Scale: Driving up CO2" *World Watch Magazine*, 10(6), November/December (1997), p. 39.

Table 35: Human migration and displacement

Total number of migrants worldwide, today	100 million
Total population of the world at the time of the classical Greek civilization	100 million
Number of people in the past decade displaced by infrastructure projects, such as road and dam construction	80–90 million
Number of people in the past decade left homeless by natural disasters, including floods, earthquakes, hurricanes, and landslides (based on an average over 25 years)	50 million
Number of people in 1981 who were landless or near-landless	983 million
Number of people expected to be landless or near-landless in 2000	1.24 billion
Number of international refugees in the early 1960s	1 million
in the mid-1970s	3 million
in 1995	27 million
Number of refugees displaced within the borders of their own countries, in 1985	9.5 million
in 1995	20 million
Number of people currently living in coastal areas vulnerable to flooding from storm surges	46 million
Number of people living in vulnerable areas if global warming produces a 50 cm rise in sea level	92 million
Number of people living in vulnerable areas if global warming produces a 1 m rise in sea level	118 million
Number of people living in vulnerable areas if global warming produces a 5 m rise in sea level	1 billion

SOURCES: Thomas Sowell, *Migration and Cultures* (New York: Basic Books, 1996). Worldwatch, "Matters of Scale: Human Migration," *World Watch* 11(5) (September/October) (1997), p. 37. Worldwatch, "Matters of Scale: The Plight of the Displaced," *World Watch* 10(1) (January/February) (1997), p. 39.

NOTES

INTRODUCTION

1. Richard Leakey and Roger Levin, *The Sixth Extinction: Patterns of Life and the Future of Humankind* (New York: Doubleday, 1995), pp. 221, 41.
2. Bertolt Brecht, *Gedichte V* (Frankfurt am Main: Suhrkamp Verlag, 1964), p. 62.
3. "Wir Werden Einsam Sein: Evolutionsbiologe Edward O. Wilson Über Artenvielfalt, Ameisen Und Menschen," *Der Spiegel* 48 (1995): pp. 193–204. NB: until several years ago, biology texts would tell you that the number of species living today might be as high as 3 million to 5 million but is probably less. Thanks to recent work in the tropical rain forests, however, biologists such as Paul Ehrlich and Edward O. Wilson now believe that we have just barely begun to catalog the Earth's present inventory of species. These two scientists have estimated that there may be as many as 50 million species on earth today, with the vast majority packed into several habitats: tropical rain forests, coral reefs, and perhaps the deep sea. Such complex and far-flung environments are very difficult to census. See Peter Douglas Ward, *Rivers in Time: The Search for Clues to Earth's Mass Extinctions* (New York: Columbia University Press, 2000), p. 28, Edward O. Wilson and F.M. Peter, eds, *Biodiversity*, 9th edn (Washington, DC: National Academy Press, 1992).
4. Ed Ayres, "The Fastest Mass Extinction in Earth's History," *Worldwatch* 11(5) (September/October) (1998).
5. Edward O. Wilson, *The Diversity of Life* (New York: W.W. Norton, 1992).
6. Peter Douglas Ward, *The End of Evolution: A Journey in Search of Clues to the Third Mass Extinction Facing the Planet Earth* (New York: Bantam Books, 1995), pp. xvi–xvii, Ward, *Rivers in Time: The Search for Clues to Earth's Mass Extinctions*.
7. Ward, *Rivers in Time: The Search for Clues to Earth's Mass Extinctions*, p. 7, Peter Douglas Ward and Donald Brownlee, *Rare Earth: Why Complex Life Is Uncommon in the Universe* (New York: Copernicus, 2000), pp. 7, 113.
8. These were the short-term effects of the first few hours and days.
9. Ward, *The End of Evolution: A Journey in Search of Clues to the Third Mass Extinction Facing the Planet Earth*, Ward, *Rivers in Time: The Search for Clues to Earth's Mass Extinctions*, pp. 7–8.
10. Stephen Jay Gould, book cover introduction to Peter Ward's *The End of Evolution*.
11. The key question in this book is not whether *Homo sapiens sapiens* does violence to nature, since it is probably not possible for him to do otherwise. *Homo sapiens* is part of nature, and in some sense, we need to do violence to other species if we are to survive and reproduce as a species. Rather, the question is first whether this violence needs to be mindless, cruel, and unnecessary, and, second, whether this sort of behavior now confronts the supreme contradiction: *Homo sapiens* cannot continue in this way and survive.

12. Stephen Jay Gould, *The Flamingo's Smile: Reflections in Natural History*, 1st edn (New York: W.W. Norton, 1985), pp. 231–2, Glendon Schubert, "Catastrophe Theory, Evolutionary Extinction, and Revolutionary Politics," in *The Dynamics of Evolution: Punctuated Equilibrium Debate in the Natural and Social Sciences*, ed. Albert Sombert and Stephen A. Peterson (Ithaca, NY and London: Cornell University Press, 1989), pp. 248–81.

13. For a discussion of extinction estimates, see Ward, *The End of Evolution: A Journey in Search of Clues to the Third Mass Extinction Facing the Planet Earth*, p. 250.

14. Ibid.

15. Wilson, *The Diversity of Life*. Edward O. Wilson, *The Future of Life* (New York: Alfred A. Knopf, 2002).

16. See Norman Myers et al., "Biodiversity Hotspots for Conservation Priorities," *Nature* 403 (2000).

17. Edward O. Wilson, *Vanishing Point: On Bjorn Lomborg and Extinction* ([Online, available: http://www.gristmagazine.com/grist/books/wilson121201.asp], 2001).

18. The 130,000-year-old earliest known example to date of a modern human being, *Homo sapiens sapiens*, was found at Omo in East Africa; skull size and shape are completely modern. Characteristic early tools of *Homo sapiens sapiens*, all from East or South Africa, include bolas for throwing at small game and flake tools.

19. Norman Myers, ed., *Biological Diversity and Global Security, Ecology, Economics, Ethics: The Broken Circle* (New Haven, CT: Yale University Press, 1991).

20. Mainstream sociology tends to view society as a system of communication (see Niklas Luhman, *Ecological Communication* [Chicago: University of Chicago Press, 1986]), and disregards its material properties. So too, neoclassical economics, which views the economy as a system of stocks and flows of money; it is only the monetary side of reality that is addressed by economic theory. At best, physical concepts are discussed as tools for the development of monetarization. These kinds of theories are not very helpful in conceptualizing the relationships between societies and their natural environments.

21. A recent *New York Times* poll, for example, found that only 1 per cent of Americans consider the environment the most important problem facing the country (ENN, July 1 1998). See Jay Hanson and Phyllis Hanson, *Brain Food: Requiem*, ed. J. Hanson, *Brain Food Mailer, Newsletter* ([Online, available: http://dieoff.org], 1998).

22. Tim F. Flannery, *The Eternal Frontier: An Ecological History of North America and Its Peoples* (New York: Atlantic Monthly Press, 2001), Francis Haines, *The Buffalo* (New York: Crowell, 1975), A.W. Schorger, *The Passenger Pigeon: Its Natural History and Extinction* (Norman: University of Oklahoma Press, 1973).

23. Jeremy B.C. Jackson et al., "Historical Overfishing and the Recent Collapse of Coastal Ecosystems," *Science* 293 (July 27) (2001). See also Archie Fairly Carr, *The Sea Turtle: So Excellent a Fishe*, First University of Texas Press ed. (Austin: University of Texas Press, 1986).

24. The term *Homo esophagus colossus* is analogous to the concept of "future eaters," coined by Tim Flannery in *The Future Eaters* (New York: George Braziller, 1995). It underscores the argument that we are indeed future eaters.

25. Ghillean T. Prance and Thomas S. Elias, *Extinction Is Forever: Threatened and Endangered Species of Plants in the Americas and Their Significance in Ecosystems Today and in the Future* (New York: New York Botanical Garden, 1978).

26. United Nations Environment Programme, Governing Council, *World Charter for Nature: United Nations General Assembly Resolution 37/7, of 28 October 1982, Environmental Law Guidelines and Principles; 5* (Nairobi: UNEP, 1983).

27. Elias Canetti, *The Agony of Flies: Notes and Notations*, trans. H.F. Broch de Rothermann from the German "Die Fliegenpein: Aufzeichnungen" (New York: Farrar, Straus, Giroux, 1994), Anita Gordon and David Suzuki, *It's a Matter of Survival* (Cambridge, MA: Harvard University Press, 1991). E.O. Wilson cited in *Der Spiegel*, "Wir Werden Einsam Sein: Evolutionsbiologe Edward O. Wilson Über Artenvielfalt, Ameisen Und Menschen."

28. Canetti, *The Agony of Flies: Notes and Notations*, p. 199.

29. David Pimentel et al., "Economic and Environmental Benefits of Biodiversity," *BioScience* 47(11) (December) (1997), Payal Sampal, "Judgement Protects Indigenous Knowledge," *Worldwatch* 11(1) (January/February) (1998), p. 8.

30. Robert Costanza et al., "The Value of the World's Ecosystem Services and Natural Capital," *Nature* 387(6630) (May 15) (1997).

31. Janet N. Abramovitz, "Putting a Value on Nature's 'Free' Services," *Worldwatch* 11(1) (January/February) (1998), pp. 18–19, Costanza et al., "The Value of the World's Ecosystem Services and Natural Capital."

32. At least one tree species became extinct in the wake of the extermination of the dodo due to its ecologically strategic role as a seed distributor or germinator. See Wolfgang Lutz et al., *Understanding Population–Development–Environment Interactions: A Case Study on Mauritius* (Laxenburg, Vienna: International Institute for Applied Systems Analysis [IIASA] in Collaboration with University of Mauritius; Sponsored by United Nations Population Fund [UNFDP], 1993).

33. World Resources Institute (WRI), *Teachers' Guide to World Resources: Biodiversity, Educational Resources* (Washington, DC: World Resources Institute, 1994), p. 3.

34. "Schlimmster Krieg Aller Zeiten," *Der Spiegel* 18 (1992), pp. 218–32.

35. See WRI, *Teachers' Guide to World Resources: Biodiversity*.

36. Costanza et al., "The Value of the World's Ecosystem Services and Natural Capital." See also Gretchen C. Daily, "Ecosystem Services: Benefits Supplied to Human Societies by Natural Ecosystems," *Issues in Ecology* 2 (Spring) (1997), Gretchen C. Daily, ed., *Nature's Services: Societal Dependence on Natural Ecosystems* (Washington, DC: Island Press, 1998).

37. David Pimentel et al., "Natural Resources and an Optimum Human Population," *Population and Environment* 15(5) (1994), David Pimentel and Marcia Pimentel, "U.S. Food Production Threatened by Rapid Population Growth," *Gaya Preservation Coalition (GPC)* Prepared for the Carrying Capacity Network, Washington, DC (1997), Pimentel et al., "Economic and Environmental Benefits of Biodiversity."

38. Abramovitz, "Putting a Value on Nature's 'Free' Services," p. 10.

39. Mark Nathan Cohen, *The Food Crisis in Prehistory: Overpopulation and the Origins of Agriculture* (London and New Haven, CT: Yale University Press, 1977). See also Mark Nathan Cohen and George J. Armelagos, *Paleopathology at the Origins of Agriculture* (New York: Academic Press, 1984).

40. Jean-Jacques Rousseau, *The Social Contract and Discourses, 1755: "Discourse on the Origin of Inequality," Response To: "Question Proposed by the Academy of Dijon: What Is the Origin of the Inequality among Mankind; and Whether Such Inequality Is Authorized by the Law"* (New York: Dutton, 1950).

41. Theodor Adorno and Max Horkheimer, *Dialectic of Enlightenment*, trans. John Cummings (New York: Herder & Herder, 1972).

42. Peter T. Manicas, *War and Democracy* (Cambridge, MA: Basil Blackwell, 1989).

1 THE HUMAN ODYSSEY: FROM BIOLOGICAL TO CULTURAL EVOLUTION

1. Elisée Reclus, *L'Homme et la terre*, 6 vols (Paris: Paris: Librairie Universelle, 1905), vol. 1, p. i.

2. Julian Huxley, *Evolution in Action* (New York: Mentor Books, 1953).
3. The origins of life, probably some 4 billion years ago, involved a series of evolutionary processes ranging from prebiotic organic synthesis of inorganic chemicals ($H2O$; N_2; CO_2; NH_3; [CH_4]); to simple organic compounds (via energy from ultraviolet radiation and light); to simple organic compounds (via concentration and polymerization); to organic macromolecules, protocells, and finally living cells. After the first emergence of life on earth it took more than 3 billion years for creatures with differently specialized cells to begin appearing in the fossil record, whereupon there was a huge explosion of diversity (the "Cambrian Explosion," of around 500 million years ago).
4. The oldest fossil records to date are one 6 million-year-old creature found in Kenya called *Orrion tungenensis* and dubbed "Millennium Man." In 2001 a new subspecies of *Aridipithecus*, called *Aridipicus ramidus kaddaba* or *Aridipus kaddaba* and dating from 5.8 million to 5.2 million years ago, was found in Ethiopia by Yohannes Haile-Selassie. Molecular studies based on Haile-Selassie's find suggest that the lineages leading to humans and chimpanzees diverged approximately 6.5 million to 5.5 million years ago, in the Late Miocene. These fossils lack the primitive canines and specialized incisors and molars of all chimpanzees, and they look like other later hominids. See Yohannes Haile-Selassie, "Late Miocene Hominids from the Middle Awash, Ethiopia," *Nature* 412 (12 July) (2001).
5. It is not with human biology but with social organizational and institutional behavior that we (collectively) have a problem.
6. Humans, if the taxonomy is correct, are the fifth great ape, next to orangutans, gorillas, chimpanzees, and bonobos, and it was only around 130,000 years ago that we reached "full" humanity. See Jared M. Diamond, *The Third Chimpanzee: The Evolution and Future of the Human Animal* (New York: Harper Collins Publishers, 1992), Richard W. Wrangham and Dale Peterson, *Demonic Males: Apes and the Origins of Human Violence* (Boston, MA: Houghton Mifflin, 1996), p. 29.
7. The genetic distance separating us from pygmy chimps (a mere 1.6 per cent) is barely double that separating pygmy from common chimps (0.7 per cent). It is less than that separating two species of gibbons (2.2 per cent). The remaining 98.4 per cent of human DNA is just normal chimp DNA. For example, human hemoglobin, the oxygen-carrying protein that gives blood its red color, is identical in all of its 287 units with chimp hemoglobin. In this respect, as in most others, we are just a third species of chimpanzee, and what differentiates us from common and pygmy chimps – our upright posture, large brains, ability to speak, sparse body hair, and peculiar sexual lives – must be concentrated in a mere 1.6 per cent of our genetic program (Diamond, *The Third Chimpanzee: The Evolution and Future of the Human Animal*, pp. 2, 23.)
8. Chimpanzees, like humans, show cultural diversity. Other endangered apes, too, such as gorillas and orangutans, show cultural diversity (as do whales and dolphins).
9. "Sex Für Frieden," *Der Spiegel* 30 (1993), p. 171, F.B.M. de Waal and Frans Lanting, *Bonobo: The Forgotten Ape* (Berkeley: University of California Press, 1997).
10. Humans, as paleontologist Stephen Jay Gould notes, are neotenous apes. In neoteny, rates of development slow down and juvenile stages of ancestors become the adult features of descendants. Many central features of our anatomy link us with fetal and juvenile stages of primates: small face, vaulted cranium and large brain in relation to body size, unrotated big toe, foramen magnum under the skull for correct orientation of the head in upright posture, primary distribution of hair on head, armpits, and pubic areas. In other mammals, exploration, play and flexibility of behavior are qualities of juveniles, only rarely of adults. Neoteny has been invoked

as an explanation for many of the differences between humans and other apes. See Stephen J. Gould, *The Mismeasure of Man* (New York: W.W. Norton, 1981), p. 333, Stephen J. Gould, *Ontogeny and Phylogeny* (Cambridge, MA: Harvard University Press, 1977), pp. 352–404.

11. Haile-Selassie, "Late Miocene Hominids from the Middle Awash, Ethiopia."

12. These earliest three known hominid ancestors were *Aridipithecus ramidus kadabba*, the oldest known possibly bipedal ape, represented by fossils from sites in Ethiopia; the better-known *Australopithecus africanus*, a small-brained upright walker from sites in northern Kenya; and *Australopithecus afarensis*, a small-brained, big-faced apelike species to which the famous "Lucy" belonged. See Ian Tattersall and Jeffrey H. Schwartz, *Extinct Humans*, 1st edn (Boulder, CO: Westview Press, 2000).

13. The 16 species of extinct humans include: (1) *Aridipithecus ramidus*, (2) *Australopithecus anamnesis*, (3) *Australopithecus afarensis*, (4) *Australopithecus bahrelghazali*, (5) *Australopithecus aethiopecus*, (6) *Paranthropus boisei*, (7) *Paranthropus robustus*, (8) *Australopithecus africanus*, (9) *Australopithecus garhi*, (10) *Homo rudolfensis*, (11) *Homo habilis*, (12) *Homo ergastus*, (13) *Homo erectus*, (14) *Homo antecessor*, (15) *Homo heidelbergensis*, and (16) *Homo neanderthalensis*. See Ibid.

14 See Simon Robinson, "How Apes Became Human: One Giant Step for Mankind," *Time* (July 23) (Online, available: http://www.time.com/time/pacific/magazine/20010723/cover1.html) (2001), pp. 54–61.

15. That is why the gerenuk, a type of antelope, for example, evolved its long neck and stood on its hind legs, and why the giraffe evolved its long neck. There is strong pressure to be able to reach a wider range of levels. Ibid.

16. Ibid.

17. Richard Leakey and Roger Levin, *Origins Reconsidered: In Search of What Makes Us Human* (New York: Anchor Books, Doubleday, 1992), J.M. Roberts, *The Penguin History of the World* (London: Penguin Books, 1993).

18. Stephen M. Stanley, *Children of the Ice Age: How a Global Catastrophe Allowed Humans to Evolve*, 1st edn (New York: Harmony Books, 1996).

19. When accounting for the evolutionary journey of human evolution we should note that, going back 2 million years ago, East Africa was home not just to lions and leopards, but to saber-toothed cats, giant baboons, and wild pigs as big as buffaloes. Archaic humans hence then were not only rudimentary foragers and hunters but also the hunted and must have invested a good deal of effort in just trying to stay out of their way. This must have shaped the evolution of our species profoundly.

20. Its actual use as an axe seems unlikely, but the name is established.

21. Diamond, *The Third Chimpanzee: The Evolution and Future of the Human Animal*, J.M. Roberts, *History of the World* (New York: Oxford University Press, 1993).

22. Roberts, *History of the World*, pp. 11–13.

23. Alan Walker and Pat Shupman, *The Wisdom of the Bones* (New York: Alfred Knopf, 1996).

24. David Price, "Energy and Human Evolution," *Population and Environment: A Journal of Interdisciplinary Studies* 16(4) (March) (1995), pp. 301–19.

25. Stephen Vickers Boyden, *Biohistory: The Interplay between Human Society and the Biosphere*, vol. 8, *Man and the Biosphere Series* (Paris: UNESCO, Pantheon, 1992).

26. Roberts, *History of the World*.

27. Ibid.

28. Diamond, *The Third Chimpanzee: The Evolution and Future of the Human Animal*, pp. 36–8.

29. Ibid., pp. 38–9.

146 Ecocide

30. *Homo erectus* spread across Asia and Europe, but became extinct everywhere except in Africa, where they continued to evolve. Eventually, a new and improved *Homo sapiens* swept once more out of Africa – this time to stay. See Chris Stringer and Robin McKie, *African Exodus: The Origins of Modern Humanity*, 1st American edn (New York: Henry Holt, 1997).

31. Ian Tattersall, *The Last Neanderthal: The Rise, Success, and Mysterious Extinction*, Rev. edn (Boulder, CO and Oxford: Westview Press, 1999).

32. If we believe that all life – in contrast to rocks and gases – shares a certain quality of sensitivity, or self-awareness, then *Homo sapiens* was an astonishing and wholly unpredictable leap forward in this respect, because human beings manifest an idea of personhood never before achieved. The exact moment of this discovery is of course problematic, as are most events in evolution, but I would date it from early summer about 60,000 years ago, when a group of Neanderthals living in present-day Iraq who lost one of their members dug a grave for him in the Shandidar Cave of the Zagros Mountain highlands, placed his body inside, and covered it with yarrow blossoms, cornflowers, hyacinths, and mallows.

33. Carson I.A. Ritchie, *Food and Civilization: How History Has Been Affected by Human Taste* (New York: Beaufort Books, 1981), p. 19, Ian Tattersall, *The Human Odyssey: Four Million Years of Human Evolution*, ed. American Museum for Natural History, Foreword by Donald Johanson (New York: Prentice Hall, 1993), p. 156.

34. Ritchie, *Food and Civilization: How History Has Been Affected by Human Taste* pp. 16–17.

35. NB: Neanderthals walked upright and had brains some 10 per cent larger than those of anatomically modern human brains.

36. Tattersall, *The Human Odyssey: Four Million Years of Human Evolution*, p. 156.

37. Forty thousand years ago anatomically modern humans in African decorated themselves with pearls made from ostrich egg shells, according to finds in Zaire. See "Siegeszug Aus Der Sackgasse: Neue Knochenfunde Vom Urmenschen Und Die Entstehung Des Homo Sapiens (3)," *Der Spiegel* 44 (1995), p. 145.

38. Ian Tattersall, *Becoming Human: Evolution and Human Uniqueness*, 1st edn (New York: Harcourt Brace, 1998).

39. *Der Spiegel*, "Siegeszug Aus Der Sackgasse: Neue Knochenfunde Vom Urmenschen Und Die Entstehung Des Homo Sapiens (3)," and "Siegeszug Aus Der Sackgasse: Neue Knochenfunde Von Urmenschen Und Die Entstehung Des Homo Sapiens (2)," *Der Spiegel* 43 (1995).

40. *Der Spiegel*, "Siegeszug Aus Der Sackgasse: Neue Knochenfunde Von Urmenschen Und Die Entstehung Des Homo Sapiens (2)." NB: Australian Aborigine art is said to pre-date the beloved French gallery by ten millennia.

41. Oceanic islands, as defined here, are those surrounded by deep water beyond the continental shelf; they have remained separate from the continent even during marine regressions of the glacial age. See Diamond, *The Third Chimpanzee: The Evolution and Future of the Human Animal*, p. 355.

42. By 1600 CE, world population had reached about half a billion, and it reached 6 billion in 2000 CE.

43. Diamond, *The Third Chimpanzee: The Evolution and Future of the Human Animal*.

44. Tim F. Flannery, *Future Eaters: An Ecological History of the Australasian Lands and People* (New York: George Braziller, 1995), pp. 100–1.

45. Circa 18,000 to 21,000 BCE, Jean Clottes, "Rhinos and Lions and Bears (Oh My!)," *Natural History* 5 (1995). NB: The best-known documents of this period are the cave paintings as in Altamira, Spain, first discovered in 1879, and in Chauvet cave in the Rhone Valley of southern France. The "Leonardo da Vincis of the ice age"

produced perspectivist portrayals of animal hordes, hunting panoramas, careful working of stone walls, and three-dimensional models of horses and lions in the cave grotto of Chauvet. A wealth of animal and abstract images, some 300 counted so far, cascades across cave walls. Each of the most spectacular mammals of the ice age Rhone Valley is there: lions, woolly rhinos, mammoths, reindeer, horses, wild cattle, bears, ibexes, a leopard, and most unusually – an owl. The Magdalenian paintings (c. 16,000–9,000 years ago) at Altamira, Spain, primarily focus on bison, which had at that time not yet been exterminated in Europe. We can infer that bison were important because of the hunt. They were hunted primarily for the food they provided, but also many other useful commodities like skin, bones, and fur could be extracted from the remains of such a large animal. The ceiling painting is of 15 large bison with a few interspersed animals including a horse. The groups of animals portrayed, particularly those on the walls such as bison, deer, wild boar, and other combinations, do not normally aggregate in nature. These pictures are of the animals only, and contain no landscape or horizontal base. See Bryant, "Extinction and Depletion from Over-Exploitation," also Flannery, *Future Eaters: An Ecological History of the Australasian Lands and People*, p. 136.

46. Ritchie, *Food and Civilization: How History Has Been Affected by Human Taste*, p. 19.
47. A "fish gorge" is a kind of fish trap. Dead falls are places where big game hunters stampeded horses, bison, or other game over a cliff. Blals are specialized hunting tools such as the instrument that shoots blow darts.
48. In 1989, Russian geologist Sergei Barteman discovered mammoth tusks littered on Range Island, an isolated island between Alaska and Siberia. Barteman found that mammoths survived there until less than 4,000 years ago, several centuries after the building of the pyramids. Mammoths survived there for many thousands of years longer than anywhere else – 7,000 years longer than on the North American mainland, for example, due to the island's isolation and to protection from human predation resulting from sea level change. However, having eluded extinction in isolation at least for that time period, they evolved into a *dwarf* variety some 4 feet tall (approximately 1.5 meters, or only one-third their original size). See the production by BBC-TV, NOVA, *Mammoths of the Ice Age* (Video), *A Nova Production by BBC-TV in Association with WGBH Educational Foundation* (South Burlington and Boston: BBC-TV and WGBH, 1995).
49. Bryant, "Extinction and Depletion from Over-Exploitation."
50. Paul S. Martin and Richard G. Klein, eds, *Quarternary Extinctions: A Prehistoric Revolution* (Tucson: University of Arizona Press, 1984), Neil Roberts, *The Holocene: An Environmental History* (New York: Basil Blackwell, 1992), p. 59.
51. Ritchie, *Food and Civilization: How History Has Been Affected by Human Taste*, pp. 19–20.
52. Brian M. Fagan, *Ancient North America: The Archeology of a Continent* (London: Thames and Hudson, 1991), pp. 126–36.
53. Diamond, *The Third Chimpanzee: The Evolution and Future of the Human Animal*, Flannery, *The Eternal Frontier: An Ecological History of North America and Its Peoples*, Flannery, *Future Eaters: An Ecological History of the Australasian Lands and People*, Martin and Klein, eds, *Quarternary Extinctions: A Prehistoric Revolution*, Peter Douglas Ward, *The Call of Distant Mammoths: Why the Ice Age Mammals Disappeared* (New York: Copernicus, 1997), Ward, *Rivers in Time: The Search for Clues to Earth's Mass Extinctions*.
54. Of all mammal genera whose members exceed 44 kg in average adult body weight, Europe has lost only 29 per cent of those living there some 200,000 years ago. This is truly remarkable when one considers how altered most European landscapes are.

It stands in stark contrast with the loss of 94 per cent of such animals in Australia. See Bryant, "Extinction and Depletion from Over-Exploitation," also Flannery, *Future Eaters: An Ecological History of the Australasian Lands and People*, pp. 136, 308.

55. Bryant, "Extinction and Depletion from Over-Exploitation."

56. Flannery, *Future Eaters: An Ecological History of the Australasian Lands and People*, p. 185.

57. Madhav Gadgil and Ramachandra Guha, *The Fissured Land: An Ecological History of India* (New Delhi: Oxford University Press, 1992), p. 73.

58. Bryant, "Extinction and Depletion from Over-Exploitation."

59. Today, we regard Africa as the continent of big mammals. Modern Eurasia also has many species of big mammals (though not in the manifest abundance of Africa's Serengeti Plain) such as Asia's rhinos and elephants and tigers, and Europe's moose and bears and (until classical times) lions. Australia/New Guinea today has no equally large mammals – in fact no mammal larger than 100-pound kangaroos. But Australia/New Guinea formerly had its own suite of diverse big mammals, including giant kangaroos, rhino-like marsupials called diprotodonts that reached the size of a cow, and a marsupial "leopard." It also had a 400-pound ostrich-like flightless bird, plus some impressively big reptiles, including a 1 ton lizard, a giant python, and land-dwelling crocodiles. All of those Australian and New Guinean giants (the so-called megafauna) disappeared after the arrival of humans. See, Jared M. Diamond, *Guns, Germs, and Steel: The Fates of Human Societies* (New York: W.W. Norton , 1997), Flannery, *Future Eaters: An Ecological History of the Australasian Lands and People*, Martin and Klein, eds, *Quartenary Extinctions: A Prehistoric Revolution*.

60. Gifford H. Miller et al., "Pleistocene Extinction of *Genyornis Newtoni*: Human Impact on Australian Megafauna," *Science* 283 (January 8) (1999).

61. Arriving in a land which had never seen hominids before, and where animals had no innate fear of humans, Flannery suggests, early humans must have felt or become, in a sense, like gods. Their impact in Australia, according to Flannery, was enormous, for they proceeded to kill all mammals larger than themselves, including the above-mentioned rhino-sized wombat, the enormous horned turtle, the razor-toothed marsupial lion, and the giant rat-kangaroo; see Tim Flannery, 'The Future Eaters' (interview) *Geographical Magazine* 69(1) (January) (1997), p. 26. The only species to survive were the quickest and the smallest – kangaroos, wallabies, koala bears, and wombats. Ninety-five per cent of all its large mammals were lost between 40,000 and 60,000 years ago. See Flannery, *Future Eaters: An Ecological History of the Australasian Lands and People*, Martin and Klein, eds, *Quartenary Extinctions: A Prehistoric Revolution*.

62. All twelve original species of moa, Aotearoa's largest bird species, are now extinct. All of these extinctions occurred within less than 500 years of Maori colonization and settlement; hence the popular song from Aotearoa: "No moa, no moa, In Old Ao-tea-roa. Can't get 'em. They've et 'em; They've gone and there ain't no moa!" These largest species were members of the family Diornithea, which included three very tall and graceful species that occurred on both the North and the South Island. With its neck outstretched, the largest moa would have reached over 3.5 meters high, towering twice as high as a man, and weighed up to 250 kilograms. The moa belonged to a very ancient group of birds known as ratites, now restricted to the southern continents, with the ostrich in Africa, the emu and cassowary in Australia/New Guinea, the rhea in South America, and the kiwi in New Zealand. Thus everything points to their being yet another group of Gondwanan origin.

63. Atholl Anderson, "Prehistoric Polynesian Impact on the New Zealand Environment," in *Historical Ecology in the Pacific Islands: Prehistoric Environmental and Landscape Changes*, ed. Patrick V. Kirk and Terry L. Hunt (New Haven, CT: Yale University Press, 1997), Ian K. Bradbury, *The Biosphere* (New York: Belhaven Press, 1991), p. 186, Richard Cassels, "The Role of Prehistoric Man in the Faunal Extinctions of New Zealand and Other Pacific Islands," in Martin and Klein, eds, *Quarternary Extinctions: A Prehistoric Revolution*.

64. Bryant, "Extinction and Depletion from Over-Exploitation." NB: Some archaeologists have argued that South America may have been settled as early as 30,000 to 40,000 years ago, but there is as yet no conclusive evidence or widely accepted confirmation of this thesis.

65. Paul S. Martin, "Pleistocene Overkill," *Natural History* 76 (1967), Martin and Klein, eds, *Quarternary Extinctions: A Prehistoric Revolution*. Bryant, "Extinction and Depletion from Over-Exploitation.", Martin and Klein, eds, *Quarternary Extinctions: A Prehistoric Revolution*, Roberts, *The Holocene: An Environmental History*.

66. Bryant, "Extinction and Depletion from Over-Exploitation", Martin and Klein, eds, *Quarternary Extinctions: A Prehistoric Revolution*, Roberts, *The Holocene: An Environmental History*.

67. Bryant, "Extinction and Depletion from Over-Exploitation,"

68. Cassels, "The Role of Prehistoric Man in the Faunal Extinctions of New Zealand and Other Pacific Islands," Diamond, *The Third Chimpanzee: The Evolution and Future of the Human Animal*, p. 356, Ward, *The End of Evolution: A Journey in Search of Clues to the Third Mass Extinction Facing the Planet Earth*, Wilson, *The Diversity of Life*.

69. Studies of fossil birds of Hawai'i and the South Pacific by Smithsonian biologist Storrs Olson have uncovered "one of the swiftest and most profound biological catastrophes in the history of the world." It was not, as one might think, caused by the arrival of Europeans with guns. By the time Captain Cook passed through in the eighteenth century, around 80 per cent of all the species of birds of the region had already been wiped out. In Hawai'i, fossils of more than 50 species of birds that are today extinct have been unearthed. As the Polynesians spread throughout the region centuries before, they brought with them dogs, pigs, and rats (a particularly large ecological jolt for islands such as Hawai'i that had no native mammals other than bats) that raided the nests of ground-dwelling birds. The Polynesians cleared land for farming. They hunted. They brought domestic chickens that may have spread diseases such as avian malaria. Wherever Polynesian artifacts appear in the archaeological record, a whole range of birds, including parrots, pigeons, and flightless geese, simultaneously vanish. Some of these species survive on a few remote islands, but others live on only in the legends of the islanders, who have names for birds they have never seen; their descriptions of these legendary birds precisely match the fossil birds that archaeologists have unearthed. See Patrick V. Kirk and Terry L. Hunt, eds, *Historical Ecology in the Pacific Islands: Prehistoric Environmental and Landscape Changes, Based on Papers Presented at the XVIIth Pacific Science Congress Held in Honolulu in 1991* (New Haven, CT: Yale University Press, 1997), S.L. Olson, "Extinction on Islands: Man as a Catastrophe," in *Conservation for the Twenty-First Century*, ed. D. Western and M. Pearl (New York: Oxford University Press, 1989), Storrs L. Olson and Helen F. James, "The Role of Polynesians in the Extinction of the Avifauna of the Hawaiian Islands," in Martin and Klein, eds, *Quarternary Extinctions: A Prehistoric Revolution*.

70. Jared M. Diamond, "Paleontology: Twilight of the Pygmy Hippo," *Nature* 359(6390) (September) (1991), Magazine *Discover*, "Early Sailors Hunted Pygmy Hippo to Extinction," *Discover* March (1993), Ross McPhee, "Digging Cuba: The Lessons of

the Bones," *Natural History* 106(11) (Dec.–Jan.) (1997), Diane Pinkadella, "Were Pygmy Hippos Hunted to Extinction?," *Earth* 2(3) (1993).

71. In Jamaica a native monkey may have survived as late as the eighteenth century. See McPhee, "Digging Cuba: The Lessons of the Bones."

72. Ibid.

73. Jared Diamond was one of the first to question whether we have not possibly overlooked minifauna extinctions. For example he comments on the enormous differences in archaeological visibility of the early human impact or "blitzkrieg." Diamond raised the question of size-related sample biases and questioned whether the samples of the fossil minifauna are rich enough to judge whether it suffered extinctions comparable to those of the megafauna. Paul Martin (in Martin and Klein, *Quaternary Extinctions: A Prehistoric Revolution*, p. 355) affirmatively noted that extinctions of interest within the last 100,000 years were not limited to large mammals. The disappearance of a large number of genera of small birds and mammals on oceanic islands during the Holocene is one case in point. See Jared M. Diamond, "Historic Extinctions: A Rosetta Stone for Understanding Prehistoric Extinctions," in Martin and Klein, eds, *Quatenary Extinctions: A Prehistoric Revolution*, p. 856. See also Olson, "Extinction on Islands: Man as a Catastrophe," Olson and James, "The Role of Polynesians in the Extinction of the Avifauna of the Hawaiian Islands."

74. Flannery, *Future Eaters: An Ecological History of the Australasian Lands and People*, p. 115, Paul S. Martin, "The Discovery of America," *Science* 179 (1973), pp. 969–74.

75. Diamond, *The Third Chimpanzee: The Evolution and Future of the Human Animal*, p. 45.

76. See Derek Bickerton, *Language and Species* (Chicago: University of Chicago Press, 1990).

77. Diamond, *The Third Chimpanzee: The Evolution and Future of the Human Animal*, p. 54.

78. Ibid., p. 56.

79. Ibid., p. 141.

80. Bickerton, *Language and Species*, p. 240.

81. Stephen Edelston Toulmin, "Back to Nature," *New York Review of Books* 9 June (1977), p. 4 (cited in Gould, *The Mismeasure of Man*, p. 325).

82. Gould, *The Mismeasure of Man*, p. 324.

83. Ibid., pp. 325–6.

2   PROBLEMATIC SOCIETY–NATURE RELATIONS BEFORE THE MODERN ERA

1. Cited in Jeremy Swift, *The Other Eden: A New Approach to Man, Nature and Society* (London: J.M. Dent & Sons, 1974) p. 13. NB: Gilgamesh was a historical figure who ruled the city-state of Uruk sometime between 2700 and 2500 BCE; he was remembered as a great warrior as well as the builder of Uruk's massive walls and temple. His exploits so impressed his contemporaries that he became the focal point of a series of oral sagas that recounted his legendary heroic deeds. Around 2000 BCE or shortly thereafter, an unknown Babylonian poet reworked some of these tales, along with other stories, such as the adventures of Utnapishtim, into an epic masterpiece that became widely popular and influential throughout southwest Asia and beyond. See James H. Overfield and Andrea J. Alfred, *The Human Record: Sources of Global History (vol. 1: To 1700)* (Boston, MA: Houghton Mifflin Company, 1994), p. 7.

2. Swift, *The Other Eden: A New Approach to Man, Nature and Society*, p. 15, J.V. Thirgood, *Man and the Mediterranean Forests: A History of Resource Depletion* (London: Academic Press, 1989), pp. 29–30.

3. The term "Neolithic Revolution" was originally coined by anthropologist Vere Gordon Childe, *Man Makes Himself* (New York: New American Library; Mentor Books, 1951).

4. Fekri Hassan, "The Dynamics of Agricultural Origins in Palestine: A Theoretical Model," in *Origins of Agriculture*, ed. Charles Reed (Chicago: Chicago Publishers, 1977), p. 589.

5. This variation, also known as "neolithic time lags" is explored by Jared Diamond, *The Third Chimpanzee: The Evolution and Future of the Human Animal*, and in Diamond, *Guns, Germs, and Steel: The Fates of Human Societies*.

6. Marvin Harris, *Kannibalen Und Könige: Die Wachstumgrenzen Der Hochkulturen* (Darmstadt: Klett & Kotta, 1990), p. 24.

7. Marshall Sahlins, "The Original Affluent Society," in *Stone Age Economics* (Chicago: Aldine Atherton, 1972).

8. Susan George, *Food for Beginners, Social Studies Historical Series* (New York and London: Writers and Readers Publishing Corporation, 1982), Marshall D. Sahlins, *Stone Age Economics*.

9. J.L. Angel, "Paleontology, Paleodemography and Health," in *Population, Ecology and Social Evolution: World Anthropology*, ed. Steven Polgar (The Hague: Mouton, 1975), Marvin Harris, *Cultural Anthropology*, 3rd edn (New York: Harper & Collins, 1991), p. 75, R. Lee, "Problems in the Study of Hunters and Gatherers," in *Man the Hunter*, ed. R. Lee and I. DeVore (Chicago: Aldine, 1969), Sahlins, *Stone Age Economics*.

10. The modern ethnographic example taken here are !Kung Bushmen in southern Africa. See George, *Food for Beginners*, p. 6.

11. Marina Fischer-Kowalski and Helmut Haberl, "Metabolism and Colonization: Modes of Production and the Physical Exchange between Societies and Nature," *Innovation in Social Science Research* 6(4) (Schriftenreihe Ökologie, Band 32. Wien/Austria; Interuniversitäres Institut für Interdisziplinäre Forschung und Fortbildung; Abteilung Soziale Ökologie) (1993), pp. 4–5.

12. Donella H. Meadows, Dennis L. Meadows, and Jørgen Randers, *Beyond the Limits: Confronting Global Collapse, Envisioning a Sustainable Future* (Post Mills, VT: Chelsea Green Publishing Company, 1992), pp. 218–21.

13. The overall pattern of archaeological excavations in Europe to date suggests that a real commitment to maritime lifeways did not precede late Upper Paleolithic times. Similarly, in the New World, early occupants (the Paleo-Indians and hypothetical pre-Clovis occupants) have not been found to use marine resources, and in most parts of North America a real commitment to maritime lifeways postdates the mid-Holocene. David R. Yesner, "Life in the Garden of Eden: Causes and Consequences of the Adoption of Marine Diets by Human Societies," in *Food and Evolution: Towards a Theory of Human Food Habits*, ed. Marvin Harris and Eric B. Ross (Philadelphia, PA: Temple University Press, 1987), p. 285.

14. Marvin Harris, *Cannibalism and Kings: The Origins of Culture* (New York: Vintage Books, 1977), p. 30.

15. Cohen, *The Food Crisis in Prehistory: Overpopulation and the Origins of Agriculture*.

16. Fischer-Kowalski and Haberl, "Metabolism and Colonization: Modes of Production and the Physical Exchange between Societies and Nature," p. 5.

17. Brian M. Fagan, *The Journey from Eden: The Peopling of Our World* (New York: Thames & Hudson, 1990).

18. Cohen, *The Food Crisis in Prehistory: Overpopulation and the Origins of Agriculture*, Gary Gray, *Wildlife and People: The Human Dimension of Wildlife Ecology* (Urbana: University of Illinois Press, 1993), p. 21. (Around 13,000 BCE the glaciers of the ice age began to melt, thus submerging the land bridges and improving the climate.

With the improvement of the climate, animal, plant, and human populations began to rise. It was also about this time when animals were domesticated for human use for the first time.)

19. Fagan, *The Journey from Eden: The Peopling of Our World*, Gray, *Wildlife and People: The Human Dimension of Wildlife Ecology*, p. 21.

20. Fagan, *The Journey from Eden: The Peopling of Our World*.

21. Gray, *Wildlife and People: The Human Dimension of Wildlife Ecology*, p. 21.

22. See Anne H. Ehrlich and Paul Ehrlich, *Earth* (New York: Franklin Watts, 1987), David Macauley, "Thinkers out of Space: Hannah Arendt on Earth Alienation; a Historical and Critical Perspective," *Capitalism, Nature, Socialism* (CNS) 3(4) (December) (1992).

23. The term "domestication" shares a root meaning with "domination" – suggesting a possible suffocating control – but it is also cognate with *domus* (house), implying an attempt on the part of humans to make something familiar to them on an everyday basis. The idea thus retains some ambiguities and ambivalence associated with this process, one many historians believe has been our single most significant historical interaction with the natural world and one of the most important events in our own psychological, biological, and social history. Domestication, too, stands in contrast to the *wild*, a term related to *will*, so that it can be said that a wild animal, plant, or human – unlike its domestic counterpart – is likely self-willed, uncontrolled, even autonomous. To this extent, there is a basis for critique built into an understanding of the process of domestication from the start.

24. A. Ehrlich and P. Ehrlich, *Earth*, p. 60.

25. The process of habitat displacement is also referred to by conservation biologists as "competitive exclusion," the displacement of one species from its habitat or ecological niche by another. When humans appropriate other species' "ecological space," it often leads to the local or even global extinction of the non-human organism.

26. Fischer-Kowalski and Haberl, "Metabolism and Colonization: Modes of Production and the Physical Exchange between Societies and Nature," in Marina Fischer-Kowalski et al. eds, *Gesellschaftlicher Stoffwechsel Und Kolonisierung Von Natur: Ein Versuch in Sozialer Ökologie* (Amsterdam: G+B Verlag Fakultas, 1997).

27. Alfred Crosby, *Ecological Imperialism: The Biological Expansion of Europe, 900–1900* (Melbourne and Cambridge: Cambridge University Press, 1986), Diamond, *Guns, Germs, and Steel: The Fates of Human Societies*.

28. Price, "Energy and Human Evolution," pp. 301–19.

29. Macauley, "Thinkers out of Space: Hannah Arendt on Earth Alienation; A Historical and Critical Perspective."

30. Rousseau's insight, however, is tragically lost to progressivist interpretations of history. From Smith onward, the philosophical mainstream ideologically argues *against* the tolerant theory insisting that powers ought to be shared and argues, instead, that the inequalities associated with exclusive property forms are desirable, contributing to "advance" and "progress"; or, more ideologically fatalistic in the late modern, late Cold War era, when the powers-that-be begin to insist point blank that "There is no alternative" (TINA).

31. David Muschamp, ed., *Political Thinkers* (Basingstoke: Macmillan Education, 1989), p. 127, Rousseau, *The Social Contract and Discourses*.

32. Chris Maser, *Global Imperative: Harmonising Culture and Nature* (Walpole, NH: Stillpoint Publisher, 1992), p. 68.

33. Rene Jules Dubos, "Franciscan Conservation Versus Benedictine Stewardship," in *A God Within*, ed. R.J. Dubos (New York: Charles Scribner Sons, 1972), p. 114.

34. Ibid., p. 115.
35. Donald J. Hughes, "Mencius' Prescriptions for Ancient Chinese Environmental Problems," *Environmental Review* 13(12–25) (1989), Donald J. Hughes, "Ripples in Clio's Pond: Menicus, Ecologist," *Capitalism, Nature, Socialism* 8(3) (September) (1997).
36. Mencius (Meng Tze), *Mencius*, trans. D.C. Lau (London: Penguin Books, 1970), p. 8.
37. Hughes, "Ripples in Clio's Pond: Mencius, Ecologist," p. 120.
38. Ibid., pp. 117–21.
39. Dated back to the eleventh to sixth century BCE.
40. Jin-qi Fang and Zhiren Xie, "Deforestation in Preindustrial China: The Loess Plateau Region as an Example," *Chemosphere* 29(5) (1994).
41. Jin-qi Fang, *Deforestation of the Loess Plateau in Pre-Industrial Time: Destruction of the Chinese Cradle*, Working Paper (Honolulu: East-West Center Program of the Environment, 1994).
42. N.H. Shi, "The Geographical Character of the Loess Plateau During the Zhou Period (100–256 B.C.)," *Journal of Shaanxi Normal University* 3/4 (1978), N.H. Shi, ed., *On Gully Control and Water Conservation on the Loess Plateau*, vol. 2, *Contributions to Historical Geography of China* (Xian: Shaanxi People's Publishing House [in Chinese], 1985), S.Y. Tian, "Hydrological Changes in Shanxi Province and Their Relations with the Alterations between Farming and Animal Husbandry in Different Historical Times," *Journal of Shanxi University* (philosophy) 1 (1981).
43. These lakes were recorded in the literature before the time of the geographer Li Daoyuan (fl. c. 500 CE), who compiled the famous book *Notes on the Book of Waterways*. See Y.Z. Chen, "Li Daoyuan fl. c. 500 A.D.," *Geographers, Bibliographical Studies* (1988).
44. Tian, "Hydrological Changes in Shanxi Province and Their Relations with the Alterations between Farming and Animal Husbandry in Different Historical Times."
45. See Georg Borgstrom, *The Food and People Dilemma, The Man–Environment System in the Late Twentieth Century* (Belmont, CA: Duxbury Press, 1973), p. 97, Donald Worster, *Dust Bowl: The Southern Plains in the 1930s* (New York: Oxford University Press, 1979), p. 4. NB: This deforestation, beginning more than 3,000 years ago, not only led to loss of biodiversity but produced centuries of silting and flooding. The creation of the Dust Bowl in the southwestern Great Plains in the United States is the first modern example of a major ecological blunder.
46. John Bellamy Foster, *The Vulnerable Planet: A Short History of the Environment* (New York: Monthly Review Press, 1994), pp. 36, 37, Eric R. Wolf, *Europe and the People without History* (Berkeley: University of California Press, 1982).
47. Robert Redfield, *Peasant Society and Culture* (Chicago: University of Chicago Press, 1956), Norman Yoffee, "Orienting Collapse," in *The Collapse of Ancient States and Civilizations*, ed. Norman Yoffee and George L. Cowgill (Tucson: University of Arizona Press, 1988).
48. G.F. Dales, "Early Despotism in Mesopotamia," in *Early Antiquity*, ed. I.E. Diakanoff (Chicago: University of Chicago Press, 1991).
49. "Hydraulic Civilization," in *Britannica Online:* Copyright (c) 1997 Encyclopedia Britannica, Inc.
50. Ritchie, *Food and Civilization: How History Has Been Affected by Human Taste.*
51. Karl W. Butzer, "Environmental Change, Climate History and Human Modification: Civilizations of the Ancient near East," in *Civilizations of the near East*, ed. J.M. Sasson, John Baines and Karen S. Robinson (New York: Scribner, 1994), Dominique Collon, *First Impressions, Cylinder Seals in the Ancient near East* (London: British Museum Publications, 1987).

52. See Karl W. Butzer, *Early Hydraulic Civilizations in Egypt: A Study in Cultural Ecology* (Chicago: University of Chicago Press, 1976), Roberts, *The Holocene: An Environmental History*, Karl Wittfogel, *Oriental Despotism: A Comparative Study of Total Power* (New Haven, CT: Yale University Press, 1957).

53. Sing C. Chew, "Ecological Relations and the Decline of Kingdoms and Civilizations in the Bronze Age 2500 BC to 1700 BC: Some Considerations on Mesopotamia and Harappa," in *The Global Environment and the Worldsystem*, ed. W. Goodfrank, D. Goodman, and A. Szasz (Santa Cruz: Draft presented at the Political Economy of the World System XXI Conference, April, Santa Cruz, CA, 1997).

54. Diakonoff 1991, cited in ibid.

55. Ellis 1976, cited in ibid.

56. Boyden, *Biohistory: The Interplay between Human Society and the Biosphere*, pp. 192–3.

57. Ibid.

58. Roberts, *The Holocene: An Environmental History*, p. 129.

59. Overfield and Alfred, *The Human Record: Sources of Global History (vol. 1: To 1700)*.

60. Roberts, *The Holocene: An Environmental History*, pp. 129–31.

61. Ibid., p. 130.

62. Archaeologist Patrick Culbert maintains a similar argument in his study of Maya agricultural intensification and collapse. See Patrick T. Culbert, "The Collapse of Classical Maya Civilization," in *The Collapse of Ancient States and Civilizations*, ed. Norman Yoffee and George L. Cowgill (Tucson: University of Arizona Press, 1988).

63. A. Ehrlich and P. Ehrlich, *Earth*, p. 157.

64. The earliest sedentary foragers so far discovered are the Natufians, who enter the archaeological record approximately 12,000 years ago in the eastern Mediterranean.

65. Richard H. Grove, *Green Imperialism: Colonial Expansion, Tropical Island Edens and the Origins of Environmentalism, 1600–1860* (Cambridge: Cambridge University Press, 1995), p. 18, G. Rollefson and I. Kohler, "Prehistoric People Ruined Their Environment," *New Scientist* 125(24) (February) (1990).

66. Grove, *Green Imperialism: Colonial Expansion, Tropical Island Edens and the Origins of Environmentalism, 1600–1860*, pp. 19–20.

67. Sing C. Chew, "Neglecting Nature: World Accumulation and Core–Periphery Relations, 2500 BC to AD 1990," in *World System History: The Social Science of Long-Term Change*, ed. Jonathan Friedman, Robert A. Denemark, Barry K. Gills, and George Modelski (London and New York: Routledge, Taylor & Francis Group, 1995), pp. 219–22.

68. Chew, "Ecological Relations and the Decline of Kingdoms and Civilizations in the Bronze Age 2500 BC to 1700 BC: Some Considerations on Mesopotamia and Harappa."

69. Ibid., p. 30.

70. Gary Gardener, "Shrinking Fields: Cropland Loss in a World of Eight Billion," *Worldwatch Paper 131* (July) (1996), p. 5, Clive Ponting, "Historical Perspectives on Sustainable Development," *Environment* 32(9) (November) (1990).

71. Dubos, "Franciscan Conservation Versus Benedictine Stewardship," p. 116.

72. Roberts, *The Holocene: An Environmental History*, p. 128.

73. A. Ehrlich and P. Ehrlich, *Earth*, p. 157.

74. Ibid., p. 158.

75. Ellen Meiksins-Wood, *Democracy against Capitalism: Renewing Historical Materialism* (New York: Cambridge University Press, 1995), p. 202.

76. Donald J. Hughes, "Ripples in Clio's Pond: Classical Athens and Ecosystem Collapse," *Capitalism, Nature, Socialism* 7(3) (September) (1996), pp. 97–8.

77. Ibid.

78. Ibid., p. 99.

79. The Peloponnesian War was fought between Athens and Sparta, from 431 to 404 BCE, and resulted in the transfer of hegemony in Greece from Athens to Sparta. It took place on the peninsula of Peloponnesus, which forms the southern part of mainland Greece, the seat of the early Mycenaean civilization and later of the powerful city-states of Argos.

80. Sing C. Chew, "For Nature: Deep Greening World-Systems Analysis for the 21st Century," *Journal of World-Systems Research* 3(3) [Online, available: http://csf.colorado.edu/wsystems/jwsr.html] (1997), p. 389.

81. Diodorus reports that the Spartans cut down all the trees in Attica during the wars. See also Thucycides, *Peloponnesian Wars*, 2.54, cited in John Perlin, *A Forest Journey: The Role of Wood in the Development of Civilization* (Cambridge, MA: Harvard University Press, 1991), p. 91.

82. Theophrastus, *De causis*, (14) 2–4, 5, cited in C.J. Glacken, *Traces on the Rhodian Shore: Nature and Culture in Western Thought from Ancient Times to the End of the Eighteenth Century* (Berkeley: University of California Press, 1967), p. 130n. See also Theophrastus, *De nentis*, in A. Loeb, ed., *Theophrastus' Enquiry into Plants* (New York, 1916), p. 379, on the changing climate of Crete.

83. Grove, *Green Imperialism: Colonial Expansion, Tropical Island Edens and the Origins of Environmentalism, 1600–1860*, p. 20.

84. Hughes, "Ripples in Clio's Pond: Classical Athens and Ecosystem Collapse," p. 99, Theodore A. Wertheim, "The Furnace vs the Goat: The Pyro Technology Industries and Mediterranean Deforestation in Antiquity," *Journal of Field Archeology* 10 (1983).

85. Hughes, "Ripples in Clio's Pond: Classical Athens and Ecosystem Collapse."

86. The earlier disappearance of forests in the Mediterranean area came about partly because the evergreen forests of the region were easier to clear than the deciduous forests further north, but more particularly because the ecological conditions were less favorable to their rapid regeneration. Among the components of these ecological conditions, along with the nature of the climate and the soil, were the ubiquitous goats that roamed the cleared areas in large numbers. It has been suggested that they effectively destroyed any seedlings that might otherwise have grown into trees to replace those that had been removed by humans (A. Ehrlich and P. Ehrlich, *Earth*, p. 186).

   As a result, much of the evergreen forest in the Mediterranean region was transformed early into the semi-natural brushwood, which is known as *garigue* or *maquis*. Some authors have suggested that deforestation in Greece and in Italy was an important factor contributing to the decline of Roman and Greek civilization (Boyden, *Biohistory: The Interplay between Society and the Biosphere*, p. 127). For a comparative study of historical attitudes toward nature, see J. Donald Hughes, *Ecology in Ancient Civilizations* (Albuquerque: University of New Mexico Press, 1975).

87. "By comparison with the original territory, what is left is ... the skeleton of a body wasted by disease; the rich, soft soil has been carried off and only the bare framework of the district left" (Plato, in *Critias*, describing the deforestation of Attica – the region around Athens – during the four centuries BCE. Plato, *Critias*, ed. E. Hamilton and H. Cairns, *Collected Dialogues*, Bollingen series 71 (New York: Pantheon Books, 1961), p. 1216. A. Ehrlich and P. Ehrlich, *Earth*, p. 159.

88. Hughes, "Ripples in Clio's Pond: Classical Athens and Ecosystem Collapse," p. 102.

89. The Romans had made citizens of other lands into slaves; they appeared to have assumed (in their colonizing quest and imperial endeavors) that they could do the same with the Earth and all her creatures. The "practicality," however, was "short-

sighted." See Donald J. Hughes, "Ripples in Clio's Pond: Rome's Decline and Fall: Ecological Mistakes?" *Capitalism, Nature, Socialism* 8(2) (June) (1997), p. 123. Roman efforts were geographically far-reaching; Rome had the ability to reach out and use resources located at great distances. Roman roads and ships brought timber from the Alps and Lebanon. Tin was brought from beyond the straits of Gibraltar. Gigantic projects like the Roman road system, which was long enough to reach the moon, show that rulers had ways of getting cooperation. No other ancient empire combined large size with social control as effectively as did Rome.

90. Paul Ehrlich and Anne Ehrlich, *Extinction: The Causes and Consequences of the Disappearance of Species* (New York: Random House, 1981), p. 159.

91. Hughes, "Ripples in Clio's Pond: Rome's Decline and Fall: Ecological Mistakes?" p. 121.

92. Cited in ibid.

93. P. Ehrlich and A. Ehrlich, *Extinction: The Causes and Consequences of the Disappearance of Species*, p. 159.

94. Ibid.

95. Kent MacDougall, *Humans as Cancer* (USA, CA: [Online, available: http://www. churchofeuthanasia.org/e-sermons/humcan.html], 1997).

96. P. Ehrlich and A. Ehrlich, *Extinction: The Causes and Consequences of the Disappearance of Species*, p. 159. NB: Wolves, bears, ostriches, lions, and other species fought against each other or against people in Rome's Colosseum. The Emperor Nero even staged Colosseum fights with polar bears catching seals. Rome's Colosseum performed grotesque mythological re-enactments of violence that provided a safety valve for the people to express collective feelings of togetherness and violence. From Constantine onward, the Christian emperors were no less violent than their pagan predecessors, however. Crocodiles, lions, and bears continued to be used in the games. Animal hunts for the gladiatorial games persisted for 200 years. Crowds and rulers were trapped in violent entertainment games and addicted to the escalation of violence. Prostitution was practiced underneath the Colosseum structures along with the fights. In 549 CE the final amphitheater games were held.

97. Ibid.

98. Ivory for the Roman Empire was brought from as far away as Java. Romans were noted for their genius for transporting live creatures from the ends of the earth. They could bring in live ostriches from North Africa and crocodiles from Egypt to Rome, and they had no difficulty in procuring oysters from Britain. See Worldwatch, "Endpiece: The Ivory Trade," *Worldwatch* 10(3) (May/June) (1997), p. 40; and Ritchie, *Food and Civilization: How History Has Been Affected by Human Taste*, p. 52.

99. P. Ehrlich and A. Ehrlich, *Extinction: The Causes and Consequences of the Disappearance of Species*, p. 159.

100. Cited in Hughes, "Ripples in Clio's Pond: Rome's Decline and Fall: Ecological Mistakes?" p. 122. Hughes observes that Romans were unaware of these destructive implications, because they thought that by killing off animals that sometimes raided their herds, they were doing a good thing. But since predators ate a far greater number of rodents and other animals that devour crops, increases in the numbers of the latter reduced agricultural production.

101. Ibid.

102. Pollution has a long history that precedes the human dilemmas of axial civilizations. Even 200,000 years ago, the pristine African "Garden of Eden" was not completely free of pollution. Fossil evidence from the skeletons of some early hominids shows that they suffered lead poisoning from "naturally" contaminated water. These particular individuals had the misfortune to live in what is now called Broken Hill

(Kabwe) in Zambia. Present-day anthropogenic pollution in the area certainly has increased by quantum leaps, being not far from one of the world's major copper-producing areas, and its first known record of serious lead pollution predates Greco-Roman antiquity. See Adam Marham, *A Brief History of Pollution* (London: Earthscan Publications, 1995).

103. The history of human lead production began about six millennia ago. Significant lead production started just about a millennium later, with the discovery of the techniques of smelting lead-silver alloys from lead sulfide ores and coupling silver from the alloys. Lead production then rose continuously during the Copper, Bronze, and Iron ages, stimulated by the introduction of silver coinage and the development of Greek civilization. A maximum of about 80,000 metric tons per year – approximately the rate at the time of the Industrial Revolution – was produced during the flourishing of Roman power and influence around two millennia ago. The use of lead was ubiquitous, and other mining districts in the Old World were known and worked, especially those in Spain, the Balkans, Greece, and Asia Minor. See Sungmin Hong et al., "Greenland Ice Evidence of Hemispheric Lead Pollution Two Millennia Ago by Greek and Roman Civilisations," *Science* 265 (1994).

104. Hughes, "Ripples in Clio's Pond: Rome's Decline and Fall: Ecological Mistakes?" pp. 122–3.

105. Ibid., p. 123.

106. Ibid.

107. Ibid., p. 124.

108. It might be supposed that Roman technology was environmentally less damaging than its modern counterparts, since it was simpler, utilizing human and animal power for the most part, and to some extent non-polluting water power. However, as Donald Hughes notes, the Romans brought their efforts to bear over centuries, and even simple technologies can be destructive when they are pursued over large territories for a long period of time, as the dependence on wood and charcoal for energy and resultant inroads into forests demonstrate. See ibid.

109. Ibid., p. 125.

110. The extent of the Roman ecological devastation of Carthage is in question. It has been referred to as a problem less of history "as it actually happened," and more as a problem of literary fabrication; i.e. as a problem of the "spurious authority of a long line of copyists": see Bennet Bronson, "The Role of Barbarians in the Fall of States," in *The Collapse of Ancient States and Civilizations*, ed. Norman Yoffe and George L. Cowgill (Tucson: University of Arizona Press, 1988), p. 197, R.T. Ridley, "To Be Taken with a Pinch of Salt: The Destruction of Carthage," *Classical Philology* 81 (April) (1986), pp. 140–6, Susan T. Stevens, "Notes and Discussions: A Legend of the Destruction of Carthage," *Classical Philology* 83 (January) (1988), Paolo Visona, "Passing the Salt: On the Destruction of Carthage Again," *Classical Philology* 83 (January) (1988), pp. 41–2, B.H. Warmington, "The Destruction of Carthage: A Refractio," *Classical Philology* 83 (April) (1988), pp. 309–10.

111. Particularly noteworthy in this context are the elegant, tiled "spewhouses" or "vomitoriums" of latter-day Rome.

112. As Mannion cautiously notes, "It may be that environmental issues were at the root of these processes." See A.M. Mannion, *Global Environmental Change: A Natural and Cultural Environmental History* (New York: Longman Scientific and Technical, 1988); and Hughes, "Ripples in Clio's Pond: Rome's Decline and Fall: Ecological Mistakes?"

113. Hughes, "Ripples in Clio's Pond: Rome's Decline and Fall: Ecological Mistakes?" p. 125.

114. The North African provinces, once highly productive granaries which provided food for the population of Rome and its large standing armies, gradually became degraded as Roman demands for grain pushed vegetation on to marginal lands, prone to erosion. Scrub vegetation spread and some intensively cultivated areas became desertified. The irrigation system the Romans used depended on watersheds that have since been deforested, and now yield less run-off, reducing the chance of restoring productivity. See WRI (World Resources Institute), "History of Use and Abuse," in *World Resources 2000–2001: People and Ecosystems: The Fraying Web of Life* (Washington, DC: Oxford University Press, 2000), pp. 6–7.

115. David E. Stuart and Susan B. Moczygemba-McKinsey, *Anasazi America: Seventeen Centuries on the Road from Center Place* (Albuquerque: University of New Mexico Press, 2000), p. 9.

116. J. Jefferson Reid and Stephanie Michelle Whittlesey, *The Archaeology of Ancient Arizona* (Tucson: University of Arizona Press, 1997), Stuart and Moczygemba-McKinsey, *Anasazi America: Seventeen Centuries on the Road from Center Place*, p. 16, Ward, *The Call of Distant Mammoths: Why the Ice Age Mammals Disappeared*.

117. Stuart and Moczygemba-McKinsey, *Anasazi America: Seventeen Centuries on the Road from Center Place*, p. 39.

118. This included the border area of the states of Utah, Arizona, New Mexico, and Colorado, with the major modern towns of Denver in the north, Flagstaff in the west, Phoenix in the southwest, and Albuquerque in closest proximity.

119. Stuart and Moczygemba-McKinsey, *Anasazi America: Seventeen Centuries on the Road from Center Place*, p. 7.

120. Julio L. Betancourt, Thomas R. Van Devender, and Paul S. Martin, eds, *Packrat Middens: The Last 40,000 Years of Biotic Change* (Tucson: University of Arizona Press, 1990), Maser, *Global Imperative: Harmonising Culture and Nature*, p. 68.

121. Maser, *Global Imperative: Harmonising Culture and Nature*, p. 69.

122. In particular, see the work of Betancourt, Devender, and Martin, eds, *Packrat Middens: The Last 40,000 Years of Biotic Change*. For a most recent work see Stuart and Moczygemba-McKinsey, *Anasazi America: Seventeen Centuries on the Road from Center Place*.

123. Stuart and Moczygemba-McKinsey, *Anasazi America: Seventeen Centuries on the Road from Center Place*, pp. 107, 109.

124. Ibid., pp. 115, 145.

125. Ibid., pp. 118–21.

126. Ibid., pp. 85–8.

127. Ibid., p. 220.

128. Ibid., p. 82.

129. Ibid., pp. 221–3.

130. Ibid., pp. 86–7.

131. Ibid., p. 200.

132. Ibid.

133. See also Timothy A. Kohler, "Prehistoric Human Impact on the Environment in Upland North American Southwest," *Population and Environment: A Journal of Interdisciplinary Studies* 13(4) (1992), pp. 255–68, Charles L. Redman, *Human Impact on Ancient Environments* (Tucson: University of Arizona Press, 1999), pp. 117–22.

134. William R. Coe, "The Maya: Resurrecting the Grandeur of Tikal," *National Geographic* 148(6) (December) (1975), Michael D. Lemonick, "Secrets of the Maya," *Time* August (1993), and "Knurrende Mägen," *Der Spiegel* 24 (1995), p. 203.

135. Glen Welker, *Mayan Civilization* ([Online, available: http://www.indians.org/welker/maya.htm], 1997).

136. US expert Patrick Culbert, in *Der Spiegel*, "Knurrende Mägen," p. 203.

137. US News and World Report, "What Killed the Mayas: War or Weather?" *US News and World Report* June 12 (1995), p. 10.

138. *Der Spiegel*, "Knurrende Mägen."

139. Ibid, Eric R. Wolf, *Sons of the Shaking Earth: The People of Mexico and Guatemala; Their Land, History, and Culture* (New York: Chicago University Press, 1959).

140. US News and World Report, "What Killed the Mayas: War or Weather?" p. 10.

141. Alan Weisman, "The Real Indiana Jones and His Pyramids of Doom," *Los Angeles Times Magazine* October 14 (1990), p. 42.

142. Van B. Weigel, *Earth Cancer* (Westport, CT and London: Praeger Press, 1995), p. 115.

143. Jared M. Diamond, "Easter's End: Easter Island," *Discover* August (1995), p. 64.

144. Ibid.

145. The present carrying capacity of the 64-square-mile island is around 2,000 persons, less than one-tenth of what is considered to be its peak population. See ibid.

146. Ibid., p. 67.

147. Ibid.

148. Ibid.

149. Sahlins, *Stone Age Economics*.

150. Already by 1650 wood charcoal was no longer used, according to archaeological research findings by French anthropologists (personal communications).

151. "Die Magie Der Osterinseln: Hollywood Entdeckt Einen Südseekult," *Geo* 6 (June) (1993), pp. 13–36.

3   THE MODERN ASSAULT ON NATURE: THE MAKING OF ECOCIDE

1. Michel de Montaigne (1533–1592), *The Essays* ("Morall, politike and millitarie discourses," translated from French by John Florio: 1603), a Scolar Press facsimile (Menston, UK: Scolar Press, 1969); in "Of Coaches," vol. 3, pp. 141–4.

2. Foster, *The Vulnerable Planet: A Short History of the Environment*, p. 43.

3. David Jary and Julya Jary, *The Harper Collins Dictionary of Sociology: Sociology from 'Anomie' to 'Zeitgeist'* (New York: Harper & Collins Publishers, 1991), p. 527.

4. By contrast, the Romans left about a third of Britain forested. See P. Ehrlich and A. Ehrlich, *Extinction: The Causes and Consequences of the Disappearance of Species*, p. 160.

5. Max Weber, *The Protestant Ethic and the Spirit of Capitalism* (New York: Scribner, 1930), Worster, *Dust Bowl: The Southern Plains in the 1930s*, p. 5.

6. Capitalism had made a number of promising starts in Italian city-states of the late Middle Ages, but these early sprouts were too divided and weak to survive in a hostile feudal environment.

7. Enrique Leff, *Ecologica y Capital*. English trans., *Green Production: Toward an Environmental Rationality*, ed. with an Introduction by James O'Connor, trans. Margareta Vilanueva, Democracy and Ecology Series (New York: Guilford Press, 1995), p. 18.

8. Max Weber, *The Protestant Ethic and the Spirit of Capitalism*.

9. Jary and Jary, *The Harper Collins Dictionary of Sociology: Sociology from 'Anomie' to 'Zeitgeist'*, pp. 527–8.

10. Max Weber, *The Protestant Ethic and the Spirit of Capitalism* (London: Routledge, 1992), p. xii, cited in Jay Hanson, "The Industrial Religion," in http://dieoff.org/page2.htm.

11. Michael Miley, "Against Nature: The Ideology of Ecocide," *Propaganda Review* 11 (1994), p. 41.

12. Mark Dowie, *Losing Ground: American Environmentalism at the Close of the Twentieth Century* (Cambridge, MA: MIT Press, 1995), pp. 10–14, Miley, "Against Nature:

The Ideology of Ecocide," p. 40, Jeremy Rifkin, *Biosphere Politics: A New Consciousness for a New Century* (New York: Crown, 1991), p. 31.

13. Rifkin, *Biosphere Politics: A New Consciousness for a New Century*, p. 35.

14. The prevailing liberal ethos and worldview are hampered by incoherent partitions. The fundamental commitments of liberal theory are reflected in two key aspects of its discursive structure. First, it is silent on issues of exploitation and community. And second, it upholds (and is hampered by) another incoherent partition: the separation of private and public sphere. Moreover, the most powerful form of collective organization in contemporary capitalism – the modern business corporation – is stripped of its communal status in liberal theory. It is ignored in neo-classical economics, treated as a quasi-individual in law, and considered "private" in political discourse. Its status as a form of social power is thereby obscured, and its reality as the terrain of class conflict is systematically slighted. Liberal political philosophy is curiously at odds with liberal economic theory.

The key thesis here is that the capitalist economy not only fosters the exercise of unaccountable power, it also thwarts those forms of political learning-through-choosing by means of which democratic societies may come to deepen their fundamental political commitments and capacities. It was liberalism that was best able to provide a viable geoculture for the capitalist world economy, one that would legitimate the other institutions both in the eyes of the cadres of the system and, to a significant degree, in the eyes of the mass of the population, the so-called ordinary people. To the critics, the innermost core of liberalism is a failed promise of happiness. Enough however still remained: it brought tolerance, human rights, the liberal state (*Rechtsstaat*), democracy, or also its minimum, parliamentary democracy. But when liberalism went out through the woods of world history to achieve more – to cut all that wild forest and to plant in its place artificial man-made paradises – it prepared also in multiple ways the end of history.

15. Anthony Giddens, *The Consequences of Modernity* (Stanford, CA: Stanford University Press, 1990).

16. Carl Von Clausewitz, Michael Howard, and Peter Paret, eds, *On War* (Princeton, NJ: Princeton University Press, 1984), P.R. Ehrlich and A.H. Ehrlich, *The Population Explosion* (Simon & Schuster: New York, 1990), Paul R. Ehrlich, *The Population Bomb* (New York: Sierra Club-Ballantine Books, 1968), Andre Gunder Frank, "The Development of Underdevelopment," in *Imperialism and Underdevelopment*, ed. R.I. Rhodes (New York: Monthly Review Press, 1970), pp. 4–17, Manicas, *War and Democracy*, L.S. Stavranos, *Global Rift: The Third World Comes of Age* (New York: William Morrow, 1981).

17. Arran Gare, "Soviet Environmentalism: The Path Not Taken," in *The Greening of Marxism*, ed. Ted Benton, Demcracy and Ecology Series (New York: The Guilford Press, 1996), p. 111.

18. Fred Hirsch, *The Social Limits to Growth* (Cambridge, MA: Harvard University Press, 1970), Worster, *Dust Bowl: The Southern Plains in the 1930s*, p. 6.

19. Environmental amenities, like pure air and water, biodiversity, or the serenity of nature, are often difficult or impossible to calculate in terms of a "price tag." Sweeping this problem aside, economists typically leave them out of cost-benefit analyses, working under the convenient assumption that their value is zero. Thus – and this lies at the core of the modern predicament – the dominant contemporary global economic system cannot flag the long-term environmental degradation from global economic and demographic growth. In other words, the contemporary framework structurally compels people to externalize (trade off) social and ecological

costs. See Martin O'Connor, *Is Capitalism Sustainable? Political Economy and the Politics of Ecology, Democracy and Ecology* (New York: Guilford Press, 1994).

20. Foster, *The Vulnerable Planet: A Short History of the Environment*, p. 124, Meadows et al., *Beyond the Limits: Confronting Global Collapse, Envisioning a Sustainable Future*, James O'Connor, "The Second Contradiction of Capitalism: Causes and Consequences," *Capitalism, Nature, Socialism (CNS)* CNS/CES Pamphlet 1. Paper given at the Conference on New Economic Analysis, Iniciativa per Catalunya, Barcelona, Spain, November 30–December 2, 1990 (1991), Mathis Wackernagel and William Rees, *Our Ecological Footprint: Reducing Human Impact on the Earth* (Philadelphia and Gabriola Island: New Society Publishers, 1996), Edward O. Wilson, "Is Humanity Suicidal? We Are Flirting with the Extinction of Our Species," *The New York Times Magazine* May 30 (1993).

21. Worster, *Dust Bowl: The Southern Plains in the 1930s*, pp. 94–95. NB: According to a Haudenosaunee (Iroquois) teaching, "We are a part of everything that is beneath us, and around us. Our past is our present, our present is our future, and our future is seven generations past and present."

22. Ibid.

23. Current environmental policies are still predominantly based on concepts of controlling and dominating nature, what could be labeled imperialism. Other colonial enterprises prior to Europe, such as Inca, Aztec, Chinese, and Islamic, share a highly instrumentalized, dominant social class-based ideological behavior pattern whereby humans tend to value nature in relation to how it can serve human interests and needs (often finding most destructive expression, for example, in pharaonic megalomania).

24. Worster, *Dust Bowl: The Southern Plains in the 1930s*, p. 97.

25. Samir Amin, "1492 – Columbus and the New World Order," *Monthly Review* 44(14) (July/August) (Special Issue) (1992), p. 10.

26. Alfred Crosby, *The Columbian Exchange: Biological and Cultural Consequences of 1492* (Westport, CT: Greenwood Press, 1972).

27. Cited in Douglas Hilt, "Rediscovering the Discoverers: The Dual Case of Columbus and Cook," in *Native American Cultures: Before and after Columbus*, ed. D. Hilt (Speech) (Honolulu: University of Hawai'i at Manoa Summer Session; Committee for the Humanities, 1994).

28. Winona LaDuke, "A Society Based on Conquest Cannot Be Sustained," in *Toxic Struggles: The Theory and Practice of Environmental Justice*, ed. Richard Hofrichter (Philadelphia, PA: New Society Publisher, 1993), p. 101.

29. The New World here includes the Americas, Australia, New Zealand, and many small islands. Syphilis probably was brought from the New World to Europe by Columbus.

30. Crosby, *The Columbian Exchange: Biological and Cultural Consequences of 1492*, Crosby, *Ecological Imperialism: The Biological Expansion of Europe, 900–1900*.

31. Ibid.

32. Malcolm Jones Jr, "When the Horse Came," *Newsweek* Fall/Winter (Special Issue: "When Worlds Collide: How Columbus's Voyage Transformed both East and West") (1991), p. 77.

33. Wolf, *Europe and the People without History*, pp. 195–96.

34. Foster, *The Vulnerable Planet: A Short History of the Environment*, p. 45.

35. Eduardo Galeano, *Open Veins of Latin America: Five Centuries of the Pillage of a Continent*, trans. Cedric Belfrage (New York: Monthly Review Press, 1973), pp. 74–5.

36. Cited in Foster, *The Vulnerable Planet: A Short History of the Environment*, p. 45.

37. Galeano, *Open Veins of Latin America: Five Centuries of the Pillage of a Continent*, pp. 74–5.

38. Fernand Braudel, *The Structure of Everyday Life* (New York: Harper & Row, 1979), p. 224, Ralph Davis, *The Rise of the Atlantic Economies* (London: Weidenfeld & Nicolson, 1973), p. 251, Foster, *The Vulnerable Planet: A Short History of the Environment*, pp. 45–6, Stavranos, *Global Rift: The Third World Comes of Age*, pp. 96–7, Immanuel Wallerstein, *The Modern World System: Mercantilism and the Consolidation of the European World Economy, 1600–1750*, vol. 2 (New York: Academic Press, 1980), p. 51, Eric Williams, *Capitalism and Slavery* (New York: Capricorn Books, 1944), pp. 30–84.

39. Gwyn Jones, *A History of the Vikings* (New York: Oxford University Press, 1968), p. 23.

40. Ibid., pp. 161–2.

41. Immanuel Wallerstein, *The Modern World System: Capitalist Agriculture and the Origins of the European World Economy in the Sixteenth Century*, vol. 1 (New York: Academic Press, 1974), p. 121, Wolf, *Europe and the People without History*, p. 158.

42. Robert Joseph Kerner, *The Urge to the Sea: The Course of Russian History. The Role of Rivers, Portages, Ostrogs, Monasteries, and Furs* (Berkeley: University of California Press, 1942), p. 8, Wolf, *Europe and the People without History*, pp. 158–9.

43. *Tithes* refers to the tenth part of goods or income paid as a tax for the support of the church or any tax or levy, especially of one-tenth.

44. Wolf, *Europe and the People without History*, p. 159.

45. Peter J. Bryant, "Chapter 3: Extinction and Depletion from Over-Exploitation," *Biodiversity and Conservation: A Hypertext Book* (University of California, Irvine School of Biological Sciences [Online, available: http://darwin.bio.uci.edu/~sustain/bio65/lec03/b65lec03.htm], 1997).

46. Ibid.

47. Wolf, *Europe and the People without History*, p. 159.

48. One ought not to forget the miners here, since their discoveries were very often what led the government to abrogate Indian treaties made previously!

49. Wolf, *Europe and the People without History*, p. 159.

50. Ibid., p. 193.

51. Ibid., p. 194.

52. Bryant, "Extinction and Depletion from Over-Exploitation."

53. Ibid.

54. In the time of Charles I, the king of England between 1625 and 1642, the rage in Europe was dashing beaver hats trimmed in ostrich feathers. Beaver hats were also used in seventeenth-century British infantry officers' uniforms. In addition, there were superstitions surrounding beaver furs that may have also contributed to their popularity. It was believed that by rubbing the oil into your hair, you would develop a remarkable memory. It was also rumored that the deaf could regain their hearing by wearing a beaver hat. The cost of such a hat was about the same as the price of a new car today. The huge demand for hats in the eighteenth and early nineteenth century caused the fur trade to boom. By 1850, the trapping had just about stopped. Few beavers remained, and the silk hat was becoming the new style. Thus many beavers owe their lives to the tiny silkworm.

55. Mark Mancall, *Russia and China; Their Diplomatic Relations to 1728*, Harvard East Asian Series 61 (Cambridge, MA: Harvard University Press, 1971), p. 12, Wolf, *Europe and the People without History*, p. 159.

56. Wolf, *Europe and the People without History*, p. 185.

57. Ibid.

58. Ibid., pp. 192–3.

59. Ibid.

60. Bryant, "Extinction and Depletion from Over-Exploitation."

61. Clive Ponting, *A Green History of the World: The Environmental Collapse of Civilisations* (London: Penguin Books, 1991).

62. Bryant, "Extinction and Depletion from Over-Exploitation."

63. William Cronon, *Nature's Metropolis: Chicago and the Great West* (New York: W.W. Norton, 1991), pp. 213–18. Cited in Foster, *The Vulnerable Planet: A Short History of the Environment*, p. 74.

64. D. Hull, "Where the Buffalo Roam Has Deadly New Caveat," *Washington Post* July 22 (1997).

65. Peter J. Bryant, "Chapter 4: Whaling and Fishing," *Biodiversity and Conservation: A Hypertext Book* (University of California, Irvine School of Biological Sciences [Online, available: http://darwin.bio.uci.edu/~sustain/bio65/lec04/b65lec04.htm], 1998).

66. Corset stays are the stiff bands that give the corset its support.

67. Bryant, "Whaling and Fishing."

68. Kyoichi Toriso, "Western Seas Whaling: A Brief History of the Whaling Hunt," *Fukuoka Style* Vol. 12 (October 31) (1995).

69. Bryant, "Whaling and Fishing."

70. Ibid.

71. "Ein Stück Schlaraffenland," *Der Spiegel* 28 (1992), pp. 190–91.

72. Stephen R. Kellert and Edward O. Wilson, eds, *The Biophilia Hypothesis* (Washington, DC: Island Press, 1993).

73. The ability to float "too easily" may be helping to drive the world's rarest whale to extinction, research has found. The remarkable buoyancy of the North Atlantic right whale not only made them the first of the great whales to be hunted to the point of extinction in the nineteenth century; but it continues to endanger the species in the late modern era because right whales have more difficulty in diving to avoid large ships. Fatal ship collisions are taking a big toll on the tiny population, with at least 16 recorded in the past 30 years. Right whales migrate up and down the waters off the east coast of North America, from their calving grounds off Florida to their feeding grounds off eastern Canada.

74. Bryant, "Whaling and Fishing."

75. The early modern whaling industry made New Bedford, Massachusetts, the predominant whaling port in the United States and one of the richest cities in the country in the mid-nineteenth century. It inspired one of America's greatest novels, *Moby Dick* by Herman Melville. Whaling also influenced global politics. The domination of the American whaling fleets in the Arctic in the latter half of the nineteenth century and the importance of Hawai'i as a supply center for these fleets, for example, created a strategic interest in these areas, which led to the purchase of Alaska in 1867 and the military "annexation" of Hawai'i in 1898.

76. Today the species is up to pre-exploitation levels (about 22,000) and has been removed from the endangered species list. However, plans to develop a salt-mining operation in Baja Mexico during the late 1990s again endangered the gray whale's breeding grounds besides those of a range of other sea life.

4   THE PLANET AS SACRIFICE ZONE

1. Karl Kraus (1874–1936), the Austrian satirist, from a speech given on November 19, 1914, in Vienna (first published in *Die Fackel*, Dec. 1914; repr. in *In These Great Times: A Karl Kraus Reader*, ed. Harry Zohn, Montreal: Engendra Press, 1976).

2. Peter Marks, "A Vision of Environment: Is Life Worth Living Here?," in *Is America Possible? Social Problems from Conservative, Liberal and Socialist Perspectives*, ed. Henry Etzkowitz (New York: State University of New York at Purchase, 1974), p. 121.

3. Rifkin, *Biosphere Politics: A New Consciousness for a New Century*, p. 9.

4. These squatters had managed to eke out a living by pasturing a cow or perhaps a few geese on the village common pastures. An English poet wrote: " 'Tis very bad in man or women, To steal a goose from off the common, But surely 'tis the worse abuse, To steal a common from the goose." Cited in Ritchie, *Food and Civilization: How History Has Been Affected by Human Taste*, p. 132.

5. Rifkin, *Biosphere Politics: A New Consciousness for a New Century*, p. 71.

6. Miley, "Against Nature: The Ideology of Ecocide," p. 39.

7. Meadows et al., *Beyond the Limits: Confronting Global Collapse, Envisioning a Sustainable Future*, pp. 218–21.

8. Donald Worster and Alfred Crosby, eds, *The Ends of the Earth: Perspectives on Modern Environmental History* (New York: Cambridge University Press, 1989), pp. 11–12.

9. Foster, *The Vulnerable Planet: A Short History of the Environment*, pp. 50–68.

10. As we can see from his engravings, *The Horrors of War*, Goya (1746–1828) was no sellout; "he didn't look the other way." Thomas H. Falk, *Elias Canetti*, ed. David O'Connell; Georgia State University, Twaynes World Author Series; German Literature (New York: Twayne Publishers, 1993), p. 31.

11. Manicas, *War and Democracy*.

12. Anthony Giddens, *A Contemporary Critique of Historical Materialism, vol. 2: Nation-State and Violence* (Berkeley: University of California Press, 1987), Eric J. Hobsbawm, *The Age of Extremes: A History of the World, 1914–91* (New York: Pantheon Books, 1991).

13. By World War II, as Manicas notes, "class war" had been "diverted toward international war." The people, habituated in the class struggle to appeals calling them to fight for their rights and for better opportunities, to strike at privilege and oppression, now were told by the leaders of the hypernationalist and irrational modern mass movement known as fascism that they must continue to fight, not as traitorous members of a class but as "patriots in a national cause." The German propaganda minister Joseph Goebbels shrewdly mobilized on chauvinist-racial grounds by invocations of "national-socialism." Class-oriented industrial production techniques of labor organization, such as the "scientific management" associated with Taylorism, became the shared ideological co-ordinates and performance principles of both the Stalinist "East" and the West. See Manicas, *War and Democracy*, p. 379.

14. Walter Benjamin, *Illuminations*, ed. Hannah Arendt, Translated by Harry Zohn (New York: Schocken, 1969), p. 242.

15. Manicas, *War and Democracy*, p. 253.

16. As the historian Eric J. Hobsbawm argues, "we have adapted to living in a society, that is by standards of our grandparents 'uncivilized.' We have gotten used to it [inhuman conditions]." He refers to the resurgence of torture, legitimated against the background of the lunacies of the Cold War, of the "accelerated descent into darkness" in the late modern period and a reversal of the progress of civility that took place from the eighteenth century until the early twentieth century, achieved overwhelmingly or entirely due to the influence of the Enlightenment. See Eric J. Hobsbawm, "Barbarism: A User's Guide," *New Left Review* 206 (July/August) (1994), pp. 44–54.

17. Hobsbawm, *The Age of Extremes: A History of the World, 1914–91*, Jonathan Schell, *The Fate of the Earth* (New York: Knopf Publishers, 1982), Edward Thompson et al., *Exterminism and the Cold War* (London and New York: Schocken Books, 1982).

18. The Bikini Atoll hydrogen bomb explosion, the largest ever, produced a mushroom cloud that rose 15 miles into the stratosphere. The fallout exposed some 229 Marshallese Islanders on Rongelap Atoll, including some US servicemen, and a crew of 23 workers on the nearby Japanese fishing boat *Lucky Dragon*, many of whom developed severe radiation sickness and died associated premature deaths. The Rongelapese were not evacuated from the islands until two days after the hydrogen bomb test. Using declassified government archival films and contemporary interviews, the Australia-based investigative journalist and cinematographer Dennis O'Rourke produced a film documentary titled *Half Life* (1986), presenting the restrained but chilling picture of a cynical radiation experiment on human populations sponsored by the military-industrial complex and condoned by Washington. Dennis O'Rourke, *Half-Life: A Parable for the Nuclear Age*, Videorecording/Film (Los Angeles, CA: Direct Cinema [86 mins], 1986), William M. Peck, *A Tidy Universe of Islands* (Honolulu: Mutual Publishing, 1997), p. 11.

19. It is really only in the twentieth century, and the late twentieth century at that, that the environmental consequences of industrial production, combined with capitalist or state socialist economic organization, have been widely and actively registered as "environmental degradation" and extended their spatial reach beyond the local or the national. The globalization of environmental degradation since the 1970s in particular, has accelerated on unparalleled and, I suggest, progressively ecocidal scale. See J.R. McNeill, *Something New under the Sun: An Environmental History of the Twentieth-Century World*, 1st edn (New York and London: W.W. Norton, 2000). And David Held et al., *Global Transformations: Politics, Economics and Culture* (Stanford, CA: Stanford University Press, 1999), pp. 390–1.

20. Donella H. Meadows et al., *The Limits to Growth: A Report for the Club of Rome's Project on the Predicament of Mankind* (New York: Universe Books, 1972).

21. William R. Catton, *Overshoot. The Ecological Basis of Revolutionary Change* (Chicago: University of Illinois Press, 1982), Meadows et al., *Beyond the Limits: Confronting Global Collapse, Envisioning a Sustainable Future*, Peter Morrison Vitousek et al., "Human Domination of Earth's Ecosystems," *Science* 277 (1997), Peter Morrison Vitousek et al., "Human Alteration of the Global Nitrogen Cycle: Causes and Consequences," *Ecological Applications* 7 (1997), Wackernagel and Rees, *Our Ecological Footprint: Reducing Human Impact on the Earth*.

22. R.A. Rappaport, *Pigs for the Ancestors: Ritual in the Ecology of a New Guinea People* (New Haven, CT: Yale University Press, 1984).

23. The story of the sowing of the ruins of Carthage with salt, apparently as a symbol of its total destruction and perhaps as a means of ensuring the soil's infertility, is well known to most students of Roman history. Indeed, in the legends of antiquity and in ancient texts and studies of antiquity, the tale of the city's being plowed and salted appears repeatedly. The famous "scorched earth" story of Carthage has it that salt was sown in the ground after the site was plowed. However, the extent of Roman ecological devastation of the site, and, in particular, the use of salt as a means of environmental terrorism, remains in question. See Ridley, "To Be Taken with a Pinch of Salt: The Destruction of Carthage," pp. 140–6, Visona, "Passing the Salt: On the Destruction of Carthage Again," pp. 41–2, Warmington, "The Destruction of Carthage: A Refractio," pp. 309–10.

24. UNEP (United Nations Environment Programme), *Global Biodiversity Assessment* (Cambridge: United Nations Environment Programme, 1995), p. 728.

25. J.T. Mark Caggiano, "The Legitimacy of Environmental Destruction in Modern Warfare: Customary Substance over Conventional Form," *Boston College Environmental Affairs Law Review* 20 (1993), pp. 1–33, 479–506, Josef Goldblatt, "The

Environmental Modification Convention," in *Environmental Warfare: A Technical, Legal, and Policy Appraisal*, ed. Arthur H. Westing (London and Philadelphia: Taylor & Francis, 1984), Arthur H. Westing, ed., *Environmental Hazards of War: Releasing Dangerous Forces in an Industrialized World* (London and Newbury Park: Sage Publications, 1990).

26. Caggiano, "The Legitimacy of Environmental Destruction in Modern Warfare: Customary Substance over Conventional Form," pp. 13, 489, Goldblatt, "The Environmental Modification Convention."

27. Laurence Badash, *Scientists and the Development of Nuclear Weapons: From Fission to Limited Test Ban Treaty, 1939–1963* (Atlantic Highlands, NJ: Humanities Press, 1995).

28. William Thompson, *Scorched Earth: The Military's Assault on the Environment, Weapons Incorporated* (Philadelphia: New Society Publishers [Online, available: http://www.earthisland.org/journal/bigmil.html], 1995).

29. Caggiano, "The Legitimacy of Environmental Destruction in Modern Warfare: Customary Substance over Conventional Form," pp. 10, 486.

30. For Marcuse, the US intervention in Vietnam (1954–75) was waging ecocide against the environment, as well as genocide against the people: "It is no longer enough to do away with people living now; life must also be denied to those who aren't even born yet by burning and poisoning the Earth, defoliating the forests, blowing up the dikes. This bloody insanity will not alter the ultimate course of the war but it is a very clear expression of where contemporary capitalism is at: the cruel waste of productive resources in the imperialist homeland goes hand in hand with the cruel waste of destructive forces and consumption of commodities of death manufactured by the war industry." Herbert Marcuse cited in Douglas Kellner, "Illuminations: Marcuse, Liberation, and Radical Ecology," *Sarah Zuko's Cultural Center Articles/Papers: Theorists and Critics* (1992).

31. Thompson, *Scorched Earth: The Military's Assault on the Environment*.

32. Ibid.

33. Ibid.

34. Ibid.

35. Ibid.

36. Ibid.

37. "Cries of Ecocide from Croatia: Ecological Destruction Caused by War," *Earth Island Journal* 7(1) (1992), p. 17.

38. Arthur H. Westing, "Threat of Modern Warfare to Man and His Environment: An Annotated Bibliography," in *Reports and Papers in the Social Sciences No. 40*, ed. International Peace Research Association (IPRA) (Paris, France: UNESCO, 1979).

39. Ruth Leger Sivard, *World Military and Social Expenditures 1996*, 16th edn (Washington, DC: World Priorities Press, 1996), p. 20.

40. Ruth Leger Sivard, *World Military and Social Expenditures 1991*, 14th edn (Washington, DC: World Priorities Press, 1991), pp. 30–1. NB: Environmental problems of long standing plague the nuclear weapons industry. Besides soil and water contamination by radioactive materials, some sites suffer contamination by conventional hazardous chemicals used in the production process. In the second half of the twentieth century, the US nuclear weapons industry has manufactured nearly 70,000 nuclear warheads. It has produced about 89 metric tons of plutonium and more than 500 tons of highly enriched uranium, the primary radioactive material in nuclear weapons. Decades of activity at US Department of Energy nuclear weapons laboratory, production, and test facilities have left an estimated 4,500 contaminated sites covering tens of thousands of acres of land.

Efforts to clean them up and bring nuclear weapons facilities into compliance with environmental laws are expected to take at least 30 years and cost more than $200 billion. In 1990 it was also reported that as many as 42 of the 177 underground tanks in the United States that are used to store waste from nuclear bomb production are in danger of exploding. Such an explosion could mean the spread of toxic chemicals and radioactive materials over large areas. The risk is due to unforeseen reactions between the chemicals stored and those introduced in an endeavor to consolidate the waste. The ferrocyanide percolating in the tanks is sufficient to cause an explosion equivalent to 36 tons of TNT. In 1957 in the Soviet Union, the explosion of such a nuclear waste storage tank spread radiation over a large area and forced the evacuation of 10,000 people, with some reports that hundreds of people later died. It has also been reported that 28 kg of plutonium (equivalent to seven nuclear bombs) escaped into the air ducts at the Rocky Flats weapons plant during its 30 years of operation: plutonium is so toxic that it is usually accounted for in gram quantities (Union of International Association [UIA] "Environmental Hazards – Nuclear Weapons Industry," *Encyclopedia of World Problems and Human Potential* (PE5698) [Online, available: http://www.uia.org/uialists/ndx/pro/pro132.htm] 1998).

41. Ed Ayres, "The Expanding Shadow Economy," *World Watch* July/August (1996), pp. 11–23.

42. Sivard, *World Military and Social Expenditures 1991*, p. 31.

43. Ibid.

44. Including the energy consumption by weapons industries could well double the total. See ibid.

45. Ibid., p. 5.

46. Thompson, *Scorched Earth: The Military's Assault on the Environment*.

47. Ibid.

48. Ibid.

49. Mike Davis, "Dead West: Ecocide in Marlboro Country," *New Left Review* 200 (1993), pp. 49–73.

50. The United States, for example, has detonated all its nuclear weapons in the lands of indigenous people, with over 600 of those tests within the property belonging to the Shoshone nation. Nuclear waste remains the largest obstacle for a peaceful atom, and native peoples are again central to the discussion. The well-equipped Hanford Nuclear Reservation is within the treaty area of the Yakima Indian nation near the Columbia River. A significant portion of the 570 square miles of land contained in the nuclear site is contaminated. Approximately 20 different indigenous peoples reside in this area. In August 1973, over 115,000 gallons of high-level liquid radioactive waste there seeped into the ground from a leaking storage tank. The waste contained cesium 137, strontium 90, and plutonium, one of the most toxic substances known to humans. At least 400,000 gallons of radioactive material have been reported as having leaked at the Hanford Reservation. See LaDuke, "A Society Based on Conquest Cannot Be Sustained," p. 105.

51. Davis, "Dead West: Ecocide in Marlboro Country," p. 50.

52. Murray Felsbach and Alfred Jr. Friendly, *Ecocide in the USSR: Health and Nature under Siege*, Foreword by Lester Brown (New York: Basic Books, 1992), p. 1.

53. See Davis, "Dead West: Ecocide in Marlboro Country," Carol Gallagher, *American Ground Zero: The Secret Nuclear War* (Cambridge, MA: MIT Press, 1993), Peter Goin, *Nuclear Landscapes, Creating the North American Landscape: Catalogue of an Exhibition* (Baltimore, MD: John Hopkins University Press, 1991), Richard Misrach, *Desert*

Canton, ed. Essay by Reyner Banham, *1st edn* (Albuquerque: University of New Mexico Press, 1987), Richard Misrach, *Richard Misrach (A Photographic Book: Landscape Photography)* (San Francisco, CA: Grapestake Gallery, 1979), Richard Misrach, *Violent Legacies: Three Cantons*, ed. Susan Sontag, 1st edn (New York: Aperture, 1992), Patrick Nagatani, *Nuclear Enchantment*, editorial essay by Eugenia Parry Janis, *Photographs by Patrick Nagatani* (Albuquerque: University of New Mexico, 1991).

54. Davis, "Dead West: Ecocide in Marlboro Country," p. 50.
55. Ibid., p. 51. See Misrach, *Desert Canton*, Misrach, *Richard Misrach*, Misrach, *Violent Legacies: Three Cantons*, Richard Misrach and Myrian Weisang Misrach, *Bravo 20: The Bombing of the American West, Creating the North American Landscape* (Baltimore, MD: John Hopkins University Press, 1990).
56. Davis, "Dead West: Ecocide in Marlboro Country," p. 73.
57. The cold deserts and sagebrush (artemisia) steppes of the Great Basin and the high plateau are floristic colonies of Central Asia (see Neil West, ed., *Ecosystems of the World*, vol. 5: *Temperate Deserts and Semi-Deserts* [Amsterdam: Elsevier, 1983]), but their physical landscapes are virtually unique (see W.L. Graf, ed., *Geomorphic Systems of North America* [Boulder, CO: Geological Society of America, 1987]). Ibid., p. 73, 60f.
58. UNCED, for example, omits any discussion of nuclear power and fails to recognize that there are no safe storage and disposal solutions to the world's growing radioactive waste problem. Discussion of the environmental impact of the military, including the nuclear and toxic contamination caused by military activities around the world, are inexplicably excluded from the Earth Summit texts. See Joshua Karlinger, *The Corporate Planet: Ecology and Politics in the Age of Globalization* (San Francisco: Sierra Club Books, 1997).
59. See also Ranee K.L. Panjabi, *The Earth Summit at Rio: Politics, Economics, and the Environment* (Boston, MA: Northeastern University Press, 1997), Adam Rogers, *The Earth Summit: A Planetary Reckoning*, Foreword by Noel Brown, Afterword by David Suzuki (Lower Lake, CA: Atrium Publishers Group, 1995), UCS (Union of Concerned Scientists), *World Scientists' Warning to Humanity*, ed. UCS (November 18) (Cambridge, MA: Union of Concerned Scientists, 1992).
60. John Kenneth Galbraith, "World Military and Social Expenditures," in *World Military and Social Expenditures 1993*, ed. Ruth Leger Sivard (Washington, DC: World Priorities Press, 1993), p. 3.
61. Jacob von Uexkuell and Bernd Jost, eds, *Project Der Hoffnung: Der Alternative Nobelpreis* (English: *Alternative Nobelprize: Right Livelihood Award Project)* (München: Raben Verlag, 1990), p. 15.
62. Immanuel Wallerstein cited in Mary Mellot, ed., *Building a New Vision: Feminist, Green Socialism*, p. 40 in *Toxic Struggles: The Theory and Practice of Environmental Justice* (Philadelphia, PA: New Society Publishers, 1993), p. 40. See also Joni Saeger, *Earth Follies: Coming to Feminist Terms with the Global Environmental Crisis* (New York: Routledge, 1993).
63. Alan Thein Durning, "The Health of the Planet," in Sivard, ed., *World Military and Social Expenditures 1991*, p. 34.
64. David C. Korten, founder and president of the International Institute for Sustainable Development, at http://iisd1.iisd.ca/50comm/panel/pan21.htm, reviewed September 2001.
65. Worldwide nation-states' expenditures on military capability to protect against "dangerous instabilities" both abroad and internally, such as the rising tide of civil wars or the prospects of some rogue nation or groups attacking US allies or interests,

for example, continue to far outweigh any expenditures that governments are willing to make to help reduce those instabilities. US legislators continue to refuse to pay the country's delinquent UN dues, to provide support for international family planning assistance, or to allocate other modest sums that could go a long way toward stabilizing what is becoming a precariously volatile planet. As is well documented, it is a range of extreme human deprivations – of food, clean water, shelter, medical services, family planning assistance, basic education, and job training – that constitutes the real threat to human security worldwide. It is those deprivations that allow demagogues to thrive, insurgencies to arise, and ethnic or ideological hatreds to fester. See Michael Renner, *Fighting for Survival: Environmental Decline, Social Conflict, and the New Age of Insecurity* (Washington, DC: Worldwatch Institute, 1996).

66. Kofi Annan, Christopher Flavin, Linda Starke and Worldwatch Institute, eds, *State of the World 2002: A Worldwatch Institute Report on Progress towards a Sustainable Society* (New York: W.W. Norton, 2002).

67. Albert Einstein, 1931, cited in Ruth Leger Sivard, *World Military and Social Expenditures 1993*, 15th edn (Washington, DC: World Priorities Press, 1993), p. 34.

68. Richard P. Cincotta and Robert Engelman, "Real Numbers: Biodiversity and Population Growth," *Issues in Science and Technology Online* (spring) (2000), J.A. McNeeley et al., "Human Influences on Biodiversity," in *Global Biodiversity Assessment*, ed. V.H. Heywood (Cambridge: Cambridge University Press and UNEP, 1995), M.E. Soule, "Conservation: Tactics for a Constant Crisis," *Science* 253 (1991), P. Stedman-Edwards, *The Root Causes of Biodiversity Loss: An Analytical Approach, Macroeconomics for Sustainable Development Office* (Washington, DC: Worldwide Fund for Nature, 1997), UNEP, *Global Biodiversity Assessment*.

69. The following analogies may help illustrate the magnitude of our numbers: if I were to look at the face of every one of the world's 6 billion people, and they were contained in a book with 0.1 mm thick pages, with ten people per page on both sides of each sheet, the book would be 19 miles thick. If I looked at ten people every second (one side of each sheet for 16 hours a day, it would take me 28 years and 6 months to get through it. By the time I finished, in the year 2026, there would be 2 billion extra people to look at, contained in a brand new 6 miles thick volume! If all of the world's current population were fit into the state of Texas – all 6 billion people – each person would get about 164 square feet as his or her own chunk. If all those people lined up, each one occupying only one foot, the queue would be very, very long, too. The queue would be about 1,680,000 km (a little more than a million miles) – approximately 42 tours around the globe. So what if the people of the world made a movie? If it showed all 6 billion people one at a time, with only 15 seconds of footage per person, this is 6.75 meters (20 feet) of film per person. There would be 40.5 million km (25.3 million miles) of negative. The film would last for 23,333,333 hours. To watch this film it would take 972,222 days or 2,661 years, 9 months, and some days – this is without sleeping, eating, or any other time out.

70. Boyden, *Biohistory: The Interplay between Human Society and the Biosphere*, pp. 243–4.

71. Arthur H. Westing, "A World in Balance," *Environmental Conservation* 8 (1981).

72. Brian Groombridge, ed., *Global Biodiversity: Status of the Earth's Living Resources* (London: Chapman & Hall, 1992). Arthur H. Westing, "Biodiversity Loss and Its Implications for Security and Armed Conflict," in *The Living Planet in Crisis*, ed. Joel Cracraft and Francesca T. Grifo (New York: Columbia University Press, 1999), p. 209.

73. W.M. Hern, "Why Are There So Many of Us? Description and Diagnosis of a Planetary Ecopathological Process," *Journal of Population and Environment* 12 (1990), Weigel, *Earth Cancer*.

74. Westing, "Biodiversity Loss and Its Implications for Security and Armed Conflict."

75. Peter Morrison Vitousek et al., "Human Appropriation of the Products of Photosynthesis," *Bioscience* May (1986), Vitousek, "Human Domination of Earth's Ecosystems."

76. For example, to replicate the pattern of grain consumption as evidenced in the United States today, by 2025 the regional requirement would be 4.5 billion metric tons of grain, or the harvest of more than two planets at earth's current output levels. UN-ESCAP (United Nations Economic and Social Commission for Asia and the Pacific), *State of the Environment in the Asia Pacific* (New York: United Nations, 2000).

77. Overwhelmingly wealthy, white, and non-immigrant.

78. In short, the bulk of today's environmental degradation is done by two groups, the top richest billion and the bottom poorest. The richest billion destroys the global environment through rapid over-consumption of resources and vast generation of wastes, while the bottom billion destroys their resources out of necessity and a lack of options. See Tom Athanasiou, *Divided Planet: The Ecology of Rich and Poor* (Boston: Little, Brown, 1996).

79. UNEP, *Global Biodiversity Assessment*, p. 793.

80. Ibid.

81. Cincotta and Engelman, "Real Numbers: Biodiversity and Population Growth," V. Walter Reid, "How Many Species Will There Be?," in *Tropical Deforestation and Species Extinction*, ed. T.C. Sayer, Jeffrey Whitmore, and International Union for Conservation of Nature and Natural Resources (London and New York: Chapman & Hall, 1992).

82. Don Hinrichsen, "Putting the Bite on the Planet: Rapid Human Population Growth Is Devouring Global Natural Resources," *International Wildlife* September/October (1994), pp. 39–40.

83. According to three scenarios published by the UN, the global population in the year 2050 will be somewhere between 7.3 billion and 10.7 billion, depending on how fast the fertility rate falls. Ninety-seven per cent of the projected future population growth will be in developing regions. Jeffrey Kluger, "The Big Crunch," *Time* April–May (2000), p. 49.

84. Cincotta and Engelman, "Real Numbers: Biodiversity and Population Growth."

85. Ibid.

86. The predicament is that people's life decisions are conditioned by socioeconomic systems in which the incentives for sacrificing the future for the present are often overwhelming. See Gretchen D. Daily and Paul R. Ehrlich, "Population, Sustainability, and Earth's Carrying Capacity: A Framework for Estimating Population Sizes and Lifestyles That Could Be Sustained without Undermining Future Generations," *BioScience* 42 (November) (1992).

87. Population growth seems to affect everything but is seldom held responsible for anything. Some of the key reasons for this predicament are: first, growth is invisible from day to day; second, there is what some political demographers refer to as "scale paralysis" – a sense of powerlessness in response to the size of the problem; third, many people are unable to comprehend such large numbers; fourth, politically, population growth is never an immediate problem, but long-range and thus to be put off; last but not least, the subject can be controversial and divisive.

88. This is not to say that either Muslim or Christian clergy are necessarily opposed to "environmental protection." With a heavily Muslim population and a severely degraded ecological landscape, Pakistan, for example, launched an environmental protection program in 1997 utilizing well-known religious leaders. More than 700 verses of the Holy Quran, according to a recent interpretation, say that saving the planet is one's duty under Mohammed (after Marilyn Bauer, *Religious Jihad Launched against Environmental Pollutants* [Environmental News Network, Inc.: Online, available: http://www.enn.com, reviewed July 1, 2002]). For a more progressive approach in Judeo-Christian religious (re)interpretations on the environment, see the UCS (Union of Concerned Scientists) video film documentary titled *Keeping the Earth: Religious and Scientific Perspectives on the Environment*, narrated by James Earl Jones (previously titled *Endangered Species and the Natural World* [UCS: Cambridge, MA]).

89. It should be stressed in this context that the reduction of the death rate remains a central imperative in family planning strategies. For example, in those countries which have succeeded in reducing the number of deaths in children, there is a decline in the birthrate within one generation. Once parents have confidence that their children will survive, the need to have many children declines. In the past, it took one or two generations for the birthrate to fall in a country after the fall of the child deathrate. Now it takes less than a generation. A fall in deathrates of children has always come before a fall in birthrates. David Morley and Hermione Lovel, *My Name Is Today: An Illustrated Discussion of Child Health, Society and Poverty in Less Developed Countries* (London: Macmillan, 1986), p. 37.

90. Lori S. Ashford and Jeane A. Noble, "Population Policy: Consensus and Challenges," *Consensus: The Nature and Consequences of Environmental Change* 2(2) (1996).

91. Christopher Flavin, "Last Days for the G-7?," *Worldwatch* 10(4) (July/August) (1997), p. 39. NB: In 2025, chronic water supply shortages will affect nearly half of the world's 7.8 billion people, if population growth follows the UN's medium projection (Katie Mogelaard, "Six Billion and Counting," *Nucleus: The Magazine of the Union of Concerned Scientists* 21[3] [Fall 1999], p. 7). A more recent UNEP study suggests that, if present consumption and development patterns continue, two out of every three persons on Earth will live in "water-stressed" conditions by the year 2025 (see UNEP [United Nations Environment Program], "Freshwater Synthesis," *Global Environment Outlook 2000* [Online, available: http://freshwater.unep.net, and http://www.unep.org/geo2000/english/0046.htm).

92. Mario Giampietro and David Pimentel, *The Tightening Conflict: Population, Energy Use, and the Ecology of Agriculture* ([Online, available: http://www.npg.org/forums/tightening_conflict.htm] 1993).

5   ECOCIDE AND GLOBALIZATION

1. Cited in Worldwatch, "Subsidies for Sacred Cows," *World Watch Magazine* 9 (1) (January/February) (1996): pp. 8–9.

2. David Goldblatt, *Social Theory and the Environment* (Boulder, CO: Westview Press, 1996), p. 199.

3. Political scientist Manfred Steger summarizes the five central ideological claims of globalism as follows: (1) globalization is about the liberalization and global integration of markets; (2) globalization is inevitable and irreversible; (3) nobody is in charge of globalization; (4) globalization benefits everyone; (5) globalization furthers the spread of democracy in the world. See Manfred B. Steger, *Globalism: The New Market Ideology* (Lanham, MD: Rowman & Littlefield, 2001).

4. Richard A. Falk, *Predatory Globalization: A Critique* (Malden, MA: Polity Press, 1999), Held et al., *Global Transformations: Politics, Economics and Culture*, Roland Robertson, *Globalization: Social Theory and Global Culture* (London: Sage, 1992), Jan Aart Scholte, *Globalization: A Critical Introduction* (London: Macmillan; New York: St Martin's Press, 2000), Malcolm Waters, *Globalization, Key Ideas* (London and New York: Routledge, 1995).

5. David C. Korten, *Rights of Money Versus Rights of Living Person, People-Centered Development Forum (PCDF)* ([Online, available: http://iisd1.iisd.ca/pcdf/1996/82korten.htm], 1996).

6. Jeff Pooley, *The Globalization of Oppression: Multilateral Corporations and the Failure of Democracy* ([Online, available: http://www.digitas.harvard.edu/~perspy/issues/1995/nov/democ.html], 1995).

7. UNRISD (United Nations Research Institute for Social Development), *States of Disarray: The Social Effects of Globalization* (London: UNRISD, 1995).

8. Neo-liberalism dates back to the liberal economic theory of the nineteenth century, which demanded far-reaching restrictions on the activities of the state in economic matters. Also known as *laissez-faire* and *laissez-passer*, it is based on the conviction that humans are active chiefly in their own interests and that there are natural rules which create harmony through the operation of the "invisible hand" of the market. If individuals were left to themselves to pursue their interests (producing, buying, and selling) then everyone would profit from the result. The laws of supply and demand would ensure the best allocation of results. The laws of supply and demand would ensure the best use of capital and labor. Historically, economic *laissez-faire* was an expression of a new form of individualism geared to industry, which in the sixteenth century turned against church and state interference in the economy and trade.

9. See Noam Chomsky, *Neo-liberalism and Global Order: Doctrine and Reality* ([Online, available: http://aidc.org.za/archives/chomsky_01.html], 1998).

10. To define civil society in this context simply as the third sector between state and market is a misleading overestimation. It would be closer to reality to speak of a mouse as the third actor between the corporate market tiger and the state rhinoceros.

11. Franz J. Broswimmer, "Botanical Imperialism: The Stewardship of Plantgenetic Resources in the Third World," *Critical Sociology* 18(1) (Spring) (1991), Jack Kloppenburg Jr, "Biotechnology to the Rescue? Twelve Reasons Why Biotechnology Is Incompatible with Sustainable Agriculture," *The Ecologist* 26(2) (1996), Brewster Kneen, *Farmageddon: Food and the Culture of Biotechnology* (Gabriola Island, BC: New Society, 1999), Marc Lappé and Britt Bailey, *Against the Grain: The Genetic Transformation of Global Agriculture* (London: Earthscan, 1999).

12. Foster, *The Vulnerable Planet: A Short History of the Environment*.

13. Ernest Mandel, *Late Capitalism*, trans. Joris de Bres (London: NLB, 1975).

14. John Tuxill, *Losing Strands in the Web of Life: Vertebrate Declines and the Conservation of Biodiversity*, ed. Jane A. Peterson, *Worldwatch Paper 141* (Washington, DC: Worldwatch Institute, 1998), p. 68. NB: The debt of all developing countries in 1971 was US $277 billion. By 1997, the amount of money required just to service the US $3.171 billion debt of all developing countries amounted to US $269 billion (Lester Brown et al., *Vital Signs 1999* [New York: W.W. Norton & Co., 1999]. See also World Watch, "Matters of Scale: Earth Day, Thirty Years Later," *World Watch* [13]2 [March/April] [2000], 25).

15. Annan et al., eds, *State of the World 2002*.

16. Robert Weissman, "Corporate Plundering of Third World Resources," in *Toxic Struggles: The Theory and Practice of Environmental Justice*, ed. Richard Hofrichter (Philadelphia, PA: New Society Publisher, 1993), p. 187.

17. Walden Bello, "Global Economic Counterrevolution: The Dynamics of Impoverishment and Marginalization," in Hofrichter, ed., *Toxic Struggles: The Theory and Practice of Environmental Justice*, p. 203.

18. David Chance, "One Quarter of the World Lives on Less Than a Dollar," *Reuter News Agency* Updated 1:19 PM ET August 1 (2000).

19. See WRI (World Resources Institute) *World Resources 1990–1991* (New York: Oxford University Press, 1990), WRI, *World Resources 1992–1993* (New York: Oxford University Press, 1992).

20. Bello, "Global Economic Counterrevolution: The Dynamics of Impoverishment and Marginalization," p. 203.

21. Cited in ibid.

22. Ibid.

23. Ibid.

24. Ibid., p. 204.

25. The amount that Indonesia received in 1990 for timber concessions, many of which were sold to wealthy timber magnates with close ties to President Suharto, was US $416 million. The amount by which the actual world-market value exceeded the price charged, and by which Indonesian taxpayers were therefore forced to subsidize the magnate's windfall, was US $2.1 billion (Worldwatch, "Matters of Scale: Subsidies: The Other Side of the Coin," *World Watch* 10[2] [March/April 2000], p. 39). But this captures merely the tip of the iceberg. Credible estimates of illegal logging in Indonesia for example suggested that 70 per cent of timber supplied to the processing sector came from illegal logging. This means that 70 per cent of the industry avoided taxes and tariffs while uncontrolledly denuding vast tracts of land. A European Union-funded global study during the late 1990s resulted in a devastating report about the destruction of tropical forests by multinational companies who bribed and bullied their way to lucrative logging concessions. The study blamed, in particular, the International Monetary Fund and the World Bank for inducing countries to sell their forests for a quick cash return to pay off debts to Western countries. Well-respected authors from the World Resources Institute (WRI) and WWF were so disturbed by what they found that they recommended a moratorium on all further logging in eleven countries: Cameroon, Gabon, Congo (Brazzaville), Central African Republic, Equatorial Guinea, and the Democratic Republic of Congo in central Africa; Belize, Surinam, and Guyana in the Caribbean rim; and Papua New Guinea and the Solomon Islands in the South Pacific rim. This moratorium, they said, should last until bribery scandals had been investigated and proper environmental standards enforced. Nigel Sizer and Dominiquek Plouvier, "Increased Investment and Trade by Transnational Logging Companies in Africa, the Caribbean and the Pacific: Implications for the Sustainable Management and Conservation of Tropical Forests," in *A Joint Report by World Wide Fund for Nature and Belgium World Resources Institute's Forest Frontiers Initiative* (Brussels: European Commission EC-Project B7–6201/96–16/VIII/FOR D/1999/6732/03, 2000).

26. Weissman, "Corporate Plundering of Third World Resources," pp. 188–9.

27. May Lee, *Land-Clearing Fires Foul Malaysia's Air* (Kuala Lumpur, Malaysia: [Online, available: http://www9.cnn.com/WORLD/9709/19/malaysia.smog], 1997).

28. Mike Davis, "The Unknown Wallace," *Capitalism, Nature, Socialism* 9(1) (March) (1998), p. 77. NB: As satellite photographs reconfirmed, in contradiction to government reports, the main source of forest fires (some 80 per cent) in Indonesia

in 1997 (some 80 per cent) came from large industrial plantation clearings, while only a small part of the human-caused fires (some 20 per cent) originated from traditional slash-and-burn subsistence farmers. Jefferson Fox, "Indonesia: The Truth Behind the Haze; Government Land Policies Promote Burning; Fires: They Sent the Message that Something is Amiss," *The Honolulu Advertiser* Sunday, December 21 (1997).

29. Kidnapping and massive forest destruction in Indonesia (especially Sumatra and Borneo) and Malaysia have killed more than 30,000 orangutans in the last ten years alone. Today, fewer than 30,000 orangutans survive. Unless the species' habitat can be preserved, it risks extinction. WWF (World Wildlife Fund), *Rain Forests on Fire: Conservation Consequences* (Washington, DC: World Wildlife Fund, 1997).

30. Ashley T. Mattoon, "Bogging Down the Sinks," *Worldwatch* 11(6) (November/December 1998), pp. 32–3.

31. WWF, *Rain Forests on Fire: Conservation Consequences*. NB: The year 1997 saw some of the worst forest fires in human history. Indonesia lost 247,000 acres of virgin tropical rain forest, much of which had probably never burned before (80 per cent of these fires were caused by a neo-patrimonial oligarchy of billionaire palm-oil plantation owners and associated investors). Brazil's burning season swallowed 5 million acres of forest. Overall, more than 12 million acres of land went up in flames in an area roughly the size of Costa Rica. In 1998, again vast stretches of tropical forest were reduced to charcoal. Another 9.6 million acres were lost in Brazil. To the north, fires raged here and there through central America, and up into the highland "cloud forests" of southern Mexico, one of the last places in that country where it was still possible to find the quetzals, jaguars, and other species that have shaped thousands of years of indigenous culture. During the 1980s, the last time an estimate was made, the fires and other forms of deforestation were releasing around 1.4 billion tons of carbon into the atmosphere annually. Deforestation accounts for roughly one-fifth of humanity's annual emissions of carbon dioxide (CO_2), the primary greenhouse gas. See Mattoon, "Bogging Down the Sinks," p. 30.

32. Between 1950 and 1997, the global economy expanded from an annual output of US $5 trillion to US $29 trillion, an increase of nearly six-fold. Growth from 1990 to 1997 alone exceeded that during the 10,000 years from the beginning of agriculture until 1950. Worldwatch, "Overshoot: Building a New Economy – the Challenge for Our Generation," *State of the World 1998*; Worldwatch Press Release, January 10 1998.

33. World Commission on Environment and Development, *Our Common Future* (Oxford; New York: Oxford University Press, 1987).

34. Catton, *Overshoot: The Ecological Basis of Revolutionary Change*.

35. An environment's "carrying capacity" is its maximum persistently supportable load.

36. Hanson and Hanson, *Brain Food: Requiem*, Wackernagel and Rees, *Our Ecological Footprint: Reducing Human Impact on the Earth*. See also William E. Rees, "Revisiting Carrying Capacity: Area-Based Indicators of Sustainability," University of British Columbia, at http://www.dieoff.com/page110.htm and "Ecological Footprints of Nations," at http://www.ecouncil.ac.cr/rio/focus/report/english/footprint/. See also: http://redefiningprogress.org/programs/sustainability/ef/.

37. Jay Hanson, *The Introduction, Increase, and Crash of Reindeer on St Mathew's Island, Brain Food: Reindeer Politics* ([Online, available: http://www.dieoff.com/page80.htm], 1997).

38. See *Convention on Biological Diversity*. (Online, available: http://www.biodiv.org/index.html) reviewed March 2001.

39. The WHO estimate of 3 billion malnourished includes people who are calorie-, protein-, vitamin-, iron-, and iodine-malnourished. As the human population

continues to increase, the number of malnourished could conceivably reach more than 5 billion in future decades. WHO, "Micronutrient Malnutrition: Half the World's Population Affected," *World Health Organization* 78 (November 13) (1996).

40. UCS (Union of Concerned Scientists), "U.S. Consumption and the Environment," *Union of Concerned Scientists Briefing Paper* (UCS Publication Department, Washington, DC) (1994), pp. 1–6.

41. Ibid.

42. Ibid.

43. Galbraith believes the economy is a kind of treadmill, designed by business interests to keep people working and consuming, regardless of what they might want if they were left to their own devices. Given this vision of the artificiality of "affluence" in Western societies, he is naturally distressed by the existence of what he sees as equally artificial poverty. John Kenneth Galbraith, "How to Get the Poor Off Our Conscience," *Harpers Magazine* November (1985), John Kenneth Galbraith, *The New Industrial State*, 2nd rev. edn (New York: Mentor Books, 1967).

44. John Bellamy Foster, "Global Ecology and the Common Good," *Monthly Review* 46(9) (February) (1995), p. 2.

45. Lewis Carroll and Mervyn Laurence Peake, *Alice's Adventures in Wonderland and through the Looking Glass* (New York: Schocken Books, 1979).

46. Foster, "Global Ecology and the Common Good," p. 4.

47. Institutionalized forms of waste and planned obsolescence are an intrinsic part of the contemporary global treadmill economy, where some people do not have enough income and some have a lot of "discretionary" income. In order to keep machines running, it is necessary to generate demand in the second group. One way to do this is to design products to wear out fast. People then will have to buy more light bulbs, cars, toasters, or TVs than they really need. Another way is to promote fashions in cars, clothes, houses, or appliances. A third way is to generate demand for useless products or for products that use a lot of resources to save a little labor, such as electric knives, toothbrushes, fingernail files, or can openers. The drug industry has been known to create "illnesses" in order to generate a public. A better way to organize production is on the basis of need rather than profit within the limits of ecological integrity.

48. Peter Schmid-Schreiber, "Wie Viele Tötliche Dosen Lassen Sie Erbrüten, Nachbar?," *Presse Spiegel der Initiative Österreichischer Atomkraftwerksgegner* 2 (February), Pressespiegelgruppe der IOEAG, Wien/Vienna (1993).

49. Foster, "Global Ecology and the Common Good," p. 4.

50. Ibid., Petra Kelly, *Fighting for Hope*, trans. Marianne Wowarth (Boston and London: South End Press and Chatto & Windus, 1984).

51. C.W. Mills, *The Power Elite* (New York: Oxford University Press, 1956).

52. Robert D. Putnam, *Bowling Alone: The Collapse and Revival of American Community* (New York: Simon & Schuster, 2000).

53. Kelly, *Fighting for Hope*.

54. Mark Achbar and Peter Wintonick, eds, *Manufacturing of Consent: Noam Chomsky and the Media, Necessary Illusions*, a Zeitgeist Film Release (Montreal: National Filmboard of Canada, 1993), Samuel Bowles and Herbert Gintis, *Democracy and Capitalism: Property, Community, and the Contradictions of Modern Social Thought* (New York: Basic Books, 1986), Samuel Bowles and Herbert Gintis, *Schooling in Capitalist America: Educational Reform and the Contradictions of Economic Life* (New York: Gintis Books, 1976), Allan Schnaiberg, *Educating for an Ecologically Sustainable Culture: Rethinking Moral Education, Creativity, Intelligence, and Other Modern Orthodoxies* (Albany: State University of New York Press, 1995), Allan Schnaiberg, *The Environment: From Surplus to Scarcity* (New York: Oxford University Press, 1980).

55. Noam Chomsky, "Studying the Media: What Makes the Mainstream Media Mainstream," *The Chomsky Archives* June (1997).
56. Ulrich Beck, *Ecological Enlightenment: Essays on the Politics of the Risk Society*, trans. Mark A. Ritter (New Jersey: Humanities Press, 1995).
57. Schnaiberg, *Educating for an Ecologically Sustainable Culture: Rethinking Moral Education, Creativity, Intelligence, and Other Modern Orthodoxies*, Allan Schnaiberg, *Education, Cultural Myths, and the Ecological Crisis: Towards Deep Changes* (Albany: State University of New York Press, 1993), Schnaiberg, *The Environment: From Surplus to Scarcity*.
58. Allan Schnaiberg, "Environmental Education," *Environment, Technology and Society* ([Online, available: http://csf.colorado.edu/envtecsoc/96s/0166.html], 1996).
59. Mass media are owned and operated by large corporate conglomerates. Populations suffering the primary consequences of environmental degeneration, mass extinction of species, and the depletion of resources are not often in the news. Headlines abound regarding contaminated drinking water, leaking landfills, and violations of federal regulations. But because these items are disconnected from larger issues, the public receives only limited analysis of the historical, political, and social determinants of environmental conditions. Sometimes the media attribute these problems to the natural and avoidable consequences of life in modern society. Media language and imagery present environmental crisis as a physical problem of technological failure, regulatory failure, overpopulation, individual ignorance, or careless behavior. Opponents are categorized as "special interests" or "extremists." Rarely do media reports make connections to a broad definition of environment that includes issues of civil rights, housing, employment, the quality of life, or the policies of global corporations. Moreover, presentations of environmental issues often divert the public's attention from their relation to social and ecological injustices. Corporate appropriation of green symbols, particularly in advertisements, tends to exacerbate the shallow, sporadic coverage offered by the media. Much literature and television programming provide a great deal of advice about how individuals can protect the environment through various personal actions. Even as it assuages our conscience and offers feelings of efficacy, emphasis on individual behavior diverts attention from political power to institutional failures.
60. Foster, *The Vulnerable Planet: A Short History of the Environment*, Kelly, *Fighting for Hope*.
61. As used here, *critique* is not (merely) criticism of ecocidal practices, but the effort to lay bare the associated presuppositions of beliefs, practices, and the like.
62. One of the characteristic historical features of capitalism as a form of social organization is the "disembedding" of the market economy from society, resulting in national and international division of labor structures that are systematically loaded against those who suffer, like playing chess on a tilting board having only pawns, no other pieces. What is needed to halt, or even to slow, progressive ecocide is incompatible with the contemporary market organization of the global economy, because the essence of a neo-liberal market economy is of course precisely the lack of democratic planning – indeed its single-minded focus on individual pursuits and profit.
63. In Fotopoulos's *Inclusive Democracy: The Crisis of the Growth Economy and the Need for a New Liberatory Project*, the subtitle sums up its thesis. The primary flaw in a growth economy, according to Fotopoulos, is concentrated power. Under capitalism such power is primarily economic; under socialism it is political. But in both cases the very concentration of power contradicts the fundamental premise of democracy, which is, above all, the diffusion of power. The solution offered is a "confederal inclusive democracy" – a mixture of political strategies, continually readjusted to maintain a wide distribution of power in all aspects of the citizens' lives. See Takis Fotopoulos, "Development or Democracy?," *Society and Nature* 7 (1997), p. 82, Takis

Fotopoulos, *Towards an Inclusive Democracy: The Crisis of the Growth Economy and the Need for a New Liberatory Project* (New York: Cassell, 1996).

64. World Commission on Environment and Development, *Our Common Future*.

65. William Greider, *One World, Ready or Not: The Manic Logic of Global Capitalism* (New York: Simon & Schuster, 1997).

66. Speech on behalf of the environment and development NGOs at the UNCED Plenary, presented on their behalf by Wangari Maathai, June 11 1992. Cited in Athanasiou, *Divided Planet: The Ecology of Rich and Poor*.

67. See David Korten, *When Corporations Rule the World* (West Hartford, CT: Kumarin Press, 1995), Korten, *Rights of Money Versus Rights of Living Person*.

68. P.R. Ehrlich, G.C. Daily, and L.H. Goulder, "Population Growth, Economic Growth, and Market Economies," *Contention* 2 (1992).

69. The global "Net Primary Production of Photosynthesis" (NPP) for example cannot be expanded nor owned. Worldwide, more than 40 per cent of terrestrial net primary productivity (of the ecosystem) is currently used directly, co-opted, or forgone because of human activities (a figure projected to double this century). If this figure is even approximately correct, we are in big trouble, because the global "net primary production of photosynthesis" (NPP) (the human appropriation of the net products of photosynthesis) cannot be expanded. What would the planet be like if humans, instead of co-opting 40 per cent, took 80 per cent? 100 per cent? See Meadows et al., *Beyond the Limits: Confronting Global Collapse; Envisioning a Sustainable Future*, Vitousek, Ehrlich, and Mason, "Human Appropriation of the Products of Photosynthesis," Wackernagel and Rees, *Our Ecological Footprint: Reducing Human Impact on the Earth*.

70. Anthony Giddens, Director, London School of Economics, quoted in the *New Statesman*, October 31 1997.

71. John O'Neill, "Cost-Benefit Analysis, Rationality and the Plurality of Values," *The Ecologist* 26(3) (May/June) (1996), p. 102.

72. Ibid.

73. In Aristotle's philosophical system theory follows empirical observation, and logic, based on the syllogism, is the essential method of rational inquiry.

74. O'Neill, "Cost-Benefit Analysis, Rationality and the Plurality of Values," p. 102.

75. Immanuel Kant, "An Answer to the Question 'What Is Enlightenment?'" in *Political Writings*, ed. H. Reiss (Cambridge: Cambridge University Press, 1991).

EPILOGUE – LIVING IN THE AGE OF ECOCIDE

1. The ozone hole is the largest ever. The seasonal hole in the ozone layer over Antarctica reached record proportions in September 1998, according to a report by the World Meteorological Association (WMO). Covering an area of 9.75 million square miles, or about 2.5 times the area of Europe, 1998's hole surpassed the previous record – set in 1993 – by about 3 million square kilometers. The rift was also the "deepest" and fastest-growing ever, said WMO expert Rumen Bojikov. It involved the destruction of more than 85 per cent of the ozone in the lower stratosphere over an area of more than 10 million square kilometers; Lisa Mastny, "Ozone Hole Is Largest Ever," *World Watch* 12(1) (January/February) (1999), p. 11.

2. UNDP (United Nations Development Programme) *Human Development Report 1998* (New York: Oxford University Press, 1998).

3. Stephen P. Hubbell, *The Unified Neutral Theory of Biodiversity and Biogeography*, Monographs in Population Biology 32 (Princeton, NJ: Princeton University Press, 2001) p. x.

4. Ayres, "The Fastest Mass Extinction in Earth's History," Wilson, *The Diversity of Life*, Wilson, "Is Humanity Suicidal? We Are Flirting with the Extinction of Our Species," Wilson and Peter, eds, *Biodiversity*.

5. Elias Canetti, *Das Geheimherz Der Uhr*. English: *The Secret Heart of the Clock: Notes, Aphorisms, Fragments 1973–1985*, trans. Joel Agee (New York: Farrar, Straus, Giroux, 1991), p. 61.

6. By virtue of the social and biological evolution of our uniquely expanded manual and verbal dexterity, we have become all-purpose animals that in principle can solve any problem. Tudge, however, in an invigoratingly syncretic look at 5 million years of human life, hastens to say that this adaptability and power do not give us the right to destroy other species. Much of his history of humanity analyzes the negative impact humans have had on the Earth ever since we mastered fire and engaged in agriculture, from the depletion of the ozone layer to the pollution of the oceans and the decimation of numerous animal species. See Colin Tudge, "Why We Must Save Animals," *New Internationalist* (Special Issue) 288 (March) (1997).

7. In *Language and Species*, Derek Bickerton, for example, shows that the possession of language alone may be sufficient to account for both our unique minds and our unparalleled success as a species. Language is more than a reflection, merely labeling our thoughts and their objects; it actually "creates" all we communicate about. Bickerton shows how a primitive protolanguage could have offered *Homo erectus* a novel ecological niche; it probably developed subsequently into the languages we speak today. But, he asks, what if our vaunted human intelligence is no more than the addition of language to the cognitive powers possessed by other creatures – and what if the process of language itself is as automatic as a spider's spinning of a web? Could language, our most successful adaptation, one day cause our failure as a species? See Bickerton, *Language and Species*.

8. The critical significance of historical ecology in this context is to provide us (at least in principle) with long-term insights and perspectives on the scope and nature of human socio-biotic impact.

9. Warfare and the activities of the military-industrial complex are estimated to account for 10 to 30 per cent of the planet's total ecological damage. Thompson, *Scorched Earth: The Military's Assault on the Environment*.

10. Neo-liberal globalization gives free rein to a world of increasingly licentious and large-scale corporate individualism. With the global mobility of capital comes the mobility of both the industrial base and the tax base that supports key national institutions. Globalization not only undercuts a nation's ability to tax mobile capital, it also undercuts a nation's ability to tax capital in order to support social welfare and environmental protection programs. Globalization thus conceived has initiated a new era of capitalism, which will change the planet probably as dramatically as the first Industrial Revolution did. For the critics, the decisive challenge is this: how to bring the destructive dimensions of market forces under control and to develop democratic, socially equitable, and environmentally sustainable alternatives. This gives rise to the worldwide call for a (re)regulation of the global economy and the struggle for an alternative globalization based on ecological democracy and ecological citizenship.

11. Stephen Jay Gould, "The Persistently Flat Earth: Irrationality and Dogmatism Are Foes of Both Science and Religion," *Natural History* 3 (1994), p. 19.

BIBLIOGRAPHY

Abramovitz, Janet N. "Putting a Value on Nature's 'Free' Services." *World Watch* 11(1) (January/February) (1998), pp. 10–19.

Achbar, Mark and Peter Wintonick, eds. *Manufacturing of Consent: Noam Chomsky and the Media.* Edited by Adam Symansky, *Necessary Illusions, a Zeitgeist Film Release.* Montreal: National Filmboard of Canada, 1993.

Adorno, Theodor and Max Horkheimer. *Dialektik Der Aufklärung: Philosophische Fragmente. English: Dialectic of Enlightenment,* trans. John Cummings. New York: Herder & Herder, 1972.

Amin, Samir. "1492 – Columbus and the New World Order." *Monthly Review* 44(14) (July/August) (Special Issue) (1992), pp. 10–19.

Anderson, Atholl. "Prehistoric Polynesian Impact on the New Zealand Environment," in *Historical Ecology in the Pacific Islands: Prehistoric Environmental and Landscape Changes,* edited by Patrick V. Kirk and Terry L. Hunt, 271–83. New Haven, CT: Yale University Press, 1997.

Angel, J.L. "Paleontology, Paleodemography and Health," in *Population, Ecology and Social Evolution: World Anthropology,* edited by Steven Polgar, 167–90. The Hague: Mouton, 1975.

Annan, Kofi, Christopher Flavin, Linda Starke, and Worldwatch Institute, eds *State of the World 2002: A Worldwatch Institute Report on Progress towards a Sustainable Society.* New York: W.W. Norton, 2002.

Ashford, Lori S. and Jeane A. Noble. "Population Policy: Consensus and Challenges," *Consensus: The Nature and Consequences of Environmental Change* 2(2) [Online, available: http://www.gcrio.org/CONSEQUENCES/vol2no2/article3.html] 1996.

Athanasiou, Tom. *Divided Planet. The Ecology of Rich and Poor.* Boston: Little, Brown, 1996.

Ayres, Ed. "The Expanding Shadow Economy," *World Watch* July/August (1996), pp. 11–23.

————— "The Fastest Mass Extinction in Earth's History," *World Watch* 11(5) (September/October) (1998), pp. 6–7.

Badash, Laurence. *Scientists and the Development of Nuclear Weapons: From Fission to Limited Test Ban Treaty, 1939–1963.* Atlantic Highlands, NJ: Humanities Press, 1995.

Bauer, Marilyn. *Religious Jihad Launched against Environmental Pollutants.* [Environmental News Network, Inc.: Online, available: http://www.enn.com, reviewed July 1, 2002]

BBC-TV, NOVA. *Mammoths of the Ice Age.* Video, A Nova Production by BBC TV in Association with WGBH Educational Foundation. South Burlington and Boston: BBC TV and WGBH, 1995.

Beck, Ulrich. *Ecological Enlightenment: Essays on the Politics of the Risk Society,* trans. Mark A. Ritter. New Jersey: Humanities Press, 1995.

Bello, Walden. "Global Economic Counterrevolution: The Dynamics of Impoverishment and Marginalization," in *Toxic Struggles: The Theory and Practice of Environmental Justice,* edited by Richard Hofrichter, 197–208. Philadelphia, PA: New Society Publisher, 1993.

Benjamin, Walter. *Illuminations*, edited by Hannah Arendt, trans. Harry Zohn. New York: Schocken, 1969.

Betancourt, Julio L., Thomas R. Van Devender, and Paul S. Martin, eds. *Packrat Mittens: The Last 40,000 Years of Biotic Change*. Tucson: University of Arizona Press, 1990.

Bickerton, Derek. *Language and Species*. Chicago: University of Chicago Press, 1990.

Borgstrom, Georg. *The Food and People Dilemma, The Man–Environment System in the Late Twentieth Century*. Belmont, CA: Duxbury Press, 1973.

Bowles, Samuel and Herbert Gintis. *Democracy and Capitalism: Property, Community, and the Contradictions of Modern Social Thought*. New York: Basic Books, 1986.

———— *Schooling in Capitalist America: Educational Reform and the Contradictions of Economic Life*. New York: Gintis Books, 1976.

Boyden, Stephen Vickers. *Biohistory: The Interplay between Human Society and the Biosphere*, vol. 8, *Man and the Biosphere Series*. Paris: UNESCO, Pantheon, 1992.

Bradbury, Ian K. *The Biosphere*. New York: Belhaven Press, 1991.

Braudel, Fernand. *The Structure of Everyday Life*. New York: Harper & Row, 1979.

Brecht, Bertolt *Gedichte V*. Frankfurt am Main: Suhrkamp Verlag, 1964.

Bronson, Bennet. "The Role of Barbarians in the Fall of States," in *The Collapse of Ancient States and Civilizations*, edited by Norman Yoffe and George L. Cowgill, 196–218. Tucson: University of Arizona Press, 1988.

Broswimmer, Franz J. "Botanical Imperialism: The Stewardship of Plantgenetic Resources in the Third World," *Critical Sociology* 18(1) (spring) (1991), pp. 3–17.

Brown, Lester R., Michael Renner and Brian Halweil. *Vital Signs 1999*. Washington, D.C.: Worldwatch Institute, 1999.

Bryant, Peter J. "Chapter 3: Extinction and Depletion from Over-Exploitation," *Biodiversity and Conservation: A Hypertext Book*. University of California, Irvine School of Biological Sciences [Online, available: http://darwin.bio.uci.edu/~sustain/bio65/lec03/b65lec03.htm] 1997.

———— "Chapter 4: Whaling and Fishing," *Biodiversity and Conservation: A Hypertext Book*. University of California, Irvine School of Biological Sciences [Online, available: http://darwin.bio.uci.edu/~sustain/bio65/lec04/b65lec04.htm], 1998.

Butzer, Karl W. *Early Hydraulic Civilizations in Egypt: A Study in Cultural Ecology*. Chicago: University of Chicago Press, 1976.

———— "Environmental Change, Climate History and Human Modification: Civilizations of the Ancient Near East," in *Civilizations of the Near East*, edited by J.M. Sasson, John Baines and Karen S. Robinson, 123–51. New York: Scribner, 1994.

Caggiano, J.T. Mark. "The Legitimacy of Environmental Destruction in Modern Warfare: Customary Substance over Conventional Form," *Boston College Environmental Affairs Law Review* 20 (1993), pp. 479–506.

Canetti, Elias. *The Secret Heart of the Clock: Notes, Aphorisms, Fragments 1973–1985*, trans. Joel Agee from the German *Das Geheimherz Der Uhr*. New York: Farrar, Straus, Giroux, 1991.

———— *The Agony of Flies: Notes and Notations*, trans. H.F. Broch de Rothermann from the German *Die Fliegenpein: Aufzeichnungen*. New York: Farrar, Straus, Giroux, 1994.

Carr, Archie Fairly. *The Sea Turtle: So Excellent a Fishe*. First University of Texas Press ed. Austin: University of Texas Press, 1986.

Carroll, Lewis and Mervyn Laurence Peake. *Alice's Adventures in Wonderland and Through the Looking Glass*. New York: Schocken Books, 1979.

Cassels, Richard. "The Role of Prehistoric Man in the Faunal Extinctions of New Zealand and Other Pacific Islands," in *Quaternary Extinctions: A Prehistoric Revolution*, edited by Paul S. Martin and Richard G. Klein, 741–67. Tucson: University of Arizona Press, 1984.

Catton, William R. *Overshoot: The Ecological Basis of Revolutionary Change*. Chicago: University of Illinois Press, 1982.

CBD (Convention on Biological Diversity). 2002. *Convention on Biological Diversity*. World Trade Centre Montréal, Québec, Canada: [Online]. Available: http://www.biodiv.org/default.asp.

Chance, David. "One Quarter of the World Lives on Less Than a Dollar," Reuter News Agency, updated 1:19 p.m. ET August 1, 2000.

Chen, Y.Z. "Li Daoyuan Fl. c. 500 AD," *Geographers, Bibliographical Studies* (1988), pp. 125–31.

Chew, Sing C. "Neglecting Nature: World Accumulation and Core–Periphery Relations, 2500 BC to AD 1990," in *World System History: The Social Science of Long-Term Change*, edited by Jonathan Friedman, Robert A. Denemark, Barry K. Gills, and George Modelski, 216–34. London and New York: Routledge; Taylor & Francis Group, 1995.

——— "Ecological Relations and the Decline of Kingdoms and Civilizations in the Bronze Age 2500 BC to 1700 BC: Some Considerations on Mesopotamia and Harappa," in *The Global Environment and the Worldsystem*, edited by W. Goodfrank, D. Goodman and A. Szasz. Draft presented at the Political Economy of the World System XXI Conference, April, Santa Cruz, CA, 1997.

——— "For Nature: Deep Greening World-Systems Analysis for the 21st Century," *Journal of World-Systems Research* 3(3) [Online, available: http://csf.colorado.edu/wsystems/jwsr.html], 1997, pp. 381–402.

Childe, Vere Gordon. *Man Makes Himself*. New York: New American Library; Mentor Books, 1951.

Chomsky, Noam. "Studying the Media: What Makes the Mainstream Media Mainstream," *The Chomsky Archives* (June) [Online, available: http://www.worldmedia.com/archive], 1997.

——— *Neoliberalism and Global Order: Doctrine and Reality* [Online, available: http://aidc.org.za/archives/chomsky_01.html], 1998.

Cincotta, Richard P. and Robert Engelman. "Real Numbers: Biodiversity and Population Growth," *Issues in Science and Technology Online* (spring) [Online, available: http://www.nap.edu/issues/16.3/realnumbers.htm], 2000.

Clausewitz, Carl Von, Michael Howard, and Peter Paret, eds. *On War*. Princeton, NJ: Princeton University Press, 1984.

Clottes, Jean. "Rhinos and Lions and Bears (Oh My!)," *Natural History* 5 (1995), pp. 30–35.

Coe, William R. "The Maya: Resurrecting the Grandeur of Tikal," *National Geographic* 148(6) (December) (1975), pp. 792–8.

Cohen, Mark Nathan. *The Food Crisis in Prehistory: Overpopulation and the Origins of Agriculture*. London and New Haven, CT: Yale University Press, 1977.

——— and George J. Armelagos. *Paleopathology at the Origins of Agriculture*. New York: Academic Press, 1984.

Collon, Dominique. *First Impressions, Cylinder Seals in the Ancient Near East*. London: British Museum Publications, 1987.

Costanza, Robert, Ralph d'Arge, Stephen Farber, Monica Grasso, Bruce Hannon, Karin Limburg, Shahid Naeem, Robert V. O'Neill, Jose Paruelo, Robert G. Raskin, Paul Sutton, and Marjan van den Belt. "The Value of the World's Ecosystem Services and Natural Capital," *Nature* 387(6630) (May 15) (1997), pp. 253–60.

Cronon, William. *Nature's Metropolis: Chicago and the Great West*. New York: W.W. Norton, 1991.

Crosby, Alfred. *The Columbian Exchange: Biological and Cultural Consequences of 1492*. Westport, CT: Greenwood Press, 1972.

———— *Ecological Imperialism: The Biological Expansion of Europe, 900–1900.* Melbourne and Cambridge: Cambridge University Press, 1986.

Culbert, Patrick T. "The Collapse of Classical Maya Civilization," in *The Collapse of Ancient States and Civilizations*, edited by Norman Yoffee and George L. Cowgill, 99–101. Tucson: University of Arizona Press, 1988.

Daily, Gretchen C. "Ecosystem Services: Benefits Supplied to Human Societies by Natural Ecosystems," *Issues in Ecology* 2 (spring) (1997).

———— ed. *Nature's Services: Societal Dependence on Natural Ecosystems.* Washington, DC: Island Press, 1998.

Daily, Gretchen D. and Paul R. Ehrlich. "Population, Sustainability, and Earth's Carrying Capacity: A Framework for Estimating Population Sizes and Lifestyles that Could be Sustained without Undermining Future Generations," *BioScience* 42 (November) (1992), pp. 761–71.

Dales, G.F. "Early Despotism in Mesopotamia," in *Early Antiquity*, edited by I. E. Diakanoff. Chicago: University of Chicago Press, 1991.

Davis, Mike. "Dead West: Ecocide in Marlboro Country," *New Left Review* 200 (1993), pp. 49–73.

———— "The Unknown Wallace," *Capitalism, Nature, Socialism* 9(1) (March) (1998), pp. 73–7.

Davis, Ralph. *The Rise of the Atlantic Economies.* London: Weidenfeld & Nicolson, 1973.

Diamond, Jared M. "Historic Extinctions: A Rosetta Stone for Understanding Prehistoric Extinctions," in *Quatenary Extinctions: A Prehistoric Revolution*, edited by S. Paul and Richard G. Klein, 824–62. Tucson: University of Arizona Press, 1984.

———— "Paleontology: Twilight of the Pygmy Hippo," *Nature* 359(6390) (September) (1991), p. 15.

———— *The Third Chimpanzee: The Evolution and Future of the Human Animal.* New York: Harper Collins Publishers, 1992.

———— "Easter's End: Easter Island," *Discover* (August) (1995), pp. 63–9.

———— *Guns, Germs, and Steel: The Fates of Human Societies.* New York: W.W. Norton, 1997.

Discover Magazine. "Early Sailors Hunted Pygmy Hippo to Extinction," *Discover* March (1993), p. 14.

Dowie, Mark. *Losing Ground: American Environmentalism at the Close of the Twentieth Century.* Cambridge, MA: MIT Press, 1995.

Dubos, Rene Jules. "Franciscan Conservation Versus Benedictine Stewardship," in *A God Within*, edited by R.J. Dubos, 114–36. New York: Charles Scribner Sons, 1972.

Durning, Alan Thein. "The Health of the Planet," in *World Military and Social Expenditures 1991*, edited by Ruth Leger Sivard, 28–42. Washington, DC: World Priorities Press, 1991.

Earth Island Journal. "Cries of Ecocide from Croatia: Ecological Destruction Caused by War," *Earth Island Journal* 7(1) (1992), p. 17.

Ehrlich, Anne H. and Paul Ehrlich. *Earth.* New York: Franklin Watts, 1987.

Ehrlich, Paul. *The Population Bomb.* New York: Sierra Club–Ballantine Books, 1968.

———— and Anne Ehrlich. *Extinction: The Causes and Consequences of the Disappearance of Species.* New York: Random House, 1981.

———— and ———— *The Population Explosion.* Simon & Schuster: New York, 1990.

————, G.C. Daily, and L.H. Goulder. "Population Growth, Economic Growth, and Market Economies," *Contention* 2 (1992), pp. 17–35.

Fagan, Brian M. *The Journey from Eden: The Peopling of Our World.* New York: Thames & Hudson, 1990.

———— *Ancient North America: The Archeology of a Continent.* London: Thames & Hudson, 1991.

Falk, Richard A. *Predatory Globalization: A Critique*. Malden, MA: Polity Press, 1999.

Falk, Thomas H. *Elias Canetti*. Edited by David O'Connell; Georgia State University, Twaynes World Author Series; German Literature. New York: Twayne Publishers, 1993.

Fang, Jin-qi. *Deforestation of the Loess Plateau in Pre-Industrial Time: Destruction of the Chinese Cradle, Working Paper*. Honolulu: East-West Center Program of the Environment, 1994.

———— and Zhiren Xie. "Deforestation in Preindustrial China: The Loess Plateau Region as an Example," *Chemosphere* 29(5) (1994), p. 983.

Felsbach, Murray and Alfred Friendly Jr. *Ecocide in the USSR: Health and Nature under Siege, Foreword by Lester Brown*. New York: Basic Books, 1992.

Fischer-Kowalski, Marina and Helmut Haberl. "Metabolism and Colonization: Modes of Production and the Physical Exchange between Societies and Nature," *Innovation in Social Science Research* 6(4) (Schriftenreihe Ökologie, Band 32. Wien/Austria; Interuniversitäres Institut für Interdisziplinäre Forschung und Fortbildung; Abteilung Soziale Ökologie) (1993), pp. 414–42.

————, ————, Walter Hütter, Harald Payer, Heiz Schandl, Verena Winiwarter and Helga Zangerl-Weisz, eds. *Gesellschaftlicher Stoffwechsel Und Kolonisierung Von Natur: Ein Versuch in Sozialer Ökologie*. Amsterdam: G+B Verlag Fakultas, 1997.

Flannery, Tim F. *Future Eaters: An Ecological History of the Australasian Lands and People*. New York: George Braziller, 1995.

———— "The Future Eaters" (interview) *Geographical Magazine* 69(1) (January) (1997).

———— *The Eternal Frontier: An Ecological History of North America and Its Peoples*. New York: Atlantic Monthly Press, 2001.

Flavin, Christopher. "Last Days for the G-7?" *World Watch* 10(4) (July/August) (1997), pp. 38–9.

Foster, John Bellamy. *The Vulnerable Planet: A Short History of the Environment*. New York: Monthly Review Press, 1994.

———— "Global Ecology and the Common Good," *Monthly Review* 46(9) (February) (1995), pp. 1–10.

Fotopoulos, Takis. *Towards an Inclusive Democracy: The Crisis of the Growth Economy and the Need for a New Liberatory Project*. New York: Cassell, 1996.

———— "Development or Democracy?" *Society and Nature* 7 (1997), pp. 57–92.

Fox, Jefferson. "Indonesia: The Truth Behind the Haze; Government Land Policies Promote Burning; Fires: They Sent the Message That Something Is Amiss," *The Honolulu Advertiser* Sunday, December 21 (1997), pp. B 1–4.

Frank, Andre Gunder. "The Development of Underdevelopment," in *Imperialism and Underdevelopment*, edited by R.I. Rhodes, 4–17. New York: Monthly Review Press, 1970.

Gadgil, Madhav and Ramachandra Guha. *The Fissured Land: An Ecological History of India*. New Delhi: Oxford University Press, 1992.

Galbraith, John Kenneth. *The New Industrial State*. 2nd rev. edn. New York: Mentor Book, 1967.

———— 1985. "How to Get the Poor of Our Conscience." *Harpers Magazine* November: [Online]. Available: http://sunset.backbone.olemiss.edu/~jmitchel/ class/poor.htm, reviewed June 2002.

———— "World Military and Social Expenditures," in *World Military and Social Expenditures 1993*, edited by Ruth Leger Sivard, 3 (Foreword and Dedication). Washington, DC: World Priorities Press, 1993.

Galeano, Eduardo. *Open Veins of Latin America: Five Centuries of the Pillage of a Continent*, trans. Cedric Belfrage. New York: Monthly Review Press, 1973.

Gallagher, Carol. *American Ground Zero: The Secret Nuclear War*. Cambridge, MA: MIT Press, 1993.

Gardener, Gary. "Shrinking Fields: Cropland Loss in a World of Eight Billion," *Worldwatch Paper 131*. Washington, DC: Worldwatch Institute, July 1996.

Gare, Arran. "Soviet Environmentalism: The Path not Taken," in *The Greening of Marxism*, edited by Ted Benton, 111–28. New York: The Guilford Press, 1996.

Geo. "Die Magie Der Osterinseln: Hollywood Entdeckt Einen Südseekult," *Geo* 6 (June) (1993), pp. 13–36.

George, Susan. *Food for Beginners, Social Studies Historical Series*. New York and London: Writers & Readers Publishing Corporation, 1982.

Giampietro, Mario and David Pimentel. *The Tightening Conflict: Population, Energy Use, and the Ecology of Agriculture*. [Online, available: http://www.npg.org/forums/tightening_conflict.htm], 1993.

Giddens, Anthony. *A Contemporary Critique of Historical Materialism; Volume 2: Nation-State and Violence*. Berkeley: University of California Press, 1987.

——— *The Consequences of Modernity*. Stanford, CA: Stanford University Press, 1990.

Glacken, C.J. *Traces on the Rhodian Shore: Nature and Culture in Western Thought from Ancient Times to the End of the Eighteenth Century*. Berkeley: University of California Press, 1967.

Goin, Peter. *Nuclear Landscapes, Creating the North American Landscape; Catalogue of an Exhibition*. Baltimore, MD: John Hopkins University Press, 1991.

Goldblatt, David. *Social Theory and the Environment*. Boulder, CO: Westview Press, 1996.

Goldblatt, Josef. "The Environmental Modification Convention," in *Environmental Warfare: A Technical, Legal, and Policy Appraisal*, edited by Arthur H. Westing. London; Philadelphia: Taylor & Francis, 1984.

Gordon, Anita and David Suzuki. *It's a Matter of Survival*. Cambridge, MA: Harvard University Press, 1991.

Gould, Stephen J. *Ontogeny and Phylogeny*. Cambridge: Harvard University Press, 1977.

——— *The Mismeasure of Man*. New York: W.W. Norton, 1981.

——— *The Flamingo's Smile: Reflections in Natural History*, 1st edn. New York: W.W. Norton, 1985.

——— "The Persistently Flat Earth: Irrationality and Dogmatism Are Foes of Both Science and Religion," *Natural History* 3 (1994), pp. 12–19.

Graf, W.L., ed., *Geomorphic Systems of North America*. Boulder, CO: Geological Society of America, 1987.

Gray, Gary. *Wildlife and People: The Human Dimension of Wildlife Ecology*. Urbana: University of Illinois Press, 1993.

Greider, William. *One World Ready or Not: The Manic Logic of Global Capitalism*. New York: Simon & Schuster, 1997.

Groombridge, Brian, ed. *Global Biodiversity: Status of the Earth's Living Resources*. London: Chapman & Hall, 1992.

Grove, Richard H. *Green Imperialism: Colonial Expansion, Tropical Island Edens and the Origins of Environmentalism, 1600–1860*. Cambridge: Cambridge University Press, 1995.

Haile-Selassie, Yohannes. "Late Miocene Hominids from the Middle Awash, Ethiopia," *Nature* 412 (July 12) (2001), pp. 178–81.

Haines, Francis. *The Buffalo*. New York: Crowell, 1975.

Hanson, Jay. *The Introduction, Increase, and Crash of Reindeer on St Mathews Island, Brain Food: Reindeer Politics*: [Online, available: http://www.dieoff.com/page80.htm], 1997.

——— and Phyllis Hanson. *Brain Food: Requiem*, edited by J. Hanson, *Brain Food Mailer, Newsletter* [Online, available: http://dieoff.org], 1998.

Harris, Marvin. *Cannibalism and Kings: The Origins of Culture*. New York: Vintage Books, 1977.

——— *Kannibalen Und Könige: Die Wachstumgrenzen Der Hochkulturen*. Darmstadt: Klett & Kotta, 1990.

——— *Cultural Anthropology*, 3rd edn. New York: Harper & Collins, 1991.

Hassan, Fekri. "The Dynamics of Agricultural Origins in Palestine: A Theoretical Model," in *Origins of Agriculture*, edited by Charles Reed, 589. Chicago: Chicago Publishers, 1977.

Held, David, Anthony McGrew, David Goldblatt, and Jonathan Perraton. *Global Transformations: Politics, Economics and Culture*. Stanford, CA: Stanford University Press, 1999.

Hern, W.M. "Why Are There So Many of Us? Description and Diagnosis of a Planetary Eco-pathological Process," *Journal of Population and Environment* 12 (1990), pp. 9–39.

Hilt, Douglas. "Rediscovering the Discoverers: The Dual Case of Columbus and Cook," in *Native American Cultures: Before and After Columbus*, edited by D. Hilt (Speech). Honolulu: University of Hawai'i at Manoa Summer Session; Committee for the Humanities, 1994.

Hinrichsen, Don. "Putting the Bite on the Planet: Rapid Human Population Growth Is Devouring Global Natural Resources," *International Wildlife* September/October (1994), pp. 36–45.

Hirsch, Fred. *The Social Limits to Growth*. Cambridge, MA: Harvard University Press, 1970.

Hobsbawm, Eric J. *The Age of Extremes: A History of the World, 1914–91*. New York: Pantheon Books, 1991.

——— "Barbarism: A User's Guide," *New Left Review* 206 (July/August) (1994), pp. 44–54.

Hong, Sungmin, Jean-Pierre Candelone, Clair C. Patterson, and Claude F. Boutron. "Greenland Ice Evidence of Hemispheric Lead Pollution Two Millennia Ago by Greek and Roman Civilisations," *Science* 265 (1994), pp. 1841–2.

Hubbell, Stephen P. *The Unified Neutral Theory of Biodiversity and Biogeography, Monographs in Population Biology 32*. Princeton, NJ: Princeton University Press, 2001.

Hughes, Donald J. *Ecology in Ancient Civilizations*. Albuquerque: University of New Mexico Press, 1975.

——— "Mencius' Prescriptions for Ancient Chinese Environmental Problems," *Environmental Review* 13 (1989) pp. 12–25 .

——— "Ripples in Clio's Pond: Classical Athens and Ecosystem Collapse," *Capitalism, Nature, Socialism* 7(3) (September) (1996), pp. 97–102.

——— "Ripples in Clio's Pond: Rome's Decline and Fall: Ecological Mistakes?" *Capitalism, Nature, Socialism* 8(2) (June) (1997), pp. 121–5.

——— "Ripples in Clio's Pond: Mencius, Ecologist," *Capitalism, Nature, Socialism* 8(3) (September) (1997), pp. 117–21.

Hull, D. "Where the Buffalo Roam Has Deadly New Caveat," *Washington Post* July 22 (1997).

Huxley, Julian. *Evolution in Action*. New York: Mentor Books, 1953.

Jackson, Jeremy B.C., Michael X. Kirby, Wolfgang H. Berger, Karen A. Bjorndal, Louis W. Botsford, Bruce J. Bourque, Roger H. Bradbury, Richard Cooke, Jon Erlandson, James A. Estes, Terence P. Hughes, Susan Kidwell, Carina B. Lange, Hunter S. Lenihan, John M. Pandolfi, Charles H. Peterson, Roberts S. Steneck, Mia J. Tegner, and Robert R. Warner. "Historical Overfishing and the Recent Collapse of Coastal Ecosystems," *Science* 293 (July 27) (2001), pp. 629–38.

Jary, David and Julya Jary. *The Harper Collins Dictionary of Sociology: Sociology from "Anomie" to "Zeitgeist"*. New York: Harper & Collins Publishers, 1991.

Jones, Gwyn. *A History of the Vikings*. New York: Oxford University Press, 1968.

Jones, Malcolm Jr. "When the Horse Came," *Newsweek* fall/winter (Special Issue: "When Worlds Collide: How Columbus's Voyage Transformed both East and West") (1991), pp. 76–7.

Kant, Immanuel. "An Answer to the Question 'What Is Enlightenment?'" in *Political Writings*, edited by H. Reiss. Cambridge: Cambridge University Press, 1991.

Karlinger, Joshua. *The Corporate Planet: Ecology and Politics in the Age of Globalization.* San Francisco: Sierra Club Books, 1997.

Kellert, Stephen R. and Edward O. Wilson, eds. *The Biophilia Hypothesis.* Washington, DC: Island Press, 1993.

Kellner, Douglas. "Illuminations: Marcuse, Liberation, and Radical Ecology," *Sarah Zuko's Cultural Center Articles/Papers: Theorists and Critics* [Online, available: http://www.uta.edu/english/dab/illuminations/kell11.html], 1992.

Kelly, Petra. *Fighting for Hope,* trans. Marianne Wowarth. Boston and London: South End Press and Chatto & Windus, 1984.

Kerner, Robert Joseph. *The Urge to the Sea: The Course of Russian History. The Role of Rivers, Portages, Ostrogs, Monasteries, and Furs.* Berkeley: University of California Press, 1942.

Kirk, Patrick V. and Terry L. Hunt, eds. *Historical Ecology in the Pacific Islands: Prehistoric Environmental and Landscape Changes, Based on Papers Presented at the XVIIth Pacific Science Congress Held in Honolulu in 1991.* New Haven, CT: Yale University Press, 1997.

Kloppenburg, Jack Jr. "Biotechnology to the Rescue? Twelve Reasons Why Biotechnology Is Incompatible with Sustainable Agriculture," *The Ecologist* 26(2) (1996), pp. 61–7.

Kluger, Jeffrey. "The Big Crunch," *Time* April–May (2000), p. 49.

Kneen, Brewster. *Farmageddon: Food and the Culture of Biotechnology.* Gabriola Island, BC: New Society, 1999.

Kohler, Timothy A. "Prehistoric Human Impact on the Environment in Upland North American Southwest," *Population and Environment: A Journal of Interdisciplinary Studies* 13(4) (1992), pp. 255–68.

Korten, David. *When Corporations Rule the World.* West Hartford, CT: Kumarin Press, 1995.

——— *Rights of Money Versus Rights of Living Person, People-Centered Development Forum (PCDF)* [Online, available: http://iisd1.iisd.ca/pcdf/1996/82korten.htm], 1996.

Kraus, Karl. *In These Great Times: A Karl Kraus Reader,* edited by Harry Zohn. Montreal: Engendra Press, 1976).

LaDuke, Winona. "A Society Based on Conquest Cannot Be Sustained," in *Toxic Struggles: The Theory and Practice of Environmental Justice,* edited by Richard Hofrichter. Philadelphia, PA: New Society Publisher, 1993.

Lappé, Marc, and Britt Bailey. *Against the Grain: The Genetic Transformation of Global Agriculture.* London: Earthscan, 1999.

Leakey, Richard and Roger Levin. *Origins Reconsidered: In Search of What Makes Us Human.* New York: Anchor Books, Doubleday, 1992.

——— and ——— *The Sixth Extinction: Patterns of Life and the Future of Humankind.* New York: Doubleday, 1995.

Lee, May. *Land-Clearing Fires Foul Malaysia's Air.* Kuala Lumpur, Malaysia [Online, available: http://www9.cnn.com/WORLD/9709/19/malaysia.smog], 1997.

Lee, R. "Problems in the Study of Hunters and Gatherers," in *Man the Hunter,* edited by R. Lee and I. DeVore, 3–12. Chicago: Aldine, 1969.

Leff, Enrique. *Ecologica y Capital.* English: *Green Production: Toward an Environmental Rationality,* trans. Margareta Vilanueva, edited and with an Introduction by James O'Connor, *Democracy and Ecology Series.* New York: Guilford Press, 1995.

Lemonick, Michael D. "Secrets of the Maya," *Time* August (1993), pp. 44–50.

Luhman, Niklas. *Ecological Communication.* Chicago: University of Chicago Press, 1986.

Lutz, Wolfgang, Jawahrall Baguant, Christopher Prinz, Ferenc L. Toth, and Anne Babbette Wils. *Understanding Population–Development–Environment Interactions: A Case Study on Mauritius.* Laxenburg, Vienna: International Institute for Applied Systems Analysis (IIASA) in Collaboration with University of Mauritius; Sponsored by United Nations Population Fund (UNFDP), 1993.

Macauley, David. "Thinkers out of Space: Hannah Arendt on Earth Alienation; A Historical and Critical Perspective," *Capitalism, Nature, Socialism* (CNS) 3(4) (December) (1992), pp. 19–46.

MacDougall, Kent. *Humans as Cancer.* USA, CA [Online, available: http://www.envirolink.org/orgs/coe/e-sermons/humcan.html], 1997.

Mancall, Mark. *Russia and China: Their Diplomatic Relations to 1728, Harvard East Asian Series 61.* Cambridge, MA: Harvard University Press, 1971.

Mandel, Ernest. *Late Capitalism,* trans. Joris de Bres. London: NLB, 1975.

Manicas, Peter T. *War and Democracy.* Cambridge, MA: Basil Blackwell, 1989.

Mannion, A.M. *Global Environmental Change: A Natural and Cultural Environmental History.* New York: Longman Scientific and Technical, 1988.

Marham, Adam. *A Brief History of Pollution.* London: Earthscan Publications, 1995.

Marks, Peter. "A Vision of Environment: Is Life Worth Living Here?" in *Is America Possible? Social Problems from Conservative, Liberal and Socialist Perspectives,* edited by Henry Etzkowitz, 116–21. New York: State University of New York at Purchase, 1974.

Martin, Paul S. "Pleistocene Overkill," *Natural History* 76 (1967), pp. 32–8.
———— "The Discovery of America," *Science* 179 (1973), pp. 969–74.
———— and Richard G. Klein, eds. *Quarternary Extinctions: A Prehistoric Revolution.* Tucson: University of Arizona Press, 1984.

Maser, Chris. *Global Imperative: Harmonising Culture and Nature.* Walpole, NH: Stillpoint Publisher, 1992.

Mastny, Lisa. "Ozone Hole Is Largest Ever," *World Watch* 12(1) (January/February) (1999), p. 11.

Mattoon, Ashley T. "Bogging Down the Sinks," *World Watch* 11(6) (November/December) (1998), pp. 28–36.

McNeeley, J.A. et al. "Human Influences on Biodiversity," in *Global Biodiversity Assessment,* edited by V.H. Heywood. Cambridge. Cambridge University Press and UNEP, 1995.

McNeill, J.R. *Something New under the Sun: An Environmental History of the Twentieth-Century World,* 1st edn. New York and London: W.W. Norton, 2000.

McPhee, Ross. "Digging Cuba: The Lessons of the Bones," *Natural History* 106(11) (December/January) (1997), pp. 50–5.

Meadows, Donella H. et al. *The Limits to Growth: A Report for the Club of Rome's Project on the Predicament of Mankind.* New York: Universe Books, 1972.
————, Dennis L. Meadows, and Jørgen Randers. *Beyond the Limits: Confronting Global Collapse; Envisioning a Sustainable Future.* Post Mills, VT: Chelsea Green Publishing Company, 1992.

Meiksins-Wood, Ellen. *Democracy against Capitalism: Renewing Historical Materialism.* New York: Cambridge University Press, 1995.

Mellot, Mary, ed. *Building a New Vision: Feminist, Green Socialism,* pp. 36–46 in *Toxic Struggles: The Theory and Practice of Environmental Justice,* edited by Daniel Hofrichter. Philadelphia: New Society Publishers, 1993.

Mencius (Meng Tze). *Mencius,* trans. D.C. Lau. London: Penguin Books, 1970.

Miley, Michael. "Against Nature: The Ideology of Ecocide," *Propaganda Review* 11 (1994), pp. 38–69 (San Francisco, CA: Media Alliance).

Miller, Gifford H., John W. Magee, Beverly L. Johnson, Marilyn L. Fogel, Nigel A. Spooner, Malcolm T. McCulloch, and Linda K. Ayliffe. "Pleistocene Extinction of *Genyornis Newtoni:* Human Impact on Australian Megafauna," *Science* 283 (January 8) (1999), pp. 205–8.

Mills, C.W. *The Power Elite.* New York: Oxford University Press, 1956.

Misrach, Richard. *Richard Misrach (A Photographic Book; Landscape Photography).* San Francisco, CA: Grapestake Gallery, 1979.

————— *Desert Canton,* edited by Reyner Banham. Albuquerque: University of New Mexico Press, 1987.

————— *Violent Legacies: Three Cantons,* edited by Susan Sontag. New York: Aperture, 1992.

————— and Myrian Weisang Misrach. *Bravo 20: The Bombing of the American West, Creating the North American Landscape.* Baltimore, MD: Johns Hopkins University Press, 1990.

Mogelaard, Katie. "Six Billion and Counting," *Nucleus: The Magazine of the Union of Concerned Scientists* 21(3) (1999), pp. 6–8.

Montaigne, Michel de, *The Essays* ("Morall, politike and millitarie discourses," translated from French by John Florio; 1603), a Scolar Press facsimile. Menston, UK: Scolar Press, 1969.

Morley, David and Hermione Lovel. *My Name Is Today: An Illustrated Discussion of Child Health, Society and Poverty in Less Developed Countries.* London: Macmillan, 1986.

Muschamp, David, ed. *Political Thinkers.* Basingstroke: Macmillan Education, 1989.

Myers, Norman, ed. *Biological Diversity and Global Security,* edited by F. Herman Borman and Stephen Kellert, *Ecology, Economics, Ethics: The Broken Circle.* New Haven, CT: Yale University Press, 1991.

—————, R. Mittermeier, C.G. Mittermeier, G.A.B. daFonseca, and J. Kent. "Biodiversity Hotspots for Conservation Priorities," *Nature* 403 (2000), pp. 853–8.

Nagatani, Patrick. *Nuclear Enchantment,* edited by Eugenia Parry Janis, photographs by Patrick Nagatani. Albuquerque: University of New Mexico, 1991.

O'Connor, James. "The Second Contradiction of Capitalism: Causes and Consequences," *Capitalism, Nature, Socialism* CNS/CES Pamphlet 1. Paper given at the Conference on New Economic Analysis, Iniciativa per Catalunya, Barcelona, Spain, November 30–December 2 1990 (1991).

O'Connor, Martin. *Is Capitalism Sustainable? Political Economy and the Politics of Ecology, Democracy and Ecology.* New York: Guilford Press, 1994.

O'Neill, John. "Cost–Benefit Analysis, Rationality and the Plurality of Values," *The Ecologist* 26(3) (May/June) (1996), pp. 98–103.

O'Rourke, Dennis. *Half-Life: A Parable for the Nuclear Age,* Videorecording/Film. Los Angeles, CA: Direct Cinema (86 min.), 1986.

Olson, S.L. "Extinction on Islands: Man as a Catastrophe," in *Conservation for the Twenty-First Century,* edited by D. Western and M. Pearl. New York: Oxford University Press, 1989.

————— and Helen F. James. "The Role of Polynesians in the Extinction of the Avifauna of the Hawaiian Islands," in *Quarternary Extinctions: A Prehistoric Revolution,* edited by Paul S. Martin and Richard S. Klein, 768–80. Tucson: University of Arizona Press, 1984.

Overfield, James H. and Andrea J. Alfred. *The Human Record: Sources of Global History, vol. 1, to 1700.* Boston: Houghton Mifflin Company, 1994.

Panjabi, Ranee K.L. *The Earth Summit at Rio: Politics, Economics, and the Environment.* Boston, MA: Northeastern University Press, 1997.

Peck, William M. *A Tidy Universe of Islands.* Honolulu: Mutual Publishing, 1997.

Perlin, John. *A Forest Journey: The Role of Wood in the Development of Civilization.* Cambridge, MA: Harvard University Press, 1991.

Pimentel, David, R. Harman, M. Pacenza, J. Pecarsky, and M. Pimentel. "Natural Resources and an Optimum Human Population," *Population and Environment* 15(5) (1994), pp. 347–69.

————— and Marcia Pimentel. "US Food Production Threatened by Rapid Population Growth," Gaya Preservation Coalition (GPC) prepared for the Carrying Capacity Network. Washington, DC [Online, available: http://www.envirolink.org/ orgs/gaia-pc/Pimentel2.html], 1997.

——— Christa Wilson, Christine McCullum, Rachel Huang, Paulette Dwen, Jessica Flack, Quynh Tran, Tamara Saltman, and Barbara Cliff. "Economic and Environmental Benefits of Biodiversity," *BioScience* 47(11) (December) [Online, available: http://www.aibs.org/biosciencelibrary/vol47/dec.97.biodiversity.html], 1997.

Pinkadella, Diane. "Were Pygmy Hippos Hunted to Extinction?" *Earth* 2(3) (1993), p. 16.

Plato. *Critias*, edited by E. Hamilton and H. Cairns, *Collected Dialogues*, Bollingen series 71 (New York: Pantheon Books), 1961.

Ponting, Clive. "Historical Perspectives on Sustainable Development," *Environment* 32(9) (November) (1990), pp. 4–9.

——— *A Green History of the World: The Environmental Collapse of Civilisations*. London: Penguin Books, 1991.

Pooley, Jeff. *The Globalization of Oppression: Multilateral Corporations and the Failure of Democracy* [Online, available: http://www.digitas.harvard.edu/~perspy/issues/1995/nov/democ.html], 1995.

Prance, Ghillean T. and Thomas S. Elias. *Extinction Is Forever: Threatened and Endangered Species of Plants in the Americas and Their Significance in Ecosystems Today and in the Future*. New York: New York Botanical Garden, 1978.

Price, David. "Energy and Human Evolution," *Population and Environment: A Journal of Interdisciplinary Studies* 16(4) (March) (1995), pp. 301–19.

Putnam, Robert D. *Bowling Alone: The Collapse and Revival of American Community*. New York: Simon & Schuster, 2000.

Rappaport, R.A. *Pigs for the Ancestors: Ritual in the Ecology of a New Guinea People*. New Haven, CT: Yale University Press, 1984.

Reclus, Elisée. *L'Homme et la terre*, 6 vols. Paris: Paris: Librairie Universelle, 1905.

Redfield, Robert. *Peasant Society and Culture*, Chicago: University of Chicago Press, 1956.

Redman, Charles L. *Human Impact on Ancient Environments*. Tucson: University of Arizona Press, 1999.

Rees, William E. *Revisiting Carrying Capacity: Area-Based Indicators of Sustainability*. University of British Columbia: [Online]. Available: http://www.dieoff.com/page110.htm, reviewed June, 2002.

Reid, J. Jefferson and Stephanie Michelle Whittlesey. *The Archaeology of Ancient Arizona*. Tucson: University of Arizona Press, 1997.

Reid, V. Walter. "How Many Species Will There Be?" in *Tropical Deforestation and Species Extinction*, edited by T.C. Sayer, Jeffrey Whitmore, and the International Union for Conservation of Nature and Natural Resources, 55–73. London and New York: Chapman & Hall, 1992.

Renner, Michael. *Fighting for Survival: Environmental Decline, Social Conflict, and the New Age of Insecurity*. Washington, DC: Worldwatch Institute, 1996.

Ridley, R.T. "To Be Taken with a Pinch of Salt: The Destruction of Carthage," *Classical Philology* 81 (April) (1986), pp. 140–6.

Rifkin, Jeremy. *Biosphere Politics: A New Consciousness for a New Century*. New York: Crown, 1991.

Ritchie, Carson I.A. *Food and Civilization: How History Has Been Affected by Human Taste*. New York: Beaufort Books, 1981.

Roberts, J.M. *The Penguin History of the World*. London: Penguin Books, 1990.

——— *History of the World*. New York: Oxford University Press, 1993.

Roberts, Neil. *The Holocene: An Environmental History*. New York: Basil Blackwell, 1992.

Robertson, Roland. *Globalization: Social Theory and Global Culture*. London: Sage, 1992.

Robinson, Simon. "How Apes Became Human: One Giant Step for Mankind," *Time* (July 23) (2001), pp. 54–61.

Rogers, Adam. *The Earth Summit: A Planetary Reckoning*, Foreword by Noel Brown, Afterword by David Suzuki. Lower Lake, CA: Atrium Publishers Group, 1995.

Rollefson, G. and I. Kohler. "Prehistoric People Ruined Their Environment," *New Scientist* 125(24) (February) (1990), p. 29.

Rousseau, Jean-Jacques. *The Social Contract and Discourses, 1755: "Discourse on the Origin of Inequality," Response To: "Question Proposed by the Academy of Dijon: What Is the Origin of the Inequality among Mankind; and Whether Such Inequality Is Authorized by the Law"*. New York: Dutton, 1950.

Saeger, Joni. *Earth Follies: Coming to Feminist Terms with the Global Environmental Crisis*. New York: Routledge, 1993.

Sahlins, Marshall. "The Original Affluent Society," in *Stone Age Economics*, 1–39. Chicago: Aldine Atherton, 1972.

——— *Stone Age Economics*. Chicago: Aldine Atherton, 1972.

Sampal, Payal. "Judgement Protects Indigenous Knowledge," *World Watch* 11(1) (January/February) (1998), p. 8.

Schell, Jonathan. *The Fate of the Earth*. New York: Knopf Publishers, 1982.

Schmid-Schreiber, Peter. "Wie Viele Tötliche Dosen Lassen Sie Erbrüten, Nachbar?" *Presse Spiegel der Initiative Österreichischer Atomkraftwerksgegner 2* (February), Pressespiegel-gruppe der IOEAG, Wien/Vienna (1993), pp. 17–18.

Schnaiberg, Allan. *The Environment: From Surplus to Scarcity*. New York: Oxford University Press, 1980.

——— *Education, Cultural Myths, and the Ecological Crisis: Towards Deep Changes*. Albany: State University of New York Press, 1993.

——— *Educating for an Ecologically Sustainable Culture: Rethinking Moral Education, Creativity, Intelligence, and Other Modern Orthodoxies*. Albany: State University of New York Press, 1995.

——— "Environmental Education," *Environment, Technology and Society* [Online, available: http://csf.colorado.edu/envtecsoc/96s/0166.html], 1996.

Scholte, Jan Aart. *Globalization: A Critical Introduction*. London: Macmillan; New York: St Martin's Press, 2000.

Schorger, A.W. *The Passenger Pigeon: Its Natural History and Extinction*. Norman: University of Oklahoma Press, 1973.

Schubert, Glendon. "Catastrophe Theory, Evolutionary Extinction, and Revolutionary Politics," in *The Dynamics of Evolution: Punctuated Equilibrium Debate in the Natural and Social Sciences*, edited by Albert Sombert and Stephen A. Peterson, 248–81. Ithaca, NY and London: Cornell University Press, 1989.

Shi, N.H. "The Geographical Character of the Loess Plateau During the Zhou Period (100–256 BC)," *Journal of Shaanxi Normal University* 3/4 (1978), pp. 1–13 (vol. 3) and 1–11 (vol. 4) [in Chinese].

——— ed. *On Gully Control and Water Conservation on the Loess Plateau*, vol. 2, *Contributions to Historical Geography of China*. Xian: Shaanxi People's Publishing House [in Chinese], 1985.

Sivard, Ruth Leger. *World Military and Social Expenditures 1991*, 14th edn. Washington, DC: World Priorities Press, 1991.

——— *World Military and Social Expenditures 1993*, 15th edn. Washington DC: World Priorities Press, 1993.

——— *World Military and Social Expenditures 1996*, 16th edn. Washington, DC: World Priorities Press, 1996.

Sizer, Nigel, and Dominiquek Plouvier. "Increased Investment and Trade by Transnational Logging Companies in Africa, the Caribbean and the Pacific: Implications for the Sustainable Management and Conservation of Tropical Forests," in *A Joint Report by*

World Wide Fund for Nature and Belgium World Resources Institute's Forest Frontiers Initiative. Brussels: European Commission EC-Project B7–6201/96–16/VIII/FOR D/1999/6732/03, 2000.

Soule, M.E. "Conservation: Tactics for a Constant Crisis," *Science* 253 (1991), pp. 744–50.

Der Spiegel. "Schlimmster Krieg Aller Zeiten," *Der Spiegel* 18 (1992), pp. 218–32.

—— "Ein Stück Schlaraffenland," *Der Spiegel* 28 (1992), pp. 190–91.

—— "Sex Für Frieden," *Der Spiegel* 30 (1993), p. 171.

—— "Knurrende Mägen," *Der Spiegel* 24 (1995): Archeology Review.

—— "Siegeszug Aus Der Sackgasse: Neue Knochenfunde Von Urmenschen Und Die Entstehung Des Homo Sapiens (2)," *Der Spiegel* 43 (1995), pp. 136–54.

—— "Siegeszug Aus Der Sackgasse: Neue Knochenfunde Vom Urmenschen Und Die Entstehung Des Homo Sapiens (3)," *Der Spiegel* 44 (1995), pp. 136–47.

—— "Wir Werden Einsam Sein: Evolutionsbiologe Edward O. Wilson Über Artenvielfalt, Ameisen Und Menschen," *Der Spiegel* 48 (1995), pp. 193–204.

Stanley, Stephen M. *Children of the Ice Age: How a Global Catastrophe Allowed Humans to Evolve*. New York: Harmony Books, 1996.

Stavranos, L.S. *Global Rift: The Third World Comes of Age*. New York: William Morrow, 1981.

Stedman-Edwards, P. *The Root Causes of Biodiversity Loss: An Analytical Approach, Macroeconomics for Sustainable Development Office*. Washington, DC: Worldwide Fund for Nature, 1997.

Steger, Manfred B. *Globalism: The New Market Ideology*. Lanham, MD: Rowman & Littlefield, 2001.

Stevens, Susan T. "Notes and Discussions: A Legend of the Destruction of Carthage," *Classical Philology* 83 (January) (1988), pp. 39–42.

Stringer, Chris and Robin McKie. *African Exodus: The Origins of Modern Humanity*. New York: Henry Holt, 1997.

Stuart, David E. and Susan B. Moczygomba-McKinsey *Anasazi America: Seventeen Centuries on the Road from Center Place*. Albuquerque: University of New Mexico Press, 2000.

Swift, Jeremy. *The Other Eden: A New Approach to Man, Nature and Society*. London: J.M. Dent & Sons, 1974.

Tattersall, Ian. *The Human Odyssey: Four Million Years of Human Evolution*, edited by American Museum for Natural History, Foreword by Donald Johanson. New York: Prentice Hall, 1993.

—— *Becoming Human: Evolution and Human Uniqueness*. New York: Harcourt Brace, 1998.

—— *The Last Neanderthal: The Rise, Success, and Mysterious Extinction*, rev. edn. Boulder, CO and Oxford: Westview Press, 1999.

—— and Jeffrey H. Schwartz. *Extinct Humans*. Boulder, CO: Westview Press, 2000.

Theophrastus, *De nentis*, in *Theophrastus' Enquiry into Plants*, edited by A. Loeb. New York, 1916.

Thirgood, J.V. *Man and the Mediterranean Forests: A History of Resource Depletion*. London: Academic Press, 1989.

Thompson, Edward et al. *Exterminism and the Cold War*. London and New York: Schocken Books, 1982.

Thompson, William. *Scorched Earth: The Military's Assault on the Environment, Weapons Incorporated*. Philadelphia, PA: New Society Publishers [Online, available: http://www.earthisland.org/journal/bigmil.html], 1995.

Tian, S.Y. "Hydrological Changes in Shanxi Province and Their Relations with the Alterations between Farming and Animal Husbandry in Different Historical Times," *Journal of Shanxi University* 1 (1981), pp. 29–37 [in Chinese].

Toriso, Kyoichi. "Western Seas Whaling: A Brief History of the Whaling Hunt," *Fukuoka Style* 12 (October 31) (1995).

Toulmin, Stephen Edelston. "Back to Nature," *New York Review of Books* 9 (June) (1977), pp. 3–6.

Tudge, Colin. "Why We Must Save Animals," *New Internationalist* (Special Issue) 288 (March) (1997), pp. 28–30.

Tuxill, John. *Losing Strands in the Web of Life: Vertebrate Declines and the Conservation of Biodiversity*, edited by Jane A. Peterson, *Worldwatch Paper 141*. Washington, DC: Worldwatch Institute, 1998.

UCS (Union of Concerned Scientists). *World Scientists' Warning to Humanity*, edited by UCS (November 18). Cambridge, MA: Union of Concerned Scientists, 1992.

———— "US Consumption and the Environment," *Union of Concerned Scientists Briefing Paper*. Washington, DC: UCS Publication Department, 1994, pp. 1–6.

Uexkuell, Jacob von and Bernd Jost, eds. *Project Der Hoffnung: Der Alternative Nobelpreis* (English: *Alternative Nobelprize; Right Livelihood Award Project*). München: Raben Verlag, 1990.

Union of International Association (UIA) "Environmental Hazards – Nuclear Weapons Industry," *Encyclopedia of World Problems and Human Potential* (PE5698) [Online, available: http://www.uia.org/uialists/ndx/pro/pro132.htm] 1998).

United Nations Dept. of Economic and Social Affairs, Population Division. *World Population Prospects: The 1998 Revision*. New York: United Nations, 2000.

———— *World Population Projections to 2150*. New York: United Nations, 1998.

UN-ESCAP (United Nations Economic and Social Commission for Asia and the Pacific). *State of the Environment in the Asia Pacific*. New York: United Nations, 2000.

UNDP (United Nations Development Programme). *Human Development Report 1998*. New York: Oxford University Press, 1998.

UNEP (United Nations Environment Programme), Governing Council. *World Charter for Nature: United Nations General Assembly Resolution 37/7, of 28 October 1982, Environmental Law Guidelines and Principles; 5*. Nairobi: UNEP, 1983.

———— *Global Biodiversity Assessment*. Cambridge: United Nations Environment Programme, 1995.

———— "Freshwater Synthesis," *Global Environment Outlook 2000* [Online, available: http://www.unep.org/geo2000/english/0046.htm]. See also [http://freshwater.unep.net].

UNRISD (United Nations Research Institute for Social Development). *States of Disarray: The Social Effects of Globalization*. London: UNRISD, 1995.

US News and World Report, "What Killed the Mayas: War or Weather?" *US News and World Report* June 12 (1995), p. 10.

Visona, Paolo. "Passing the Salt: On the Destruction of Carthage Again," *Classical Philology* 83 (January) (1988), pp. 39–42.

Vitousek, Peter Morrison, A. Ehrlich, and P. Mason. "Human Appropriation of the Products of Photosynthesis," *Bioscience* May (1986), pp. 368–74.

———— et al. "Human Domination of Earth's Ecosystems," *Science* 277 (1997), pp. 494–9.

———— et al. "Human Alteration of the Global Nitrogen Cycle: Causes and Consequences," *Ecological Applications* 7 (1997), pp. 737–50.

Waal, F.B.M. de and Frans Lanting. *Bonobo: The Forgotten Ape*. Berkeley: University of California Press, 1997.

Wackernagel, Mathis and William Rees. *Our Ecological Footprint: Reducing Human Impact on the Earth*. Philadelphia, PA and Gabriola Island: New Society Publishers, 1996.

————, Larry Onisto, Alejandro Callejas Linares, Ina Susana López Falfán, Jesus Méndez García, Ana Isabel Suárez Guerrero and Ma. Guadalupe Suárez Guerrero. *Ecological*

Footprints of Nations: How Much Nature Do They Use? – How Much Nature Do They Have? University of British Columbia: [Online]. Available: http://www.ecouncil.ac.cr/rio/ focus/report/english/footprint/, reviewed June 2002.

Walker, Alan and Pat Shupman. *The Wisdom of the Bones.* New York: Alfred Knopf, 1996.

Wallerstein, Immanuel. *The Modern World System: Capitalist Agriculture and the Origins of the European World Economy in the Sixteenth Century,* vol. 1. New York: Academic Press, 1974.

———— *The Modern World System: Mercantilism and the Consolidation of the European World Economy, 1600–1750,* vol. 2. New York: Academic Press, 1980.

Ward, Peter Douglas. *The End of Evolution: A Journey in Search of Clues to the Third Mass Extinction Facing the Planet Earth.* New York: Bantam Books, 1995.

———— *The Call of Distant Mammoths: Why the Ice Age Mammals Disappeared.* New York: Copernicus, 1997.

———— *Rivers in Time: The Search for Clues to Earth's Mass Extinctions.* New York: Columbia University Press, 2000.

———— and Donald Brownlee. *Rare Earth: Why Complex Life Is Uncommon in the Universe.* New York: Copernicus, 2000.

Warmington, B.H. "The Destruction of Carthage: A Refractio," *Classical Philology* 83 (April) (1988), pp. 309–10.

Waters, Malcolm. *Globalization, Key Ideas.* London and New York: Routledge, 1995.

Weber, Max. *The Protestant Ethic and the Spirit of Capitalism.* New York: Scribner, 1930.

———— *The Protestant Ethic and the Spirit of Capitalism.* London: Routledge, 1992.

Weigel, Van B. *Earth Cancer.* Westport, CT, and London: Praeger Press, 1995.

Weisman, Alan. "The Real Indiana Jones and His Pyramids of Doom," *Los Angeles Times Magazine* October 14 (1990), pp. 13–20, 39–42.

Weissman, Robert. "Corporate Plundering of Third World Resources," in *Toxic Struggles: The Theory and Practice of Environmental Justice,* edited by Richard Hofrichter, 186–96. Philadelphia, PA: New Society Publisher, 1993.

Welker, Glen. *Mayan Civilization* [Online, available: http://www.indians.org/ welker/maya.htm], 1997.

Wertheim, Theodore A. "The Furnace vs the Goat: The Pyro Technology Industries and Mediterranean Deforestation in Antiquity," *Journal of Field Archeology* 10 (1983), pp. 445–52.

West, Neil, ed. *Ecosystems of the World,* vol. 5: *Temperate Deserts and Semi-Deserts.* Amsterdam: Elsevier, 1983.

Westing, Arthur H. "Threat of Modern Warfare to Man and His Environment: An Annotated Bibliography," in *Reports and Papers in the Social Sciences No. 40,* edited by International Peace Research Association (IPRA), 7–8. Paris, France: UNESCO, 1979.

———— "A World in Balance," *Environmental Conservation* 8 (1981), pp. 177–83.

———— ed. *Environmental Hazards of War: Releasing Dangerous Forces in an Industrialized World,* edited by Oslo International Peace Research Institute (PRIO), and United Nations Environment Program (UNEP). London and Newbury Park: Sage Publications, 1990.

———— "Biodiversity Loss and Its Implications for Security and Armed Conflict," in *The Living Planet in Crisis,* edited by Joel Cracraft and Francesca T. Grifo, 209–16. New York: Columbia University Press, 1999.

Williams, Eric. *Capitalism and Slavery.* New York: Capricorn Books, 1944.

Wilson, Edward, O. *The Diversity of Life.* New York: W.W. Norton, 1992.

———— "Is Humanity Suicidal? We Are Flirting with the Extinction of Our Species," *The New York Times Magazine* May 30 (1993), pp. 24.

———— *Vanishing Point: On Bjorn Lomborg and Extinction* [Online, available: http://www.gristmagazine.com/grist/books/wilson121201.asp], 2001.

—— and F.M. Peter, eds. *Biodiversity*, 9th edn. Washington, DC: National Academy Press, 1992.

Wittfogel, Karl. *Oriental Despotism: A Comparative Study of Total Power.* New Haven, CT: Yale University Press, 1957.

Wolf, Eric R. *Sons of the Shaking Earth: The People of Mexico and Guatemala; Their Land, History, and Culture.* New York: Chicago University Press, 1959.

—— *Europe and the People without History.* Berkeley: University of California Press, 1982.

World Commission on Environment and Development. *Our Common Future.* Oxford and New York: Oxford University Press, 1987.

WHO (World Health Organization). "Micronutrient Malnutrition: Half the World's Population Affected," *World Health Organization* 78 (November 13) (1996), pp. 1–4.

WRI (World Resources Institute). *World Resources 1990–1991.* New York: Oxford University Press, 1990.

—— *World Resources 1992–93.* New York: Oxford University Press, 1992.

—— *Teachers' Guide to World Resources: Biodiversity, Educational Resources.* Washington, DC: World Resources Institute, 1994.

—— "History of Use and Abuse," in *World Resources 2000–2001: People and Ecosystems: The Fraying Web of Life,* 6–7. Washington, DC: Oxford University Press, 2000.

Worldwatch. "Subsidies for Sacred Cows," *World Watch* 9(1) (January/February) (1996), pp. 8–9.

—— "Endpiece: The Ivory Trade," *World Watch* 10(3) (May/June) (1997), p. 40.

—— "Overshoot: Building a New Economy – the Challenge for Our Generation," State of the World 1998; Worldwatch Press Release, January 10 1998.

—— "Matters of Scale: Subsidies: The Other Side of the Coin," *Worldwatch Magazine* 10 [2] (March/April 2000), p. 39.

WWF (World Wildlife Fund). *Rain Forests on Fire: Conservation Consequences.* Washington, DC: World Wildlife Fund, 1997.

Worster, Donald. *Dust Bowl: The Southern Plains in the 1930s.* New York: Oxford University Press, 1979.

—— and Alfred Crosby, eds. *The Ends of the Earth: Perspectives on Modern Environmental History.* New York: Cambridge University Press, 1989.

Wrangham, Richard W. and Dale Peterson. *Demonic Males: Apes and the Origins of Human Violence.* Boston, MA: Houghton Mifflin, 1996.

Yesner, David R. "Life in the Garden of Eden: Causes and Consequences of the Adoption of Marine Diets by Human Societies," in *Food and Evolution: Towards a Theory of Human Food Habits,* edited by Marvin Harris and Eric B. Ross, 285–310. Philadelphia, PA: Temple University Press, 1987.

Yoffee, Norman. "Orienting Collapse," in *The Collapse of Ancient States and Civilizations,* edited by Norman Yoffee and George L. Cowgill, 1–19. Tucson: University of Arizona Press, 1988.

INDEX

Compiled by Auriol Griffith-Jones

Note: Italic page numbers refer to chapter openings; bold page numbers refer to the Glossary (pages 106–18) and Tables (pages 119–40); notes (pages 141–78) are indicated by *n* or *nn* (for more than one note on the page)